EZ · JIM LANDIS · JIM McANANY · BOB SHAW · GARY PETERS · JO

· ROGER BOSSARD · ED HERRMANN · WILBUR · LT

JIM KAAT · STEVE STONE · MIKE SQUIRES · ERIC SODERHOLM ·

SA · RICHARD DOTSON · HAROLD BAINES · GREG LUZINSKI · EDI

TTLE · GREG WALKER · BOBBY THIGPEN · KENNY WILLIAMS · DO

HOMAS · JOEY CORA · GENE LAMONT · DARRIN JACKSON · JEF

COOPER · A.J. PIERZYNSKI · JERMAINE DYE · SCOTT PODSEDNI

E MINOSO · JIM RIVERA · LUIS APARICIO · AL LOPEZ · JIM LAND

MOOSE SKOWRON · PETE WARD · TOMMY JOHN · ROGER BOSSA

CY FAUST · CHUCK TANNER · ROLAND HEMOND · JIM KAAT · STI

HERM SCHNEIDER · BRITT BURNS · TONY LA RUSSA · RICHARD D

· TOM PACIOREK · HAWK HARRELSON · RON KITTLE · GREG WALK

OBIN VENTURA · CRAIG GREBECK · FRANK THOMAS · JOEY COR

· MARK BUEHRLE · AARON ROWAND · DON COOPER · A.J. PIERZ

JERRY REINSDORF · BILLY PIERCE · MINNIE MINOSO · JIM RIVER

ARY PETERS · JOEL HORLEN · KEN BERRY · MOOSE SKOWRON · P

VOOD · BILL MELTON · CARLOS MAY · NANCY FAUST · CHUCK T

ERIC SODERHOLM · JIM ANGIO · ED FARMER · HERM SCHNEIDE

· GREG LUZINSKI · EDDIE EINHORN · VANCE LAW · TOM PACIO

WHAT IT MEANS TO BE A WHITE SOX

WHAT IT MEANS TO BE A
WHITE SOX

THE SOUTH SIDE'S GREATEST PLAYERS
TALK ABOUT WHITE SOX BASEBALL

FOREWORD BY
OZZIE GUILLEN

BOB VORWALD

TRIUMPH
BOOKS

This book is available in quantity at special discounts for your group or organization. For further information, contact:

Triumph Books
542 South Dearborn Street
Suite 750
Chicago, Illinois 60605
(312) 939-3330
Fax (312) 663-3557
www.triumphbooks.com

Printed in U.S.A.
ISBN: 978-1-60078-278-7
Design by Nick Panos
Editorial production and layout by Prologue Publishing Services, LLC
Photos courtesy of Getty Images unless otherwise indicated

*To the ballplayers. Thank you for your excellence on the field,
for giving so generously of your time, and for all the wonderful stories
and memories you shared for this project.*

CONTENTS

FOREWORD

What It Means to Be a White Sox

MANY CONSIDER ME THE FACE OF THE WHITE SOX, and it is a title I wear proudly. I am the luckiest man in baseball because I get to manage the team I want to manage, in the city where I want to manage. I am also fortunate because my owner, general manager, and players have always supported me. Nothing is better than that.

After the final out of the 2005 World Series, I didn't show a lot of emotion. I just hugged my family and thanked God that I was fortunate enough to be the guy who helped bring home a World Series championship for owner Jerry Reinsdorf and the generations of White Sox fans who had waited so long for a title.

Two days later we celebrated with the entire city of Chicago at a downtown parade. I have seen a lot of rallies and celebrations, but I have never seen anything like that. The fans screamed and cheered for hours and hours that October day—that's not easy to do. Millions of people came out, and I can still close my eyes and hear the noise from that magical celebration in my ears. My kids like to replay the footage from the World Series and celebration, and every time I see it, I get tears in my eyes.

Eighty-eight long years since the last championship, the White Sox were again winners of the World Series. And with that spectacular rally, finally, the baseball world was seeing the passion, pride, and tradition of the Chicago White Sox franchise, traits I have known about and believed in since I arrived on the South Side 20 years ago as a rookie shortstop.

My journey with the White Sox started in 1985. I was traded for Cy Young–winner LaMarr Hoyt, which put pressure on me to succeed immediately. Arriving in a big-league clubhouse was amazing. I found myself surrounded by a number of superstars, including Harold Baines, Carlton Fisk, Tom Seaver, and Greg Walker. Once I made the ballclub, I never wanted to leave. The manager was Tony La Russa, who along with coaches Jim Leyland and Eddie Brinkman, made me feel very comfortable. They gave me the opportunity to play the game, and play it the way I loved.

From the minute I first stepped on the field, I played differently than other players. I loved to have fun, always played with a smile on my face.

That season, my rookie year, Hall of Famer Tom Seaver was pitching for us and going for his 300th career win. All of a sudden, in the middle of the game, I called timeout and went to the mound to talk to Seaver. I guess it took a lot of guts to do that in my rookie year, but that's me, that's who I am, and that's how I grew up.

As I continued to play for the Sox, people started comparing me to the great Luis Aparicio. No matter who plays shortstop for the White Sox, they are not going to be able to fill his shoes, so I never even thought about the comparison. I just wanted to do the best I could to represent my team the right way. I do think I helped people remember Luis Aparicio though, and that is something I was proud of and considered an honor.

My playing days with the White Sox were some of the best times of my life. We had some really good teams in the early 1990s, winning the division in 1993. We had incredibly talented young players, like Jack McDowell, Alex Fernandez, Jason Bere, Frank Thomas, Robin Ventura, and Lance Johnson. Unfortunately, we ran into a veteran and talented Blue Jays team in the playoffs and, despite competing well, lost in six games.

Following the 1997 season, I wasn't able to come to an agreement with the White Sox and played the rest of my career elsewhere. And honestly, I was angry. I wanted to stay in Chicago, and I wanted to stay with the White Sox. I would have taken a pay cut to stay with the team, because I had spent half of my life in the city, and my family was happy here. It was like starting a new life with a different club, in a different city. And there was not another team I played for that was like the White Sox. I told myself it was time to move on, but it was difficult.

What was not difficult was coming back as a manager in 2004. I knew exactly what I would face. I convinced general manager Kenny Williams that I was the right guy for the job because I always believed that I would be the manager of the White Sox. It was—and is—my dream job. This was the team I played for, and I knew the owner, the general manager, the players,

Ozzie Guillen was an American League All-Star in 1988, 1990, and 1991 and won the American League Gold Glove at shortstop in 1990. He became manager after the 2003 season and was named the American League Manager of the Year for 2005 after leading the White Sox to their first World Championship since 1917.
Photo courtesy of AP Images

the fans, and the media. I also knew the parking lot attendants, the vendors in the stands, all the workers behind the scenes who make the White Sox great. Having already established relationships with all these people made it so much easier for me to manage here.

Following my first season in 2004, I gave Kenny my opinion of the ball-club, and he made some changes to improve the team and its chemistry. The 2005 season was easy for me as a manager. We were playing so well, and I knew every time we took the field, we had a chance to win. The talent was there, and everyone worked so well together, so it was no surprise to me that we won it all.

Every day I come to work, I realize how lucky I am because I'm doing something I love. I am still passionate about my job, and I'm never going to say, "Oh, it's okay, we'll get them tomorrow," after we lose a game. If I were a fan of a team, and I heard a manger talk like that, I would be disappointed. Fans, especially White Sox fans, deserve better. I will always be very honest and push my players to get the best out of them.

The entire 2005 season and winning the World Series as a manager were so enjoyable, I really want to do it again before my career is over. Nobody can take that feeling away from you. I have accomplished a lot in this game, been selected to All-Star Games, won Gold Gloves, but nothing tops the feeling of being part of the best team in baseball.

Ozzie Guillen came to the White Sox on December 6, 1984, in one of the greatest trades in team history. The Padres sent Guillen, Luis Salazar, Tim Lollar, and Bill Long to the Sox in exchange for LaMarr Hoyt and two minor leaguers. Guillen immediately won the starting shortstop job, committing just 12 errors in 150 games and was named the 1985 American League Rookie of the Year. He was an American League All-Star in 1988, 1990, and 1991 and won the American League Gold Glove at shortstop in 1990. He left the Sox as a free agent after the 1997 season. Guillen ranks fifth on the team's all-time list with 1,743 games played and in 2000 he was named to the White Sox Team of the Century.

Ozzie was named the 37th manager in Sox history on November 3, 2003. The Venezuelan native was the American League Manager of the Year for 2005 after leading the White Sox to their first world championship since 1917.

ACKNOWLEDGMENTS

THANK YOU SO MUCH TO ALL the individuals whose stories follow. Each of them shared their time and memories, and I can't thank them enough.

The first person I talked to about my proposal for *What It Means to Be a White Sox* was Scott Reifert, vice president of communications for the White Sox, and having his blessing got this project off the ground. Scott's advice and insight were a great asset throughout this process, and I can't thank him enough for everything. I also want to thank top Sox Bob Grim and Brooks Boyer for all their help.

Sox PR gurus Pat O'Connell and Bob Beghtol helped me get time with the current players and coaching staff throughout the season. Christine O'Reilly in the Sox's community relations department offered access and encouragement at every turn. Danielle Disch, Lou Hernandez, Ray Garcia, and Marty Maloney took turns working through my various requests and deserve a great deal of thanks.

I also want to give special thanks to White Sox chairman Jerry Reinsdorf. Twenty minutes after committing to roughly $60 million in salary when the White Sox acquired Jake Peavy just before the 2009 trade deadline, Jerry strolled into the conference room at U.S. Cellular Field for our scheduled interview. After we wrapped up, I wished him good luck, and he came back with, "I hope I know what I'm doing." With the franchise running at such a high level, I think it's pretty obvious he does. Jerry's commitment to keeping former players in the White Sox family was lauded by almost every person I interviewed for this project, and deservedly so.

Marty Wilke of WGN-TV deserves a big shout-out here for always listening to my ideas and giving me the go-ahead to work on this project.

Jon Walgren, Jim Angio, Marc Brady, Doug Stanton, and the entire WGN Sports crew do a great job of covering Chicago baseball, and I thank them for all their help. Jeanette Rivera-Rosa and Bridget Gonzales run the WGN production department, and I'd be lost without them.

Wyn Griffiths, Jim Tianis, Joe Pausback, Mike Clay, and Greg Gressle all took time from their busy schedules on game days to get many of these interviews on tape. These guys aren't just cameramen, they love the game of baseball and everything about it.

Steve Byrd and the team at STATS, LLC, are a great resource. Being able to look up every baseball number imaginable on STATS PASS is a lifesaver.

Mitch Rogatz, Tom Bast, and Don Gulbrandsen of Triumph Books are part of a great team. They have always been willing to listen to my ideas, offer solutions to any problems, and are wonderful to work with. The entire Triumph staff makes this process very doable and enjoyable.

Jack Rosenberg was the longtime sports editor at WGN-TV and has been an unbelievable mentor to me since 1982. Rosey is one of the giants of the Chicago sports scene, and being able to count on his memories and advice was a huge help.

Finally, I am blessed to have three baseball-loving sons and a wife who puts up with all four of us and, in her own way, loves the game of baseball as much as we do. Mark, Michael, and Jack, thank you for your encouragement and for putting up with all my tales. Karen, thanks for putting up with me, period.

INTRODUCTION

OCTOBER 28, 2005—The sun shone brightly on the city on this Friday morning as the citizens of Chicago prepared to pay tribute to the Chicago White Sox some 36 hours after they had completed a four-game sweep of the Houston Astros to win their first World Series since 1917. No one dared anger the baseball gods by doing any premature planning, so the parade route was unveiled only the night before, and local media outlets worked feverishly to set up broadcast locations throughout the projected path of the caravan. The spectacle and crowds that followed exceeded everyone's wildest expectations.

If the city itself didn't know what to expect, the returning champions were soon overwhelmed as they embarked on the ride of their lives. "This is the most amazing day of my life," said Jerry Reinsdorf as the lead double-decker bus pulled away from U.S. Cellular Field and headed east on 35th Street. "I never knew we had so many fans. You never really realize until you get to win something like this," marveled Paul Konerko. Sox GM Kenny Williams felt the same way: "This is overwhelming to have this kind of support. We always knew if we brought a title here, it would mean a lot, but this is unexpected."

This Chicago celebration was different. It wasn't the freezefest of stalled buses that greeted the Bears in 1986 or the remote appearances that marked the Grant Park Bulls victory rallies in the '90s. This motorcade snaked through the city and allowed fans across the South Side to stand on the street corners and wave to their heroes. Once the parade reached the Loop, 13 tons of ticker tape rained down on the players and their families as they drove past.

A.J. Pierzynski bellowed at the crowd with his megaphone. Jermaine Dye, clad in a bright white sweat suit, basked in his Series MVP status. Bobby Jenks sported an ear-to-ear grin while waving his valuable right arm to the masses.

Aaron Rowand, Geoff Blum, and Joe Crede laughed together in the front of their bus. Ozzie Guillen showed off his new Sox jacket and raised his arms in the manner of a conquering hero. Orlando "El Duque" Hernandez chomped on a cigar and shook his fists to acknowledge the throngs of fans jammed along LaSalle Street.

As the double-decker buses made their way up LaSalle, several blocks north, the then–junior U.S. Senator from Illinois loitered on the periphery of the main stage and basked in the glow of the revelry. Wearing his now-familiar black Sox cap, Barack Obama was still a bit bleary-eyed from staying up into the night in Washington, D.C., to watch the White Sox win Game 3 in 14 innings along with fellow Senator Dick Durbin and Mayor Richard M. Daley. "We had Cracker Jacks, peanuts, and, I won't lie, a couple of light beers," laughed Obama. "The team itself represents the best of Chicago." Durbin concurred. "We watched until 2:20 in the morning, but the ending was right," he said.

A stage was set up at the corner of LaSalle and Wacker, complete with a Jumbotron and Nancy Faust banging out "Na Na Hey Hey Kiss Him Good-bye" on the organ. After the team and staff were introduced and took the stage, Hawk Harrelson handled the emcee duties and made sure Frank Thomas, who had missed much of the season and all of the playoffs with an injury, was included in the revelry. Cheers, laughter, and joy rang out through Chicago's downtown as video montages relived the excitement of each round of the postseason and various players took the mike to share their thoughts with the assembled multitude.

Five days after hitting a grand slam against the Astros, Paul Konerko stepped to the mike and said, "I've got something here for Mr. Reinsdorf. Jerry, come on up here. Everybody kept asking me the last couple days what I did with that last ball from the last out. Well, it's going to this man right here, because he earned it." And he reached into his pocket, pulled out a baseball, and handed the treasure to Sox chairman Jerry Reinsdorf. Talk about a moment for the ages.

The team that had won the first and last game of the season 1–0, a perfect homage to its "Go-Go" past, was finally world champion.

FOR THE WHITE SOX, 2005 WAS NOT AN END, but a beginning. Not the culmination, but a launching pad. Ask anyone in the team's organization about winning that World Series, and the first thing you'll hear is how important it is to do it again. Achievement trumps satisfaction, hunger dominates complacency, and results are worth more than promise.

At various places in U.S. Cellular Field, the White Sox's mission statement is prominently displayed:

Passion—for the game, for the fans of the game, for winning.
Pride—in our city, in our community, in our championships, in winning.
Tradition—of passion, of pride, of commitment, of winning.

Those words are not peppy slogans dreamed up by a marketing firm. It's the way the Sox play the game and run the franchise at every turn. It's a code of responsibility for anyone wearing a White Sox uniform and the hallmark of one of baseball's most respected franchises.

It's the responsibility that comes with the history of a team that had an incredible run of 17 straight winning seasons, from 1951 to 1967. With seven out of 10 in the first decade of the new century, things are off to a good start. It's a place where loyalty is not blind, but is highly valued and used to build on the successes of the past. White Sox baseball is the fire of Ozzie Guillen, the grace of Billy Pierce, the strength of Harold Baines, the courage of Minnie Minoso, the quickness of Luis Aparicio, the power of Frank Thomas, and the guile of Mark Buehrle. These men and many others were kind enough to talk about their time on the South Side, and their stories paint the true picture of what the White Sox are all about.

These good guys wear black, play grinder ball, and will win or die trying. It's in their DNA, and their fans—from the president of the United States to the mayor of Chicago to anyone who has ever sat in the upper deck—expect no less each and every day. Ed Farmer grew up rooting for the White Sox, pitched for them for several years, and now calls their games on the radio, so he understands better than most. "It goes with the territory here," he said. "These fans demand excellence. That's as it should be." It's White Sox baseball. In the stories that follow, you'll see why.

WHAT IT MEANS TO BE A WHITE SOX

The
FORTIES

BILLY PIERCE

PITCHER

1949–1961

IWAS WITH THE TIGERS, AND THEY TRADED ME to the White Sox before the '49 season. I was very disappointed. There was a reason for my disappointment, though. When I was with the Tigers in 1948 and we came to Chicago to play the White Sox, at night the aroma from the stockyards was terrible! I had talked to the Tigers and told them there were only two teams I didn't want to go to: Philadelphia, because the fans were tough; and Chicago, because the smell was terrible. I said that was one place I didn't want to go. Now, as the years went on, it was one of the greatest ballparks ever, but not in 1948.

In 1951 Minnie Minoso joined us. We already had Chico Carrasquel and Nellie Fox for a couple of years. Our team materialized into a team that thought we could win. We had good pitching, we had good defense, and we had speed. That's when people started to call us "Go-Go." People think of the '59 team as the "Go-Go Sox," but it really started in '51. It was a team that was in first place at the All-Star break over the Yankees, who were always the team to beat in those years. Frank Lane got us more different ballplayers than you can remember. When the June trading deadline came, you never unpacked your bags because you didn't know who might be gone. [Pitching coach] Ray Berres had a cottage, and a bunch of us went up there on an off-day. We got back and said, "What happened?" only to find out two guys had been traded. That year was the start of the good White Sox teams of the '50s.

2

You build a ballclub one way or another, and in Comiskey Park at that time, it was a park built for singles and speed. The fences were a long way away, and we didn't have too many guys who could hit them. The only team that could was the Yankees in those days. We knew that. I've always said, when you know you are not going to get too many runs, you are pitching hard to every batter. I think it makes you a better pitcher, without a question.

In 1955 I lost four games 1–0, two of them in one week. One of my proudest things in baseball was my earned-run average that year of 1.97. I was the only pitcher with an ERA under 2.00 for a good period of years there. You remember certain things, and that was one I've always been proud of.

The Yankees series were always great. We'd have 50,000 plus there. People would be crammed in the aisles because there were not the fire laws we have today. The fans were on our side, and it was always exciting. They were the great Yankees, and we were the underdogs. It was like the World Series.

I pitched against Whitey Ford many times. I think someone figured out I ended up with a 9–6 record against him. The Yankees beat me more than I beat them, but I happened to beat Whitey more times. It's was always a challenge pitching against Whitey Ford, but I always tell everyone it was the other eight guys that were the challenge, because Whitey wasn't a good hitter! They were fun games because the atmosphere was so great. The fans were right there, and you couldn't ask for anything more.

It was also a great thrill to start the All-Star Game three times. My first one was in 1953, and my wife was having our first child at the time. To get into the game was one thing, but to be selected to start was really the culmination of my goals in pitching. Then to be able to start the 1955 and '56 games was also a big thrill each time.

On June 27, 1958, I had a perfect game going into the ninth against the Senators. It was a 1–0 game, but we scored two runs in the eighth. I got the first two hitters out in the ninth, and the pitcher's spot was coming up, so they put in a pinch-hitter. I knew Ed Fitz Gerald was a first-ball, fastball hitter, so Sherm Lollar called for a curveball, and I threw it down and away. Fitz Gerald reached out and hit it for a double down the right-field line. I remember Albie Pearson came up next, and I struck him out, so there was no perfect game and no no-hitter, but I did win a shutout. We were happy to win that game, but as the years go by, I would have picked a different pitch to throw.

4

Pitchers Billy Pierce (left) and Early Wynn talk prior to the 1958 All-Star Game at Memorial Stadium in Baltimore. Pierce established himself as one of the premier pitchers in the American League, compiling a 186–152 record with a 3.19 ERA over 13 seasons with the White Sox.

I was fortunate to have Carrasquel, Aparicio, and Fox behind me, but also guys like Jim Landis and Jim Rivera in the outfield. You can't just have good infielders, you need that outfield help, and we had a great defensive package over the years. When you're a pitcher, you can't ask for much more. When the ball is hit, there's a good chance it will be caught. Back in those days, our guys would do anything they could do to catch the ball, and that's all you could ask for. They would dive for it, Jim Landis would climb the fence, Rivera would make catches like he did in the World Series, and Luis and Nellie would turn double plays. They did everything you would want them to do. Being a pitcher, you know the guys behind you would give you everything they had.

I wasn't big, but there were a lot a players like me. Heck, Whitey Ford was even shorter than me. Bobby Shantz was quite little. It's not always about size. Today they say you can only throw 100 pitches. I pitched 16 innings one time and must have thrown 160 pitches. I had 193 complete games. That's just the way it was. It's changed now. I can see what they're doing with setup men, but I can't get it in my mind that when a guy pitches six innings, it's a quality start. That's hard for me to hear, the word "quality" there, because when we got the ball, we would keep it until the game ended. There are some great pitchers now, but I was really thrilled in 2005 when the White Sox pitchers had four straight complete games in the playoffs. It proved it can be done.

We always had tough teams around us in Cleveland and New York, and there were many times when we lost the pennant in the last month of the season. Nineteen fifty-nine was a different year. We beat Cleveland four in a row in a big series there, and I'll never forget the night when we clinched. They had a man on in the ninth with Vic Power up, who always hit great against us. Gerry Staley was out on the mound, and Power hit it good but right at Luis, who stepped on second base, threw it to first, and we won the pennant.

For a moment there, it was, "What?" then, "Oh man, we won the pennant!" I was warming up because Tito Francona was up next and I thought I might have to pitch to him if Power did something. But the double play ended the game, and we won the pennant.

When the Sox won the World Series in 2005, the whole South Side was very excited. That's where I live, and to see our team win the Series after all those years, you can't ask for anything more. The way they won it in four straight was great. It takes the breaks and things to fall right. They won the

5

close ballgames and there was a lot of similarities between the '59 team and that team in how we won one-run games. That's what it takes to win.

When they dedicated a statue of me at U.S. Cellular Field, it was one of the proudest days of my life. Naturally, getting married, having my children and grandchildren—nothing can beat that. Now my grandchildren can go out and see my statue, and that's big. I'm very thankful to the ballclub for doing it. It's something that will be there for a long time that my kids can see, and it's a big thrill, no doubt about it.

Being associated with the White Sox, I think about how our team materialized in the '50s and then winning the pennant in 1959. Since I quit playing baseball, they retired my number and then put my statue up. What more could a ballplayer ask for? They have done more for me than I could ever ask for. I'm just thankful now that the aroma from the stockyards is gone and I came over here to play for the White Sox. It's the greatest break I ever had.

Billy Pierce came to the White Sox from the Detroit Tigers before the 1949 season and quickly established himself as one of the premier pitchers in the American League. The southpaw compiled a 186–152 record with a 3.19 ERA while anchoring the Sox staff for 13 seasons. He posted back-to-back 20-win seasons in 1956 and 1957 and led the American League with a 1.97 ERA in 1955 (his record was only 15–10 due to the fact that he lost four 1–0 games that year). Pierce pitched in four All-Star Games (seven selections) for the American League, starting three times (1953, 1955, and 1956).

In 1987 his No. 19 was retired by the team, and in 2000 Pierce was elected to the White Sox Team of the Century. On July 23, 2007, a statue of Pierce was dedicated on the center-field concourse at U.S Cellular Field. He is still with the Sox as a community relations representative.

The
FIFTIES

MINNIE MINOSO

OUTFIELDER

1951–1957 ★ 1960–1961 ★ 1964 ★ 1976 ★ 1980

IT SEEMS LIKE JUST YESTERDAY TO ME when I came to the White Sox. It was May 1, 1951, against New York, and I was playing third base. I had always been Orestes Minoso, but from that day on I was "Minnie." Who changed it? I don't know. I've become a citizen and changed everything to Minnie Minoso.

Some people take life for granted, but I want to appreciate everything I've been given. First, I would have to thank the great fans for everything, because you can't do anything without them. They make you behave yourself when you think of the fans. You'll behave yourself if you think of them. I think that always helped me, and I want to thank the fans for that.

My first at-bat was here in Chicago in 1951. The batter in front of me got a base hit. I came to the plate in the first inning and hit one out of the ballpark for a home run. We lost the game to the Yankees 8–3, but I enjoyed it so much. I said, "What did I do?"

In the beginning, I thought the whole world was against me. They didn't have any other black ballplayers here. I was never afraid, though. I would always think that I could do anything I had to do. I would take it like a man. They hated me and called me names, but I never did anything about it. I remember getting hit with a pitch one time, and it hurt, but I wasn't about to show it. I picked up the ball, and the pitcher yelled, "Don't throw the ball back to me." I said, "You can't hurt me with that garbage you throw." It did hurt, but I wasn't going to show it. If you cried, you were giving in. This is the way it used to be, and I am proud. I still thank God every day for giving me the assistance not to fight or go after anybody. I don't think people wanted to see that.

It was tough not to be Rookie of the Year that year. I won't criticize anybody for that, but I might hurt inside. Too many times they give these awards to guys who played on the winning team and not to the player who had individual accomplishments. What can you do? The writers gave it to Gil McDougald of the Yankees because the writers were from New York. The *Sporting News* gave me a trophy for their Rookie of the Year. You have to be the best ballplayer you can, and the fans will know. The White Sox gave me a day in my honor, anyway.

I used to write letters to Frank Lane for my contract. I'd call him "Papa Number 2." You didn't have any agents at that time, and he was the general manager. I hired my cousin to write the letter. In my second year we traded letters, and then Frank came to Cuba, where I was playing winter ball. I came running in from left field, and he had the contract there for me. I was making $7,000 my first year and wanted $20,000. He offered $17,000. He told me that's all they could give me. I told him if they gave me $20,000, they would never have to give me another raise. He wouldn't do that and told me I would have many more good years. I signed it, but they gave me bonuses of a couple hundred dollars when I hit a home run or got a game-winning hit. I probably got another $6,000 in bonuses. He was always good to me.

I would get closer to the plate, stay there, and wait for one pitch. Sometimes pitchers would hit me and try to move me back. Pitchers today do the best they can from the middle of the plate out, but no one pitches inside. There's only a few. Randy Johnson and Pedro Martinez are about the only guys I see lately who will take the inside part of the plate. You're not trying to hurt anybody, but the pitcher needs that half of the plate. If they come inside, batters shouldn't think they have to go fight.

On the bases, I always had the green light. You have to take the same lead, whether you are going to steal or not. I'd get on first base, and the crowd would chant, "Go, Minnie, Go!" I had pretty good speed, but it had to be the right time. You can't steal bases for yourself, it has to be when it can help the team. Nothing makes me madder than to see someone steal third with two outs or other plays like that. Getting into scoring position by stealing second, that's what it was about. I respected the game.

Outfielder Minnie Minoso (left) and owner Bill Veeck enjoy a laugh in the Comiskey Park dugout in 1957.

I was traded to Cleveland in 1958. I was supposed to come back in 1959, but they didn't do the deal until the next year. I gave Cleveland 100 percent and always respected the uniform I wore. When I came back the next year, Bill Veeck gave me a World Series ring, and I still have it.

My first day I came back was Opening Day in 1960, and I'll never forget it. It was a back-and-forth game. I hit a grand-slam home run in the fourth inning to give us a big lead. The Athletics came back and kept getting runs until it was a tie game. In the bottom of the ninth, I led off. I worked the count to 3–0 before I watched a strike go by. Then I hit a 3–1 pitch into the upper deck to win the game. I came back to Chicago and hit two home runs! People said, "That's our man!" I still am.

I'll never forget Comiskey Park because that's where I started. You can never forget a place like that. You can't compare old parks to new parks. We had one of the greatest parks of all time.

As for the Hall of Fame, I want to know why through three committees—the writers, the veterans, and the special Negro Leagues committees—what reason they have for not naming me. What did I do wrong? There are a few guys with fewer years and less records than I have who were named to Cooperstown. I won't mention names out of respect. What's the matter with me and what did I do wrong? I want to be in Cooperstown. Compare my record to the different people there.

Jerry Reinsdorf called me "Mr. White Sox," and that was nice. Now I have people come up to me and want me to sign things with "Mr. White Sox." I've never changed. I'm the same guy who used to work on a ranch and played ball—I'm the same guy I've always been. I'm going to die in this organization and am happy to be here until my last day.

In many ways, the arrival of the Go-Go Sox coincided with the arrival of Orestes "Minnie" Minoso, who broke the White Sox's color barrier in 1951 after being acquired from the Cleveland Indians. The young outfielder burst onto the scene with a .324 average, 31 steals, and 74 RBIs. Minoso led the American League in steals his first three seasons and put together his finest year in 1954, with 19 homers, 116 RBIs, 119 runs, and a .320 batting average. He was an American League All-Star with the Sox from 1951 through 1954, 1957, and 1960. He also made the team while with the Indians in 1959. He won three Gold Gloves in 1957, 1959, and 1960. (The Gold Glove awards didn't originate until 1957, or Minoso would have undoubtedly won more.)

Minoso was traded back to the Indians along with Fred Hatfield on December 4, 1957, in exchange for Early Wynn and Al Smith. He was traded to the Sox again on December 6, 1959, along with three other players for Norm Cash, Johnny Romano, and Bubba Phillips. The Sox traded Minoso to St. Louis on November 27, 1961, for Joe Cunningham and signed him again on April 8, 1964, before releasing him in July of that year. Bill Veeck arranged for Minoso to play several games as a designated hitter in 1976 and again in 1980 to allow him to be a five-decade major leaguer.

Minoso's No. 9 was retired by the White Sox in 1983, and he was named to the Team of the Century in 2000. On September 19, 2004, the White Sox unveiled a statue of Minoso in the center-field concourse at U.S. Cellular Field. He works with the Sox as a community relations representative.

JIM RIVERA

OUTFIELDER

1952–1961

ROGERS HORNSBY WAS THE MANAGER of the St. Louis Browns at the time, and Mr. Veeck owned the Sox. The White Sox needed a catcher, so they traded me for Sherm Lollar, then bought me back, and that's how I got back to the White Sox.

Playing the Yankees in those days was always tough, and it was the same with the Cleveland Indians. If you could get one game out of three, it was cause for celebration at the time. Playing at Comiskey Park was fantastic. You could see the game no matter where you sat. Everybody enjoyed coming there, plus we had a good team with the Go-Go Sox. Everybody hustled, and the people wanted to see what kind of ballplayers we were.

The name "Jungle Jim" was given to me by Howie Robbins of the *Chicago Sun-Times*. We were playing the Dodgers in spring training down in Vero Beach. In those days, it was [Minnie] Minoso, [Luis] Aparicio, and me, and every time we got on base, we could steal on our own without permission from Al Lopez. Don Newcombe was pitching, and I knew he didn't have a good curveball, but he had a good slider and fastball. I was waiting for the slider and got on base with a single. Now, when I got on base, I was swinging my arms, and the guy said, "Look at him. He looks like he's in the jungle."

I was good at stealing and wasn't afraid to slide. I was one of the first to slide head-first, which I started doing in the minors. What happened was one day we were playing in San Diego, and I hit a ball to left-center field. When

As a member of the Go-Go Sox, Jim Rivera led the American League with 25 stolen bases in 1955.

I came around first base, I saw the ball coming in on the left, so I dove to the right side of the bag. The second baseman turned around, and I wasn't there, I was on the other side. It was so easy and nice.

I always had the thought that if I could steal second, a single got me in. In those days, the White Sox were hitless and not a good hitting team at all. We'd get someone on, and then Nellie Fox or Aparicio would get them over or we would steal second base. Then Sherm Lollar or Larry Doby would get a single to drive them in. We had to make our own runs.

In 1959 we were feeling kind of high. We had been in second or third place every year and then ended up playing the Dodgers in the World Series.

I was really proud of the clinching game in Cleveland, because that night Al Smith was batting in front of me and hit a home run to put us up two runs. Then I came up and hit a home run off Mudcat Grant, and our homers clinched the pennant. That was the greatest thrill I ever had. The reception when we got back was fantastic. Everybody was blowing horns, and there were firecrackers going off. It's a wonder somebody didn't shoot somebody, but everybody had a ball.

In the Series, [Sandy] Koufax, [Don] Drysdale, all those guys made for a great team. I think we could have beaten them if they played in a regular park, because we were hitting the ball off the fence in left field, but it was so short, as a runner you couldn't go from first to third. You had to stop at second base. We lost three games where Larry Sherry was pitching against us in relief, all of them on double-play balls.

In Game 5 I did make a great catch. The inning before, Al Lopez took out Al Smith, who had been in right, because the Dodgers started a left-hander. Since I hit lefty, I wasn't in there. I was on the bench, and Lopez took Smith and put him in left field and then put me in the game in right field. Charlie Neal was up, and I knew him from playing winter ball in Puerto Rico. He hit a lot of balls to right-center field and center field and was not a pull hitter. Bob Shaw was pitching, and Neal hit one to right-center. I was lucky enough to make that catch and save the game. We won it 1–0.

We opened in D.C. in 1961, and I caught the first ball thrown out by President Kennedy. Hank Aguirre was in front of me. All the presidents who threw the ball from the seats could hardly get it anywhere. I watched enough TV to know that President Kennedy had played plenty of touch football. I knew he could throw. When they told everybody to get out on the field because the president was going to throw out the first ball, there was Hank in front of me, and he was 6'5". I couldn't see the president at all, but I was waving. I knew he would throw it long, so I moved back. Here came the ball, Aguirre jumped up, but I pushed him and caught the ball! I ran in, and the

FBI guys stopped me and said, "Hey, Jungle, where are you going?" I told them I wanted the president to sign the ball for me, so they said it was okay. It's a true story—he signed the ball for me, and I said, "Is that your signature? It don't look too good." Vice president Johnson signed it, too, so I ended up with two presidents' signatures on it.

Manuel "Jungle Jim" Rivera was signed by the White Sox on July 23, 1951, traded to the Browns in November, then returned to the White Sox on July 28, 1952. His reckless head-first slides wowed the Comiskey crowds, as did his unmatched play in right and center field. His best offensive year was in 1953, when he hit .259 with 11 homers, had 78 RBIs, scored 79 runs, and led the American League with 16 triples. Rivera was a natural spark plug as one of the most important cogs of the Go-Go Sox and led the American League with 25 stolen bases in 1955. He was released by the White Sox on June 10, 1961.

LUIS APARICIO

SHORTSTOP

1956–1962 ★ 1968–1970

I CAME FROM A BASEBALL FAMILY. Both my father and uncle played in Venezuela. One thing I can never forget is my mother when I told her I was going to quit school and be a ballplayer like my father. She said, "If you want to go be a ballplayer, fine, but don't ever be No. 2 to anybody." That's one thing I never forgot.

I got a lot of help from all the people at spring training. Everybody was very nice to me and tried to take care of me. I didn't have any trouble with anybody, and they got me used to it.

It was hard to replace Chico [Carrasquel]. He was the guy who helped me out more than anybody else in baseball. Frank Lane used to be the general manager of the White Sox, and Chico was the shortstop. I was supposed to sign with Cleveland. When he saw me, his opinion was that I was too small for baseball. Chico told Mr. Lane that he had a kid in Venezuela who he knew could play the game. I was very happy to sign with the White Sox.

At home, we used to play baseball in the street whenever we had the chance. The police were chasing me all over! I think that's where I got my speed, running away from the police. I was a lucky man because of all that came to me. When I got the opportunity, I did my best. I never forgot that I was never going to be No. 2 to anybody. In Memphis in 1955, my second year in the United States, I was in the Double A league. I was always running since I was a kid. The other players on the team really helped me.

16

I got a lot of help from everybody, not just Nellie [Fox]. Sherm Lollar used to be our catcher, and his locker was next to mine. He was always talking to me, and I tried to listen and do the best I could with whatever he told me. Chico was the one. He took me under his arm like I was his son. I told myself I would try to do the best I could for him.

My first manager was Marty Marion, and the first time he saw me, I had a little problem trying to get the ball out of my glove on a double play. He got my glove and said, "That is too big a glove." Then, boom, he threw it away. He got me a smaller glove, and it took me a little time to get adjusted to it. I asked him why [I had to have a new glove], and he told me I was taking too much time to get the ball out of my glove because it was too big. I didn't feel it when I got the ball, but when I got the small glove, I knew right where the ball was.

I was in a ballpark in Caracas when I was named Rookie of the Year. It shocked me. There were so many guys fighting for it. They said, well, the guy from Venezuela got it. I was in the ballpark, and there were about 25,000 people there. It was like the end of the world!

Everybody tried to beat the Yankees, but to me, everybody was the same. I got some really good advice from a second baseman named Billy Martin. Everybody was running into me at second base to try and stop the double play. The way they would do it was to hit me. Billy said, "Kid, you're going to have to learn how to throw the ball from down here. When you hit one or two guys, they're going to leave you alone. They will slide way before they get to you." So I hit a couple of guys with my throws, including Mickey Mantle, and then there were no more slides into me at second base.

In 1959 we got to my first World Series. Everybody tried to win. We didn't have many good hitters. Well, there were good hitters, but we had no power. We just played good baseball and had a great manager who was really smart.

Everybody was excited to win the pennant. We had some veteran guys like Lollar, Early Wynn, Jim Rivera, and we had some young kids, too. They told them how to act, and we went to Cleveland to play the game. I just tried to get a cab and get home quick. It was 2:00 or 3:00 in the morning. I've never seen so many people that early in the morning on the street. It was really nice.

When we got to the World Series, we had never seen the guys before. They told us they were going to be tough and their pitching was tough. You had to beat [Don] Drysdale, [Sandy] Koufax, all those guys, and we got beat.

Luis Aparicio's best offensive season was in 1959, when he scored 98 runs, and finished second to his infield companion, Nellie Fox, in the AL MVP voting.

The second time I faced them I was with the Orioles, and we beat them four in a row.

I liked everything at old Comiskey. As soon as I got my uniform on, I forgot about everything and just thought about the game.

When I was traded to the Orioles, it was hard for me because I was raised in this organization. I had played a lot of years in the big leagues before I got traded. When I got traded, a couple of the older guys told me it would be hard, but that I'd get along with my new teammates. Brooksie [Robinson] tried to be familiar with everybody, and it was fine.

When I was traded back to Chicago, everybody was fine. When I came back here, it was like I came back home. At Comiskey, when they put the turf on the infield, we worked out on it a couple times before the season started. The only difference I saw was that the ball got to you too quickly. I tried to find out how I was going to do it, so I played a little deeper. I always had a strong arm, so it was no problem.

It was luck that I never got hurt. I played every day, and that's what you do in the big leagues. I never got hurt badly. I broke my finger, but it didn't stop me from playing. It's unbelievable. I didn't know baseball could be so good to you. Everybody still knows me. When I go through the airport, they look at me and say, "I've seen that face before." We're just human beings. God gave me something, and I took it.

Chicago has really great fans. They get to you. I don't want to speak for everybody, but when you see fans like that, you just go break your head for them. That's what I think. I think everybody thinks the same way. Every game was great for me, and I thank God for giving me the chance to play this game.

Luis Aparicio was signed by the White Sox as a free agent in 1954 and took over the starting shortstop position from fellow Venezuelan Chico Carrasquel in 1956. Aparicio was the American League Rookie of the Year and immediately put the "go" in the Go-Go Sox by leading the American League in steals for the next nine seasons.

He was traded to the Orioles along with Al Smith on January 14, 1963, in exchange for Pete Ward, Hoyt Wilhelm, Dave Nicholson, and Ron Hansen and won a World Series with the O's in 1966. He returned to the Sox on November 29, 1967, along with John Matias and Russ Snyder in exchange for Don Buford, Bruce Howard, and Roger Nelson. He hit .264, .280, and .313 for the Sox in his three return seasons on the South Side. On December 1, 1970, he was traded to the Red Sox for Mike Andrews and Luis Alvarado and played three seasons in Boston before retiring. Aparicio won nine Gold Gloves in his career and appeared on 10 American League All-Star teams.

Aparicio was inducted into the Hall of Fame in 1984, and his No. 11 was retired by the Sox that year. In 2000 he was named to the White Sox Team of the Century, and in 2006 the team dedicated a statue at U.S. Cellular Field featuring Aparicio and Fox turning a double play.

AL LOPEZ

MANAGER

1957–1965 ★ 1968–1969

THERE WERE TWO CLUBS THAT I ALWAYS PULLED FOR: one was Chicago and the other was Cleveland. Both were clubs that I managed, and I managed with nice people who were fine people to work for. The fans were good to me in both Cleveland and Chicago.

They started the Go-Go Sox even when Paul Richards was there. They had Minoso and Jim Rivera, and they were running guys. After we came there, we kind of capitalized on that. I think it helped our attendance quite a lot, and the people liked it. I did, too. I like that kind of baseball, instead of just the one pop out of the ballpark. It's exciting to see the home run, but the guy just jogs around. I'd rather see a triple, myself, because the ball is in play all the time.

When I went to Chicago, we had some really fine ballplayers already on the club. We had [Sherm]Lollar and [Luis] Aparicio and [Nellie] Fox, who were three outstanding ballplayers. We had really good pitching and were lucky enough to acquire Early Wynn and Al Smith from the Cleveland club for Minnie Minoso, and that made us a better ballclub when we won the pennant in 1959. We came up with a young boy named Jim Landis in center field who really gave us strong defense down the middle for good protection. We made a deal for a boy by the name of Bob Shaw who really helped us that year. We didn't expect any wins, and I think he won 18 games for us that year.

Manager Al Lopez managed the Sox for a total of 11 seasons, compiling 840 wins against 650 losses for a .564 winning percentage.

Shortstop is a very important position. You have to have a guy who's very steady at shortstop, and we had Aparicio. It's one of the key positions on a baseball club. You have to have good defense to have good pitching.

We had only one guy in the lineup who had a little power, and that was Sherm Lollar, who hit fourth for us. Outside of that, we depended mostly on speed. We adjusted because that was our club. We'd try to get Aparicio on one way or another, then would give Nellie Fox a take sign until Luis had the chance to steal second base. It was like a two-base hit every time he got on. I think he stole almost 60 bases that year and almost never got thrown out, which was tremendous. We'd wait until he got the chance to steal, because we had him on his own. Whenever he felt like he had a jump, he would go.

I'd have to give Nellie the take sign, because he was always ready to hit. He'd go after the first pitch he could unload on, so we would have to make him take pitches. It was successful and proved to be really good. We had a lot of one-run ballgames, and I think that's why my stomach still bothers me! It turned out all right, though. That was a wonderful year. I wish we could have won the World Series.

From 1949 to 1964, only two teams interrupted the Yankees' inevitable march to the American League pennant, and both were managed by former major league catcher Al Lopez, who won the title with Cleveland in 1954 and the White Sox in 1959.

"El Señor" was hired by the White Sox in 1957, and his first two teams won 90 and 82 games while finishing second. In 1959 he led the Sox to a 94–60 record, and their first World Series since 1919, where they lost to the Los Angeles Dodgers 4–2. Over the next six seasons, his teams never won fewer than 85 games. In 1963 they began a three-year stretch where they won 94, 98, and 95 games, yet were second each year.

He returned to the Sox in 1968 for a short stint, managing 47 games in 1968 and 17 in 1969 before retiring. He also played 19 seasons as a player, from 1928 through 1947, and caught a then-record 1,918 games. Lopez was elected to the Baseball Hall of Fame in 1977 by the Veterans Committee. In 2000 he was named the manager of the White Sox Team of the Century. He died on October 30, 2005, in Tampa at the age of 97, just four days after the White Sox won the World Series.

This interview was done for WGN-TV in September 1983 and is used with permission.

JIM LANDIS
OUTFIELDER
1957–1964

I WAS FORTUNATE TO END UP A CHICAGO WHITE SOX. In our day, there was no draft. I wanted to go to junior college to further my education and, actually, I wanted to be a P.E. teacher. I went to junior college in Richmond, California, and heck, we only played about six baseball games that first year, but a White Sox scout was following us early in the season. He came up to me and asked me if I wanted to play some pro ball. I'd said, "Yeah. Who for?" He told me it was the White Sox, and right then and there I was signing. Let me tell you, in those days I got a big fat bonus of $2,500, and, boy, was I thrilled!

I started as a third baseman. That's where I played all through my high school career. I started in Class D baseball in Wisconsin Rapids. That's right, people don't remember we went all the way down to Class D ball, but I played third that first year. I'm not really sure who in the organization thought I should go to the outfield. I went to spring training with the Class A team, and Don Gutteridge—it might have been he who decided to move me, but I don't remember—was there coaching. When they changed me, there was a guy there named Johnny Mostil, who had been a great center fielder with the White Sox and was then a roving scout. And all spring, he and Gutteridge worked my fanny off, day in and day out. There were a few times somebody had to come out and tell them, "Hey, the kid's had enough."

They worked me to death, and I was thinking some of the time, *What's going on here?* But as I look back, that was the key to my success.

After playing a season in D ball and one in A ball, I went into the service for two years. I was at Fort Ord and was on a championship Army team. We won the all-service series, but Billy Martin did something, and next thing I knew, Congress decided that everybody who had nine months to go in the service had to be transferred. I didn't go overseas but got sent to Alaska. I don't know whether that was lucky or not, but I played some ball up there. When I came out of the service, I went into Double A ball.

When I got to the big leagues in 1957, I would say that in my first game I didn't even realize where I was. I was so nervous, it was unbelievable, and to top it off, I had to face a tough left-hander in the late Herb Score. He only threw about 100 mph! I think I popped up weakly, struck out, and although we won the game, I went to the clubhouse thinking, *My God, I'd better get my lunch pail ready. If this is the big leagues, I'm in trouble.* I was definitely out of my league with Herb Score. That was before the accident where he got hit in the eye with a line drive. He had won 16 as a rookie and 20 the next year, so he was a great star at that time.

Fortunately, it got a lot easier after that. It took me a while to wake up, but maybe it took me a lot longer than it should have. They sent me out to Triple A that first season to get me going again, but when I came back the next year, I stayed, and everything started to happen. I was in right field at first. Larry Doby was our center fielder at the time, so I started in right field, but before too long, they traded Larry and moved me over to center.

We had no idea what we were going to do in 1959. Our skipper, Al Lopez, made a few remarks about how confident he was in our ballclub. As a player, especially at that particular time, you had to know how darn good the Yankees were. They were winning it every single year, so we didn't know if we were as good as the Yankees. But we found out by playing some pretty good baseball early and felt more and more confident as the season went along. That Yankees club that we beat out that year was the same one that had been winning and then won the pennant the next year. I don't think we were lucky. At the time, I said "Wow," but as I look back at our club, we sure had a great team with some really good pitching.

Cleveland was our big rival that year. Luckily, we had a really good record against them, and that was really our winning margin for the pennant. At the end of August, we went in there and swept a four-game series. When you

Jim Landis' best offensive season was in 1961, when he hit 22 homers, drove in 85 runs, and finished with a .283 average.

talk about confidence—not being cocky but confident—that's when we really took off. Everybody knows we weren't a great hitting ballclub: get on with a bunt, move the runner along, hit a sacrifice fly—that's how we did it. I think we won something like 35 one-run games. If you do that, you know you've got darned good pitching and defense. We managed to score enough runs to win those games.

I had a really good game in that Cleveland series, and there was one play I remember where I went from first to third on a single to left. You don't normally do that, and I was thinking, *What did I just do?* It was a big play of the ballgame because Minnie Minoso was in left, and when he booted the ball, I scored the winning run on that play.

It was poetic justice that we clinched the pennant in Cleveland, and there was no greater thing than the welcome we got coming home that night. The fans were all out at the airport to meet us. What a great feeling that was.

The World Series didn't come too fast after that, in fact, it was probably the opposite. I wish we had started the Series sooner, but the Dodgers and Milwaukee Braves had a playoff. I've always felt that if we could have gone right at it, that would have helped, because it took some of our edge off. I'm not trying to make excuses, because they beat us, but that delay hurt.

The Dodgers had great pitching. I faced Sandy Koufax in that series and played with him in winter ball in Puerto Rico. We had rooms next to each other and were together a lot, then I ended up facing him in the World Series. He was only 8–6 that year, but it was proved then and later on what a talent he turned out to be.

Playing in the Coliseum in Los Angeles was hell. Fifty-some rows up and there was no hitting background in center field. It was a devil to play there and to see there. I actually lost a fly ball that hit me in the toe and was lucky it hit me there. It was tough to hit, because all you could see were white shirts in the outfield behind the pitcher.

Johnny Podres hit me in the head in Game 6 of the World Series. He really hit me square, and I lay there for a while before I got up. Everything turned out, but I was shocked to find out later that he was throwing at me. He told me later when I saw him and he was a pitching coach for the Phillies that he felt like he needed to shake their ballclub up in a fashion. Well, it sure shook me up.

I wasn't a natural center fielder. I worked on it, going from that first spring where Gutteridge and Mostil had me working on all kinds of different things. I always worked on going back to the fence each way, all kinds of stuff. Whatever it was, I went through every drill I could to get better.

I loved playing at Comiskey. The size of the ballpark and the dimensions were great. Of course, the walls were concrete, but you can't have everything. Yankee Stadium was hard, because there were certain places, like in left-center, where you'd have to run forever. Center field was deep, too. The walls wouldn't goof you up, it was just covering all that territory. At the end of my career, I played in the Astrodome. They had a hard time at first with the roof and covering it with a paint so you could see the ball. A lot of players were losing fly balls there. You had to be careful trying to cut off a ball because of the turf, and you pretty much had to head straight to the wall any time one was hit to the gap. I stood in left field one day with another guy during batting practice, and we were rolling balls to first base. I couldn't believe how the ball just kept going and going and going. You had to learn pretty fast there.

Playing in the 1962 All-Star Game in Washington was special for me. Both teams stayed in the same hotel, so I went out to get on the bus, and I looked up to see my idol, Stan Musial, sitting there. Man, I jumped into the seat next to him and spent the ride out to the ballpark rattling his brain and trying to learn. What a wonderful feeling that was! The other thing that was funny that day was that, when I did get in to hit, I faced my old friend and teammate, Bob Shaw. That was a weird feeling.

Nineteen sixty-four was a hard one to take. We won a lot of games at the end of the season but still finished one game behind the Yankees. Moose Skowron is my friend, and had so many rings with the Yankees right up until 1962, then he won it with the Dodgers in '63, and he was with us and we lost it by one game. He was a little sad about that one, and I don't blame him.

I never hated anybody as a player. In our day, you got fined for talking to players on other teams. I played with Roger Maris and John Blanchard of the Yankees when we were all in the minors. I would sneak into their clubhouse early sometimes to shoot the breeze with them. Heck, I'll admit, I was in awe of Mickey Mantle and some of the things he did. One time I was in center field and I heard his bat break, then watched as the ball went out for a home run that had to go at least 385 feet.

I had so many great teammates. One of my favorite roommates was Sammy Esposito, a reserve infielder, who was a really class guy. Nellie Fox, Billy Pierce, Jim Rivera, Minnie Minoso—all those guys were so darned good to me. They were all older than I was and they all took care of me. It was just a great, great group of guys. We'd be on the road, get dressed after a game, and before you knew it, eight or 10 guys would all go to dinner together.

They had a nice deal in Chicago for those of us who were named to the White Sox Team of the Century. I looked around, and it was a great feeling to see so many of my teammates with me on that team. When they won it in 2005, the Sox invited some of us back for the first two home games of the World Series. That was a nice feeling, and it was extra nice for me because my son Craig is an agent, and Paul Konerko and Jon Garland were his clients. That was an extra good feeling to see them do so well, especially when Konerko hit that grand slam. More importantly, it was time for the White Sox to break through and win the whole thing. That was great.

Jim Landis patrolled center field for the White Sox as one of the premier defensive outfielders in baseball from 1957 through 1964. He won five consecutive Gold Gloves for outfield play in 1960 through 1964 and was an American League All-Star in 1962. He hit .292 with six runs scored in the 1959 World Series.

The Sox traded Landis to the Kansas City Athletics on January 20, 1965, as part of a three-team trade with the Athletics and Indians that brought Tommy John and Tommie Agee to the White Sox. Landis played with the Cleveland Indians in 1966, then finished his career with Houston, Detroit, and Boston in 1967. In 2000 he was elected to the White Sox Team of the Century.

JIM McANANY

OUTFIELDER

1958–1960

MY FIRST GAME WAS AGAINST THE YANKEES, and Whitey Ford was pitching. I got my first hit off him. Needless to say, my legs were shaking when I got into the box. On the first ball I played in the outfield, I threw Bill Skowron out at home plate, so that was a good start. Back then, you had better perform or you were out of there. It was like hallowed ground when the Yankees came to play. It was a thrill. My dad used to say that I'd rather be lucky and have sawdust for brains. It worked out well. I started out good, and that's the important thing.

I lockered between Nellie Fox and Sherm Lollar. That was a great experience for me. Both of them were such class guys and really helped me out, as did all the guys on the team at the time. Early Wynn and all those guys took me under their wings and made it so much easier for me. We were never in a hurry to get out of the clubhouse. We talked over the game and what we could do to improve. We were really a close group of guys and really didn't have stars. Everybody just did their job, no matter what it took.

I knew my job was going to alternate with Jim Rivera. He would face right-handers, and I would face left-handers. That worked out great. I had the role of hitting eighth, and my job was to get the pitcher out of the way that inning. Mr. Lopez didn't want the pitcher leading off an inning, so he would say, "I don't care what you do, just get on base or do what you have to do." Hit and run, moving the runners over, that was critical. We'd get a

Jim McAnany (seated) joins teammates (from left) Jim Rivera, Luis Aparicio, Jim Landis, and Billy Pierce at a 50th reunion for the 1959 White Sox at U.S. Cellular Field. *Photo courtesy of Bob Vorwald*

run, and our trainer would say the gloves would come out of the ground. That's how we approached it—one game at a time and one play at a time. Just do your job.

At Comiskey, the fans were great. You could stand out in right field and smell the hot dogs. That's the one thing I remember is how that smell permeated through the grandstand. I loved it.

My favorite game in 1959 was against Kansas City. We played a double-header, and I had a triple with the bases loaded in both games. We always had trouble with Kansas City for some reason even though they were a last-place team. I did well and was really happy that I was able to contribute. We had Early Wynn and Billy Pierce, who were so steadfast.

It was hard to believe when we clinched in Cleveland. Afterward, it was bedlam. The majority of the guys on the team were older than I was and had been around and never experienced that. I was so happy for them, and that was the main thing. You could see it on their faces. We came into the old Midway Airport, and it was something. There were so many people there so late at night. It was a dream come true. Those are the things you dream about and you never think it will come true, but it did.

The World Series came and then we got to face that "easy" pitching with [Don] Drysdale, [Johnny] Podres, and [Sandy] Koufax. It was a great experience. The Coliseum was really something with more than 90,000 people. Normally, I played right, but Al [Lopez] put me in left because he thought it would be easier with a short left field. It was a really a thrill. I dreamed about that as a kid, and it all came true.

I didn't have a long career, but I wouldn't have traded it for anything. I thought my career was successful, because back then just being able to get to the major leagues was something. Then, to be able to play, and play in a World Series, heck, guys play for years and never get into a World Series. I felt privileged. What a great bunch of guys they were. We were close. There was a saying in the minor leagues that if you won, you went out and celebrated, and if you lost, you went out and got loose! We had a great time. Everybody rooted for everybody, and they were all stars in their own right. I wouldn't trade it for anything.

31

Jim McAnany's major league career lasted only 93 games, but his timing was perfect. McAnany gave the Sox a much-needed spark with his outfield play in 1959. He was called up from the minors in midseason, played 67 games for the Sox, and hit .276. Injuries and military duty curtailed his career after that season. He was taken by the Los Angeles Angels in the 1960 expansion draft and never played for them, but finished his career with 18 games for the Cubs in 1961–1962.

BOB SHAW
PITCHER
1958–1961

I HAD PLAYED IN CUBA WITH MINNIE MINOSO. We played in Puerto Rico and won the Caribbean World Series. I came back after being the Most Valuable Player in Cuba and was with Detroit, where Jack Tighe was the manager. The 1958 Tigers got off to a really bad start. They had traded for Billy Martin to play shortstop, and around the 15th of June they were going to send me down. I asked them if I would get my $1,000 bonus, and they said no. I asked if they were going to bring me back up, and they said they didn't know. I asked if I could go play in Cuba, and they said they didn't know.

I walked around the hotel a few times, then called my dad and told him I didn't think I had a future in the Detroit organization. I was going to come home and, by coming home, I wasn't going to make any money. You gamble, and there's times in your life when you might make a decision that could be catastrophic, but I went home. I was taking a shower about five days later, and my mother knocked on the door and told me I was traded to the White Sox. It was the biggest break of my life. I got with Al Lopez and [pitching coach] Ray Berres, and they really helped me mechanically. Al brought me along slowly. It turned out to be a good decision—what can I say?

When I got to the Sox in June, Al pitched me in long relief, then he gave me tougher jobs with innings at the end of the game. Finally, they felt I was developed enough where I was ready to start, and I started in Boston. I'm happy to say I won that game, and I do remember Ted Williams was on their ballclub. That got me rolling, and I was fortunate to get off to a good start with the Sox.

Early Wynn was my roommate and was quite a character. I learned so much from him. He was involved in bowling alleys in Venice, Florida, and he bought his suits in Baltimore, and I tagged along. He taught me not to give in to the hitters. He was a mean, tough guy who'd say, "Hey, look. That up and in is part of your strike zone and don't be afraid to move the hitters back." He also helped me in regard to the rosin bag. Every kid who sees a rosin bag picks it up. Well, we went out one night to have dinner, and he said, "You know what? Why don't you try not using the rosin bag?" At first the ball is slick, then as it gets hot, it gets tacky. I never used the rosin bag, and then one year I was second in fewest walks allowed and one year I led the league. It's interesting what you can learn from other players. Wynn was a big help to me.

When we went to Cleveland in '59 for the big series in August, I do remember they walked me. I got to first base, and there was sand between first and second. They put sand in there to negate our speed so our feet would come out from under us. The other thing they did was water down the infield to stop our singles from going through and let the outfield grow to stop the doubles in the gap. It happened that Minnie Minoso was with the Indians. He went back on a fly ball that jumped out of his glove and went over the fence for a home run. We won that game 7–3. There were, like, 75,000 people in Municipal Stadium, so I was very happy to get us off and running in that series, and then we swept. [Dick] Donovan and Wynn also won, so we left in pretty good shape.

The game where we clinched in Cleveland, I came in to relieve Wynn, then Gerry Staley came in and threw a double-play ball in the ninth inning to win it. Everybody went crazy, and when we came back, seeing all of those people at the airport was the thrill of a lifetime.

I started Game 2 of the World Series at Comiskey. It was a packed house, the flags were flying, and from my perspective, I didn't want to let them down and pitch a bad ballgame. What happened was—and it sounds like an excuse but it's not—the scouting report on Charlie Neal was to pitch him away. I did, and he hit two home runs off me. We ended up losing 4–3. One went over the center-field wall, and the other, which you see all the time, was where Al Smith went back and the guy in the stands was reaching for the ball and knocked his beer over, so it fell on Al. I'm the culprit because I gave up that home run.

33

Bob Shaw tells a few tales from 1959 while at the 2009 SoxFest fan convention.
Photo courtesy of WGN-TV

The L.A. Coliseum was really a football stadium, and people may not remember they had a short left-field fence that was protected by a 30-foot net. It was hard to pitch there because guys could hit a pop fly over it for a home run or they could pop it off the net. Wally Moon hit what they called "Moon shots" with an inside-out swing that would go right off that net. In the fourth inning of Game 5 we had runners on, and the Dodgers elected to go for a double play. We got the run, but no one knew that would be the end of it. No other runs were scored after that, and we won 1–0.

It's interesting how life works. I lost the second game of the Series 4–3, and in this game I walked a guy in the seventh or eighth inning, then Gil Hodges hit a tremendous shot. People say it missed the left-field foul pole by one inch. If he had hit that thing one inch over, I'd have been a bum the rest of my life because I would have lost two Series games 4–3 and 2–1. It was a break for me—I was fortunate. My mom and dad flew in for the game and were back up in the 125th row or something.

Also that day Al Lopez put Jim Rivera in the game, then the next hitter cranked one into right-center field. Jim took off like heck and reached out to catch it. That saved my butt also. You don't think about taking a shutout late into the game. As I developed as a professional, I learned to concentrate on the positive and what I had to do to each hitter, such as keeping the ball away from a right-hander so he couldn't pull it.

I had made $10,000 that year and was the winningest pitcher in the American League, near the top of the ERA leaders, and was third in the Cy Young voting. I held out in 1960. They offered me $15,000, and I held out. I finally signed in Bill Veeck's apartment—he was giving me beer, and I was pouring it into the plants. I finally signed for $22,500. My salary went from $22,500 to $25,000 to $30,000 to $35,000 to $40,000 to $43,000 to $46,000, and that's what I made in my last year in 1967. That was pretty good money then, but you could still relate to the working guy. I know there is the story that I yelled at fans that year, but I don't remember that and don't know why it always comes up.

I threw a sinker/slider and had to keep the ball down. I was not over-powering and relied on command. I had good control. I didn't throw my curveball a lot, but did use my change-up. I tried to keep it down and pound it at them. I never walked many hitters. I could give up six or seven hits, but only give up a run or two, because I didn't give up many home runs or walk guys. Control was it for me.

I loved pitching at Comiskey because the fences were way out, they were concrete, and they were high. Ray Berres was a great pitching coach, and we led the American League in ERA for many years in a row.

I was single with a girlfriend. The media had me down on Rush Street every night, but that wasn't true. I took vitamin and mineral supplements back when no one was doing the health thing. I did a lot of calisthenics and ran a great deal. I did that for psychological reasons. I thought I would eat properly, take the supplements, and be healthy. And for that, I was considered odd.

I got traded quite a bit in my career. I'd have a good year, then I'd get off to a slow start or something else and I'd be traded. I'd much rather have stayed with the White Sox. When you're traded, you can't cry or complain. It's done, so I would just get in my car and drive. You just go about your life, but it was great to be with the White Sox.

I denied using a spitball for years. Finally, Gaylord Perry came out with this book called *Me and the Spitter*, and there on page seven or whatever, it said, "Bob Shaw taught me the spitball." Well, then things were out. I managed for many years and I always denied it. I taught Tony Cloninger the spitter, and he won 20 games that year. When I was a pitching coach in Milwaukee, I taught Bill Champion, but he never really utilized it. The answer is that I learned it from Frank Shellenback, who taught me to put the slippery elm in your mouth, how to prepare the ball, how to work it into the leather. I learned it from Frank, who was the last guy to legally throw the spitball.

I was with the Giants at the time and was in 60 games. At the end of the year, I was tired and I couldn't get anybody out. The pitching coach put emery paper in my locker, and the trainer put slippery elm in my locker, so I got the message that I needed help. Then I ended up doing it. The umpires would come to me before the game and say, "Don't roll it on the ground or throw it over my head. Don't embarrass us." I loaded up mine pretty heavy, and it would just fly off the ball. You couldn't miss it. If they asked for the ball, I would rub it off and throw it in, so they never threw out one of my balls.

We don't have anything to be ashamed of from our World Series, because most of the games were one-run games except the last one. We're happy for those 2005 players because we know what it's like when you lose. We were all happy for the fans, for the ownership, and especially the players when they won it.

The White Sox acquired Bob Shaw along with Ray Boone from Detroit on June 15, 1958, for Bill Fischer and Tito Francona. After a short stint in the bullpen, Shaw moved into the rotation and became the No. 2 starter in 1959, posting a sparkling 18–6 record with a 2.69 ERA and three shutouts. Shaw went 13–13 in 1960, and was traded to the Athletics on June 10, 1961, as part of an eight-player deal.

The
SIXTIES

GARY PETERS
PITCHER
1959–1969

ISIGNED AS A FIRST BASEMAN/OUTFIELDER and had pitched maybe once in my life. I never really played any organized ball in western Pennsylvania. The first organized baseball I ever played was semipro baseball with my father when I was 13 or 14. I think I pitched one game back then.

The White Sox signed me, and I was sent to Holdrege, Nebraska, to be in the rookie league, and J.C. Martin was there as the first baseman. J.C. got a bunch of money to sign—well, whatever passed for a bunch of money in those days, probably $10,000—so he was going to be the first baseman. I played right field for about a third of the season, and all the young pitchers on our rookie team got sore arms. Frank Scalzi was the manager and said, "You've got a good arm from right field, and I need you to pitch a couple of games. Have you ever pitched before?" I told him maybe one game in semi-pro. All I could do was throw hard, and I had no idea about a breaking ball. I pitched a pretty good game and never got back to right field. I became a pitcher from then on, but I always took batting practice and I always liked to hit, so I stayed around the cage.

I was in Triple A for a number of years, but that was because of Billy Pierce. I couldn't take his job because he was having such good years! Back in those days I had a winning record at Triple A, but when I look back, I probably wasn't ready to do what I did when I got to the big leagues. I started late as a pitcher, and all those years in the minor leagues, I didn't know how to throw a curveball. I threw a fastball, slider, and change-up for my pitches.

When I got to the big leagues [for a full season] in 1963, the only reason I got a start was because Juan Pizarro got sick. That's the only reason I got out there. I was out of options. I was out of everything. They were going to get rid of me. Well, Pizarro got sick, and I started a game against Kansas City early in 1963, about a month into the season. I won the game, hit a home run, and then won 11 in a row after that. That's how I got established.

I won the Rookie of the Year that year, and Pete Ward got second place, so I always tell him I keep the trophy polished for him! He lives in Portland, and I live in Sarasota, so we're a long way away, otherwise he'd be coming over to my house to try and steal it, I'm sure. I always tell him, "Don't worry, Pete. I'm keeping your trophy nice and clean!"

Those teams were fun to play on. In '63 the Yankees beat us by a few games, and in '64 they beat us by a game. In '67 we were in it all season and lost out at the end. It's no fun playing the second half of the season when you're losing. It's always fun to compete, so those were really good teams to play on. We didn't score a lot of runs, but we didn't make many errors, either. I won 20 games in 1964, then I got hurt.

I always jumped in to take batting practice whenever I could, and because I could pinch-hit, they let me take batting practice with the extra men on the road. Normally, pitchers didn't hit on the road, they just hit at home. Today, when pitchers hit in BP, they don't work on their hitting. I see a game once in a while, and the pitchers are playing some sort of long-ball game or something, not really working on hitting for the situation. I always took BP seriously and I'm glad I did. It seems like I had a salary dispute with the White Sox, and one year we were $1,000 apart. I brought up my pinch-hitting, and they gave me the money, so I guess I earned an extra $1,000 for pinch-hitting.

I did some pinch-hitting from time to time and got hurt one time in 1968. I had pitched the first game of a doubleheader, and Eddie Stanky was our manager. We got some guys on base at a time when our pitcher had been in trouble early. I was in the clubhouse at the time putting ice on my arm. The batboy came in and said, "Eddie wants you out on the field right now." It was the third inning. I threw on my uniform and went out there, but I was stiff. There were runners on first and second and, as a left-handed hitter, I wanted to pull the ball to move over the runners. I tried to pull a pitch and got about three steps toward first base when I got a spasm in my back. I ended up in

An American League All-Star in 1964 and 1967, Gary Peters was also a strong hitter who finished his career with 19 home runs.

traction for two or three days. I had rotated my pelvis a little bit, but I put up with that all year and kept pitching. I had to do a lot of therapy in the winter to work on that. I still look in the mirror from time to time—my pelvis is a little off, and I don't think you can fix that. I almost retired after that.

They had a Green Stamps Day once at the park for the players, and my wife loved that one. I hit a three-run homer and beat Minnesota when they were giving away stamps if you did something good during the game, so I got a lot of books. I remember that because I have a film at home of my wife riding around with our kids in convertibles or something before the game. It was S&H Green Stamps, and my wife was very happy about that. According to her, that was my best-ever win.

Back then the Yankees and White Sox were like the Yankees and Red Sox are now. We were neck and neck every year. The Yankees had all those great hitters, but nobody realized how good they were fundamentally, and they never made a mental mistake. Moose Skowron always tells me that when he got to the big leagues, Hank Bauer scared the life out of him by telling him not to make any mental mistakes or he wouldn't be there anymore.

I pitched against Whitey Ford I don't know how many times, and I don't think the Yankees ever scored three runs off me, but I never beat him. We just couldn't score off him, and they never made errors. When Mel Stottlemyre came up, I beat him a few times. I beat the Yankees, but never Whitey. He was just too good against us.

We used to give Gene Bossard a hard time. When he'd come out to tend the field during batting practice, we would bounce balls off his legs, but we knew that in Chicago, we had the best grounds crew anywhere—they still do. Roger [Bossard, Gene's son and the current head groundskeeper] is well-known throughout the country as one of the premier groundskeepers, and he has worked at it.

They kept it wet, no doubt about it. Jim Fregosi was with the Angels and said it was like a rice paddy in front of home plate. Every club tailored their ballpark, though. We'd go out and play the Angels, and they had some guys who could run, so it was like concrete in front of home plate. If they hit a ball down, it would go up in the air like a pop fly, and they'd be on first before it came down. Guys would slope the baselines and all kinds of things. It was slow at Comiskey, but that's because the grass was twice as high in front of home as anywhere else. Then they went and put artificial turf in the infield. We had three ground-ball pitchers and were all wondering why in the world they did that. At the same time, they lowered the mound; so both of those things really hurt our staff.

I did like to have fun. Probably the best gag I ever pulled was at spring training. I lived in Sarasota, and we had spring training down there every year. We had a guy named Deacon Jones, who was a first baseman and one of the best pure hitters I ever saw. He was not an outdoorsman at all, and I knew he was kind of afraid of stuff. One morning I was coming to the ballpark and there was a bobcat coming across the road. I had a .22 in my car and shot it. It was a big cat, probably 35 pounds. I always got to the park early, so I went to Deacon's locker. They used to always have your shirt hanging on your locker when you got there, so I took Deacon's shirt down, put the bobcat up there, put his shirt on it, and had that bobcat looking right out of the locker. About half the guys in the clubhouse knew what was going on, so they made sure to stand around when Deacon got there. He took one look

41

at that bobcat and took off screaming, because I had the cat's mouth open, and it looked pretty gruesome!

Al Lopez and Eddie Stanky were not alike. They were both really good managers, but Al was the best manager I played for. He was of the old school, where he wasn't friendly with the players. You could go talk to him, but he wasn't friendly with you. Some of the older guys didn't like him, but I never knew why. Nellie Fox was a fun-loving guy, and he would always make fun of Al. He could mimic him, and Al knew it and didn't like it. He thought Nellie was trying to undermine him. I told him later it was all in fun, but he just wouldn't listen to me about it. He handled the press and players really well. He was a good psychologist.

We were ahead of the Yankees one time 2–1 or something like that. Elston Howard came up with some men on base in the ninth inning. Al came out and told me to make him hit a slider low and inside. I had a good slider, and I told Al, "I don't like to pitch him there because he likes the ball down there. I'd rather throw the ball up waist high, throw him a runner." He told me to set him up outside, then throw a good slider down and inside. Well, we did that, and he hit a rope into the left-field bleachers to beat us. I went into the dugout, and Al pretty much told me to stick my slider where the sun didn't shine. Then he asked J.C. where the slider was, and I wished J.C. had said it was a hanger, but he didn't. He told Al I threw it right where I was told to, and Al came back and yelled at me again. That was the only time he ever got mad at me.

I got along well with Stanky because I was an older player. I wasn't afraid to pitch inside, and he liked that. He terrorized some of the younger players to the point where they didn't perform up to where they could because they were afraid. They were afraid he was going to yell at them or afraid he was going to fine them, but you can't play ball like that. He could be a little fearsome when he got mad.

It was hard to leave when I was traded to the Red Sox. I knew the town and the people so well. Back in those days, the only reason it wasn't hard to go was the salary. Everything was a battle with the White Sox, and the Red Sox were probably one of the best-paid teams. When I got traded, [Red Sox general manager] Dick O'Connell called me and asked me how much money I needed to be happy, so I just picked some number out of thin air, and he said okay. My wife was mad at me for not picking a higher number. In Chicago I mostly dealt with Ed Short and with Hank Greenberg my first year. Those guys had a budget, and I understood that.

The White Sox fans are great. I attend card shows up in Chicago sometimes, and it's amazing how many fans remember me. They're getting older and older, but they remember me! I still get a lot of letters, and we laugh about it, because it used to be, "I saw you pitch this game." Then it was, "I saw you pitch this game when I was a kid." Now it's, "My grandfather told me you were a great pitcher." You know you're getting old when you get those letters!

Left-hander Gary Peters was signed by the White Sox as an amateur free agent in 1956. Peters sparkled in his first full season in the majors in 1963 with a 19–8 record and league-leading 2.33 ERA. He beat out teammate Pete Ward to win the AL Rookie of the Year Award that year, then led the league with 20 wins the next year while posting a 2.50 ERA. After a down year in 1965, Peters went 12–10 and led the league with a 1.98 ERA in 1966 and 16–11, 2.28 in 1967 for the punchless Sox. An injury caused a 4–13 year in 1968 and, after going 10–15 for a sub-.500 team in 1969, he was traded to the Red Sox on December 13 along with Don Pavletich for Jerry Jameski and Syd O'Brien.

Peters was an American League All-Star in 1964 and 1967. He was also a strong hitter who finished his career with 19 home runs and 102 RBIs. In 2000 Peters was named to the White Sox Team of the Century.

JOEL HORLEN
PITCHER
1961–1971

I WENT TO OKLAHOMA STATE UNIVERSITY, and we went to Omaha for the College World Series and ended up winning it in 1959. The White Sox's scouting director, Jack Sheehan, introduced himself when we checked into the hotel. He told me, "Look, you're not going to see me the rest of the World Series, but I want you to make me a promise that we're the last team you will talk to." I made him that promise and won a couple games. There were a couple clubs hounding me pretty much every day, and I was glad for the attention! After it was over, I had a bunch of appointments with four or five clubs at the hotel, then about 3:00 in the morning, I knocked on Mr. Sheehan's door. He said, "I thought you had forgotten about me." I told him they were the last team I was going to talk to. He had ordered me a hamburger and soda and, of course, the hamburger was cold and the soda was warm. They offered me a bonus spread over six years, and I signed right then and there.

I only spent a couple of years in the minors. They weren't going to call me up in '61 until September 1, but they had some injuries, so I was called up in late August. I had my car and family in San Diego, so I put them on an airplane and sent them to Texas. I flew to Minneapolis and got there the day before the team got there, because they were coming in from Washington. We had a split doubleheader where we played at noon and then again at night. They fed us after the game, and we just lay around the clubhouse between games. I wasn't supposed to start until the next day. Cal McLish started the second game, but they had me warm up, and I came in for the fourth inning. I think I pitched four innings. We got a bunch of runs and went ahead, so I got my first win.

My jersey was blank. Since I wasn't supposed to pitch until the next day, I guess they figured they had time to sew on my number. I'd been wearing my warm-up jacket all day long because I didn't want anybody to start hollering at me or anything from the stands. When they told me to warm up, I had to take my jacket off, and people down in the bleachers were giving me all kinds of grief. I got to the mound, and the umpire took one look at me, then got Al Lopez to come out. Lopez had to point me out on the lineup card he had. The ump finally said we could play ball. Well, I had been standing out there and was ready, then [Minnesota manager] Sam Mele came out on the field, and I saw him point at me to the umpire then throw up his hands, like, "Who the heck is this guy?" The umpire went over and told him. In the meantime, Nellie Fox was talking to me on the mound and telling me about the first hitter up, who was Zoilo Versalles. Nellie told me Versalles hit the ball back through the middle a lot, and on the second or third pitch I threw, he hit a hard grounder right back at me, and I was able to get it and throw him out.

I didn't chew tobacco or gum, but I did chew tissue. My roommate and I had gone to a movie. It was an exciting Western, and I was eating a big box of buttered popcorn while I watched. I had some tissues there to wipe my hands on and ended up sticking a few in my mouth by accident after the popcorn was all gone, and that's how it started. I tried chewing tobacco earlier when Nellie was there and threw up every time, so I figured that wasn't for me.

The whole staff bore down more because we weren't an offensive team. Every pitch might mean the game, so you were really concentrating hard on making good pitches to every batter. I was 13–9, I guess, in '64. It got to be where the pitchers went out to the mound, and we'd say, "Don't give up a run or you'll lose your chance for a tie!" It made us better pitchers.

The gifts from Eddie Stanky started in '67 when he was giving a pair of alligator shoes to Tommie Agee and Don Buford every time they were at second base and took third on a ground ball to shortstop or third. That was unheard of in those days for a runner to advance after the throw went to first base, but it got us more runners to third. Eddie told the pitchers if we gave up 21 ground balls in a game, it didn't matter if they were hits or not, he would buy us a $300 suit. I ended up getting five suits that year. Eddie didn't have a great reputation, but I think he made me a better pitcher. I concentrated more and became a little smarter.

There was a lot going on at Comiskey. The ground was watered very soft in front of home plate, but I don't know if the grass was any longer or not. The balls felt cool to me at times—they stored them underground behind the umpire. When he wanted to get more, he had to trip this little lever and a bucket would come up and get the balls out.

The All-Star Game that year was nice. I was getting dressed for the game, and Carl Yastrzemski was sitting at his locker reading a newspaper. I walked up in front of him and I guess he saw my name on my shower shoes. I only weighed about 165 pounds by July and was skin and bones. He said, "This is the blankety-blank body that's been getting me out all these years?" I told him, "Yup, and I'm going to keep getting you out, too!"

I didn't follow the pennant race in the papers that year. I just knew where we were each day. We just went out there and had a great staff that year. We all pitched very similarly with hard sinkers and cut fastballs. I threw sliders early in my career, but it wasn't a good pitch for me, so I gave it up and learned how to change my grip to cut a fastball from Marv Grissom.

When I threw the no-hitter that year, I had my normal stuff. I was keeping the ball down a lot better. There were only a few balls hit to the outfield in that game. I had a lot of ground balls. Whoever had pitched before me had hit Bill Freehan. You had to pitch him inside, because he liked the ball away where he could extend his arms. I was trying to get a sinker inside and hit him that game and just knew when I came up I was going to get it. Bill and I had played in some golf events together, and I knew him a bit. When I came to the plate, I said, "You okay, Bill?" He called me about 10 dirty names, and I knew what was coming! The first one was at my head, and I got out of the way. The second one was at my ribs, and I don't know how I got out of the way of that one. I thought the first one would be it and wasn't expecting another one. The third pitch came at my legs, and I got my left leg out of the way, but it hit me on the inside of my knee, right on the bone. I went down in a heap, then got up and hobbled to first base. I had no thought of leaving the game. They were going to have to drag me off the mound. After the game, I got a call on the clubhouse phone from Dave Wickersham, the pitcher who hit me. He said, "Joe, I'm sorry I hit you, but I had to. If I hadn't, our manager was going to fine me $100."

Joel Horlen made his major league debut in 1961 and finished second in the Cy Young voting in 1967. He finished his career with a 3.11 ERA.

I was a little nervous at the end, but I was just trying to win a game. I had a decent lead in the game, I could just let it go. I was fortunate that my fastball really moved a lot late. I could move it both inside and out. I just tried to stay in my game plan. Most hitters have weaknesses, and that's what we concentrated on, going at those areas. When I got it, I threw my glove up in the air and didn't know where it was right away. I finally got it back about 30 minutes later. I think the clubhouse guy brought it back. I have it in my house now.

The last game of the year I was pitching for my 20th. I left when we were ahead against Washington. Somebody hit a ground ball to Tommy McCraw, and he dropped it when he was making the tag, and that's how we lost that game. We were disappointed we couldn't finish it that year, but that's baseball.

When the artificial turf came in, I do think it affected me a little bit. The ground balls got to be harder and got through the infield. It sure didn't help us any at all.

I never threw to a certain spot. When I hear that now, I think to myself when you do that, you're not getting your maximum out of the ball. I did some minor league coaching for 10 or 12 years, and I told all of them I didn't want to hear any spot pitching stuff. I'll show you some grips that will get your ball to move, and we'll go from there. Just keep the ball low, that's the main thing.

Being a player rep was definitely a problem when I was traded. We were in spring training in 1972, and I had held out for a while so I was a bit late getting there. They had our 40-man roster and another 12 invitees in a meeting. Stu Holcomb was the general manager at the time, and he got up to make a speech about why there should be no strike and he was saying some things that were just impossible to happen. He guaranteed everybody in that room they would qualify for the pension, which at that time was five years. I got up and said, "Mind if I ask for a show of hands of everyone in here who has five years?" Well, there were only about five guys who could put their hands up. He went on and told us a majority would get 10 years, and I got up again. This time when I got the show of hands who had 10 years, I was the only one. The next day, I was on the waiver list.

I still went to Dallas to represent the White Sox at the players' meeting, and Reggie Jackson stopped me to tell me Charlie Finley was trying to trade for me. He gave me Charlie's personal phone number, and I called him. Charlie told me the strike would last 10 days, which it did, and he would send me a ticket to Oakland. I pitched five innings in an exhibition game to show them I was healthy, and he gave me a contract similar to what I had made the year before. I was happy to finish there and get into the World Series that year.

It's been very gratifying. The Sox had me back to throw out the first pitch on Opening Day one year and had me back for an All-Star gathering. I've been to the SoxFest in January and really enjoyed that. They have thousands of people come through there, and I had a great time seeing all the fans who remembered me playing. It was a great time in my life.

Right-hander Joel Horlen was signed by the White Sox as a free agent in 1959. He made his major league debut in 1961 and earned a spot in the rotation during the next season. His breakout year came in 1964, when he went 13–9 with a 1.88 ERA. In 1967 Horlen led the American League with a 2.06 ERA and six shutouts during a 19–7 campaign, but still finished second in the Cy Young voting to Boston's Jim Lonborg. On September 10 of that year, Horlen no-hit the Tigers at Comiskey Park. With the Sox team on the decline, he struggled through four straight losing seasons, from 1968 through 1971.

He was released by the White Sox on April 2, 1972, and was quickly picked up by the Oakland A's, where he was part of a world championship team and then retired. Horlen's career mark of 116–117 doesn't do him justice—his 3.11 career ERA does.

KEN BERRY

OUTFIELDER

1962–1970

WHEN I SIGNED WITH THE SOX, I was playing football at Wichita State and had finished my freshman year. Freshmen weren't eligible then, so I got to play four freshman games, and that was it. In the summer I had been in western Kansas playing baseball, and there were four of us off my team who were signed to professional contracts.

I really didn't size up who was ahead of me in the system, whether through stupidity or what. My approach was to put my nose to the grindstone, go out and do my job, and not worry about anything else. It ended up that my second year I was in Visalia, California, for Class C ball, about the equivalent of low A nowadays. At the Sox team in Savannah, Georgia, Dean Look decided to go play in the NFL and quit. They moved me to his spot in Savannah, which was a jump of several levels. If I'd been only focusing on the guy in front of me, maybe I wouldn't have gotten that break. I jumped over him, kept going, and never even gave it a thought. I just did my job.

"The Bandit" nickname came from a game in Indianapolis. The park there used to be 480 feet to center field, and there was a flag pole out there. I made a catch by that pole one night on a ball hit by Jimmy Wynn, and they started calling me "the Bandit" from then on.

The next year I was in Triple A, and at the end of the year they always brought up the guys who were on the 40-man roster. So in September of '62, '63, and '64 I came up. I remember facing a soft-tossing left-hander who was pitching me away, and I hit a weak ground ball between first and second that got all the way into right field. That was my first hit.

In 1964 I was the MVP in Triple A and had a pretty good year. When I came up, Al Lopez put me in the lineup. Jim Landis wasn't really tearing it up with the bat, and defensively they felt like we were pretty equal. He put me in there, and we won 10 of 11 at the end. The Yankees had to beat Cleveland in a couple doubleheaders and beat us by a game to get to the World Series. I was just out playing and didn't realize that I could have very easily been in the Series that year. I finished pretty strong for that short period of time.

They traded Landis after that season. Nobody talked to us about anything like that, and they had a great deal of power over us. When it was time to negotiate your contract, you had to do it yourself without an agent—if you didn't like the offer, it was stay home. Free agency came around the year after I retired.

I don't think I felt any pressure, but I guess I tried a little too hard at times. I had a neck injury from high school football and didn't realize at the time how bad it was. It caused me a lot of trouble with neck spasms, and I made some errors at first because I couldn't turn my head. I finally found a Japanese chiropractor in Chicago, and he used muscle interruption to put pressure on the spasming muscles and held it in order to make the spasms subside. Once I started going to him, my problems started to go away. In the second half of the season I hit better and performed the way I could.

The front office was on me to get going or they would send me back. Al Lopez didn't say too much. He wanted you to hit the cutoff man and make the routine plays, bunt when he wanted you to, and all that. I liked him, but we could have been more active. I had 11 or 12 managers in my career, and when I started managing and coaching, I took a combination of things from the three or four of those I liked best and drew on those. I liked Chuck Tanner for being so positive and upbeat. He was the only manager I had who came out of the dugout to pat me on the back if I moved a runner from second to third with nobody out. Del Crandall used the delayed steal, and I learned how to use that a lot. Eddie Stanky taught me the most about the little things in baseball and was the toughest to play for. He was very critical, but the guys wanted to play hard for him. He would pay close attention to who was hot and make sure we didn't let that guy beat us. I wanted to be positive, aggressive, and do the little things to win when I was

51

Along with having been an American League All-Star in 1967, Ken Berry was the technical adviser for the 1988 movie *Eight Men Out*.

managing. I think Major League Baseball has strayed from that approach now, with too much emphasis on the big poppers instead of speed, defense, and pitching. I think those three keep you in games.

We came close to winning the pennant for Eddie in 1967. I led the team with a .241 batting average, but we played at Comiskey and all that went with it.

I've heard Hawk Harrelson talk on the air about being with the Red Sox and coming to play at "the Swamp." We had all these sinker-ball pitchers and didn't have a lot of quickness and speed in the infield, but if you could slow the ball down, they would get it and make the play. Everyone forgets about that when they make fun of the light-hitting White Sox. I used to hit balls hard up the middle, and the ball would just die. I had Gary Bell laughing at me one night when I hit three balls hard off him right up the middle and the ball went "splat" every time, so he was able to field it and throw me out at first base. It was good for our team, but it cost us on offense as individuals, especially when we had to negotiate our contracts. They said, "You only hit around .240." Well, they kept the balls in a cold, damp place so they wouldn't go anywhere, then they wet down the field so you couldn't get a hit, so we had a problem there as hitters. I'm not bitter, but it probably hurt my stats considerably, playing there as long as I did.

Then we traded Al Weis, Don Buford, Tommie Agee, and Tom McCraw—four fast runners and good defenders—and got Rocky Colavito, Tommy Davis, and Kenny Boyer, who were all older sluggers going into the twilight of their careers. That was it. We were a team with good pitching but no speed and defense. That would be the reason we struggled.

When the Sox traded me to California, I have to say Roland Hemond made a great trade. He got Jay Johnstone to take my place in center and a good pitcher in Tom Bradley. They got Dick Allen and had hired Chuck Tanner, so that was a winning combination.

I managed the Sox team in Birmingham for a two-year period. What I was most proud of was putting Craig Grebeck in the lineup as my fourth-place hitter on what turned out to be a championship team in 1989. I didn't really have a clean-up hitter. I remember Craig telling me one time that summer if he lost another pound, he'd be under 140! But I needed somebody there who made contact and would put the ball in play so I could start the runner and do aggressive things. He was my MVP hitting behind Robin Ventura, who was hitting third.

I was the technical adviser for the movie *Eight Men Out*. I had managed in Appleton, Wisconsin, that year, and our team lost outright at the end. Don Leppert was a friend of mine and was managing the Twins club. He had to go to the Instructional League and couldn't do it, so he put me in touch with the director, and I agreed to work on the movie. I showed up in Indianapolis in mid-September and worked for about three weeks on the film, went home for a week, then came back to finish it up. I'm also in the beginning of the movie as the heckler. The casting director saw me on the set throughout the movie and asked me if I wanted to be in it. I was going to be the guy who threatened Lefty Williams' life in the hotel and learned that part, but when she heard me yelling at the players on the field all the time, she changed her mind and gave me the heckler part. My old teammate, Dick Kenworthy, is sitting next to me in the film. He was living in Indianapolis, and I called him and asked him if he wanted to be in a movie with me. He was the little round-faced guy with the derby hat. That was how I had a movie career.

Ken Berry was signed by the White Sox as a free agent before the 1961 season. He joined the team at the end of the 1962, '63, and '64 seasons and became the Sox's regular center fielder in 1965. Berry was an American League All-Star in 1967.

"The Bandit," who was known for his leaping catches over the center-field fence at Comiskey Park, earned a Gold Glove in 1970. After hitting .276 with 50 RBIs that season, he was traded to the California Angels along with Syd O'Brien and Billy Wynne for Tom Bradley, Tom Egan, and Jay Johnstone. He played three seasons with the Angels, then spent single years in Milwaukee and Cleveland before retiring after the 1975 season.

He continued to work in baseball in many capacities and managed the Sox's Double A affiliate in Birmingham for two seasons, posting an 88–55 record in 1989 and going 77–67 in 1990. Berry also teaches baseball at his Hit-A-Way camps in his hometown of Topeka, Kansas, each winter.

MOOSE SKOWRON
FIRST BASEMAN
1964–1967

WHEN I WAS SEVEN YEARS OLD, my grandfather shaved off all my hair. I got outside, and all the older guys started calling me "Mussolini," who at the time was the dictator of Italy. As the years went on, it just became Moose.

Billy Jurges was scouting for the Chicago Cubs, and I was at a workout at Wrigley Field. It was raining, and I was the last guy to hit in batting practice. He wouldn't let me hit because he had to put the tarpaulin on the field. Well, I made the big leagues, and Jurges was with the Washington Senators. He said, "Moose, you talk to everybody at first base, but you don't talk to me." I said, "I hate you. I don't like you!" He was around here a few years ago and said, "Moose, are you still mad at me?" I said, "You bet your fanny I am!" That guy wouldn't let me hit. Thank God, I guess, because I would have never won anything if I signed with them.

I came up with the Yankees. Hank Bauer and Gene Woodling came up to me when I first started in 1954 in spring training in St. Petersburg, Florida. They got me in a room and said, "Moose, don't monkey around with our World Series money. We're used to winning every year and getting that eight grand bonus, so take care of yourself and abide by the rules." They said a few others things I can't repeat, too!

We knew the team we had to beat was the White Sox. Cleveland had a good pitching staff, and the White Sox had a great staff, but the Indians had better hitting. We'd come to Chicago and draw more than 150,000 people for the

Above: Five retired players appear in Chicago, on March 10, 1976, with owner Bill Veeck wearing the new uniforms for that season: (from left) Bill "Moose" Skowron, Moe Drabowsky, Jim Rivera, Veeck, Dave Nicholson, and Dan Osinski. *Photo courtesy of AP Images*

Left: Skowron already had five World Series wins when he joined the White Sox in 1964. *Photo courtesy of Richard Lindberg*

weekend. Billy Pierce would face Whitey Ford all the time. We'd come several times a year for Friday, Saturday, then a Sunday doubleheader.

I remember when I came to old Comiskey for the first time. I had to change in the john because they didn't even have lockers in the visiting clubhouse. I usually had 10 or 12 people at the game. I would use my four tickets, then get some from Mickey Mantle and Roger Maris. I'd give Roger mine when we went to Minnesota and give them to Mickey in Kansas City for their families.

There was a big fight one time when Art Ditmar hit Larry Doby. Ditmar said something to him, Doby said something back, then Larry ran to the mound. I tackled Doby, and Billy Martin beat the hell out of him. Walt Dropo pulled off my pants because he thought I was in there hitting him. Then Dropo and Enos Slaughter got into it, and Dropo scratched his face and ripped his uniform. I still have pictures of that one at home.

I was a hard worker. Wally Pipp came up to me at a Yankees Old-Timer's Game and said, "Hey, kid, c'mere, I want to talk to you. Don't ever get a headache. I was out one night and maybe had a few cocktails. I took the day off the next day, and Lou Gehrig took my place. I never played first base for the Yankees again." So I learned from him. I played every day when my name was in the lineup. I didn't care.

You want to talk about slumps? I went 0-for-40, then 1-for-20 right after that and somehow still finished the season hitting .319. Nobody talked to me when I wasn't hitting. Then when I got hot, the sportswriters came around, and I told them to buzz off since they didn't give me a pat on the back when I was down.

In 1963 I had a bad year after being traded from the Yankees to the Dodgers. I stunk. What can I say? I think being in the National League for the first time, I was trying too hard. I got hot at the end, though, and we won the World Series.

The most disappointing thing for me after getting traded to the White Sox in 1964 was that we didn't win the pennant and go to the World Series. I had the chance to win three straight titles with three different teams, the Yankees, Dodgers, and White Sox. We won nine in a row to end the season but lost to the Yankees by a game. It was a crazy incident that got the Yankees started. We had just swept four games from them at Comiskey, and they were on their bus fighting traffic to get to the airport. Phil Linz was an infielder and was in the back of the bus playing a harmonica. Yogi Berra was the manager up front and yelled at Linz to stick that thing. Mickey Mantle was there, and when Linz asked him what Yogi said, Mickey told him, "He wants you to play it louder." Yogi and Linz got into a fight. I was a Chicago boy who grew up only 25 minutes from Wrigley Field. Playing on the South Side was great, even if we didn't win it that year.

Our manager, Eddie Stanky, had a meeting and said, "I don't want anybody talking to the Yankees players." I said he was just jealous because he never got to play for them. I was playing first base, and Mickey got on with a hit. He said, "Moose, how are the wife and kids doing? Moose! I'm talking to you." I put my glove up to my face and said, "Mickey, I can't talk to you. It will cost me 50 bucks." He said, "After all the money I made for you in all those World Series, I'm not worth 50 dollars?" There was Stanky in the dugout, waving at me so I'd know I was getting fined! He was a heck of a manager, though, and he taught us a lot about the rules.

In 1967 Gary Peters, Joel Horlen, and the other pitchers cornered me and said, "Moose, we want you to play first base." I knew it was going to be my last year, and Tom McCraw was at first hitting about .210. I led the club in a lot of departments the three previous years, and I told Eddie I wanted to play. He said, "Moose, it's my prerogative who plays." I said, "Eddie, I don't know what that word means!" I got traded to the California Angels the next day.

The guy who gave me the most trouble was Jim Bunning. He's a senator now and sends me letters asking for donations. I won't send him a thing. I had good luck against Bill Monboquette and, believe me, I'd send him some money! He'd hand a curve to me, and I'd hit it for a home run. The Sox gave me a ring in 2005, and I gave it to my daughter. I wear my 1961 Yankees ring, which to me was the greatest team of all time. We hit 240 home runs. I sure wish they would have had a designated hitter back then, because I could have prolonged my career.

I wish I played ball today. I'd be a multimillionaire. I made a half-million dollars in 17 years and I was in eight World Series. The winning share in those Series in the '50s was $8,000 for the winners and $4,000 for the losers. Today, it's more than $300,000 for winning and $200,000 for losing.

If you hit a home run like a guy like [Alfonso] Soriano, who watches the ball sail over the fence, in our time, if Don Drysdale or Bob Gibson was pitching, you would end up in the hospital. They wouldn't take that stuff. Mickey Mantle used to hit a lot of long home runs, but when he ran around the bases, he always had his head down. Today is different. Now you can't pitch inside to anybody because you might hurt them.

I got hit in the head one day. Ike Delock from the Boston Red Sox hit me after I hit a home run off him. Ted Williams told me the story. When Ike came back to the bench, he said, "When Moose comes up again, I'm going to hit him right between the eyes." He hit me right in the head. I went to first base, and Casey Stengel asked me if I could read the scoreboard. I read the scoreboard and said, "God, please let my roommate, Bob Cerv, hit a grounder to shortstop, and they hand it to second so I can go in there and break up that double play." Gene Mauch was playing second base, and I broke his leg. He never played another game in the major leagues. I didn't do it on purpose, but we were taught to break up double plays. Now these guys are afraid to slide because their agents tell them they might get hit.

I have a great job with the White Sox as an ambassador. Mr. Reinsdorf hired me 10 years ago. I love my job, doing things like visiting suites, calling bingo for the senior citizens, and showing up at events. I'm at the park every game. Jerry Reinsdorf is just great. I enjoy being around all the fans. The day I have to worry is the day they don't say hello to me or want my autograph. I'm 78 years old, have a pacemaker, I've had a double bypass, wear hearing aids, and I'm still going. That's all that counts. This is my home.

Bill "Moose" Skowron had 10 seasons, eight World Series appearances, and five world championships under his belt when he joined the White Sox on July 13, 1964, after being traded from the Washington Senators with Carl Bouldin for Joe Cunningham. He hit .293 with 38 RBIs in 73 games that year and followed with 18 homers, 78 RBIs, and a berth on the American League All-Star team. After slumping to .249 in 1966, Skowron was traded to the California Angels on May 6, 1967, for Cotton Nash and cash.

He joined the White Sox as a roving ambassador in 2000 and continues to entertain everyone at the ballpark with his treasure trove of baseball stories and love of the game.

PETE WARD
THIRD BASEMAN/OUTFIELDER
1963–1969

WHEN I WAS TRADED TO CHICAGO, I really didn't know anything about the White Sox. I had spent four years in the Orioles' organization, and the trade was a tremendous break for me. I don't think I would have played too many games at third base for Baltimore, because they had somebody blocking me there by the name of Brooks Robinson. It was a tremendous opportunity for me, and that's the way I looked at it. I got to play for Al Lopez and the great group of guys they had there. The ballplayers were great guys. When I was first there, they had Nellie Fox, Sherm Lollar, Jim Landis, and a really good pitching staff.

Opening Day in 1963 was in Detroit and was a real thrill for me. It was my first game for the Sox, and in the seventh inning I hit a three-run home run off Jim Bunning. I always tell people that was the highlight of my career and it tailed off after that! I was just on cloud nine, and it was a tremendous thrill for me. We came from behind to win, all in my first game with the White Sox.

My roommate with the Sox was Ron Hansen, and I actually roomed with him on three different major league ballclubs. We came up with the Orioles at the end of 1962, and I roomed with him there, then we were involved in the same trade to Chicago and roomed together. We both ended up with the Yankees and were roommates there, so that was kind of a different thing.

We had some young guys like Dave Nicholson and J.C. Martin, [Joel] Horlen and [Gary] Peters, Juan Pizarro, with Eddie Fisher and Hoyt Wilhelm in the bullpen. We really had good pitching. We were solid all the way around, but back then the Yankees were a little bit better, and the Orioles were, too, one year.

Al Lopez was a tremendous manager for me. I actually got off to a really bad start. The first three weeks or so, I was hitting next to nothing. I had a couple of home runs, but I was probably hitting about .220 and making some errors. Al called me into his office about a month into the season. We had Charley Smith backing me up in case I didn't make it, and I thought when Al called me into his office, I might be getting sent out. Uh-oh. Al talked to me about throwing the ball, making sure I got it across the seams and letting it go and not to worry if it went into the stands. If I didn't get it across the seams, he told me it had a tendency to sail. Then he said, "That's okay, that's it. Go get 'em." I said, "What about my hitting?" He said, "Pete, you've hit everywhere you ever played and you'll hit here. Sometimes, it takes a little bit of time." That was his reaction, and it really pumped me up. Quite frankly, there are many managers who wouldn't leave a guy in the lineup who was hitting .220 and making a lot of errors. I turned it around from there and ended up with a .295 batting average. I really owed that to him. There were a lot of managers who I'm sure would have told me they were going to give me a little rest.

I was second in the Rookie of the Year voting to my teammate, Gary Peters, and he gives it to me about that all the time. I see him about once a year at a baseball dinner in New York, and he'll always say, "Hey, Pete, I just want you to know I polished all your trophies yesterday!" The camaraderie on that ballclub was just terrific. A few years ago, I told Gary at that dinner that I had just taken up golf and I really liked it. He said, "You ought to like it. All you have to do is hit it, and you don't have to catch it or throw it!" We had a great bunch of guys like him, and we enjoyed playing together.

I never thought of my batting stance as different. In the minor leagues, I had batted with my hands spaced two or three inches apart, then when I got to Triple A, I wasn't hitting as many home runs, so I went on down to a conventional stroke. I went to a banquet in Chicago a few years ago and was surprised when people brought up my stance. I know I wiggled the bat a lot, but that was my way of getting ready.

Nineteen sixty-four was a great year. That was when the Yankees had the fight on their bus over Phil Linz playing the harmonica. They had just gotten swept four in a row by us in Chicago, and we thought maybe we had put some distance on them, but they had that incident and got it back together. We won 10 of our last 11 and nine straight to end the year, but we still lost to them by a game. That was a really good race.

I was in a car accident the next year. We got rained out of an April game in Washington, so we flew back to Chicago and got into town just in time to see the Blackhawks in a playoff game at Chicago Stadium. Coming back from the game, the car I was in got rear-ended. Nick Kladis was a close friend of mine and was driving. Nobody did anything wrong, we just got hit in bumper-to-bumper traffic, and Tommy John was with us, too. The amazing thing about it is that we weren't really hit that hard. It must have been just a bad location. I didn't think I'd have a problem, but the next day I had a sore neck, and it just kept coming back. It bothered me quite a bit that season.

I was supposed to be on the cover of *Sports Illustrated* that year, but Muhammad Ali bumped me off. He won his title fight, and they had time to get the pictures on, so I got taken off. They brought me copies of it after I got knocked off that I still have.

Eddie Stanky and Al were just different, but both were good managers. Eddie was different psychologically than Al was. He was very smart, but sometimes he would agitate rather than motivate. When he got the job, we were all very happy. We didn't know him, because he had played a long time before we did, but we looked forward to it. He was a very smart baseball man, smarter than all of us—there was no doubt about that. A lot of us really liked playing for him. I was very fortunate because he and Al were the best managers a guy could play for. When I got traded to the Yankees, I got to play for Ralph Houk, who was cut from the same mold as Lopez.

In 1967 there were four teams in a great race. It could have been our year because we were right there all season. We went into Kansas City at the end of the year, and I can still remember walking into that ballpark. The A's were running football pass patterns in the outfield during their batting practice, so they were really loose. Danny Cater was out of their lineup and so was Bert Campaneris, but they took it to us and beat us both games. Then we lost the last series to Washington, so it was the sixth- and 10th-place teams that got us.

I went to Vietnam on a goodwill tour in the off-season. Tug McGraw, Denny McLain, Ron Taylor, and I all went. Bob Elson came with us, too.

Pete Ward finished second to teammate Gary Peters in the voting for American League Rookie of the Year, with 22 homers, 84 RBIs, and a .295 batting average.

They took us all over the place, and we wore our hats, met a lot of people, shook a lot of hands, and said hello to anyone we could.

When I was traded to the Yankees after 1969, all I can say is that if you were going to get traded, it was nice to get traded to the Yankees. I was look-ing forward to it, but it felt funny coming back into Chicago to play a game there. It was the end of my career there. Basically all I did was play a few games at first base and pinch-hit. I wasn't the player I was when I first came up. I think Ed Short, the general manager, was doing me a favor.

My memories of Chicago are tremendous. For my last few years of my Sox career, I lived only four blocks from the park and was familiar with the neighborhood. I walked to work, except when I playing poorly, I was afraid to! Comiskey Park was big and a lot of times it was damp. Whatever could be done was done for the pitchers by the grounds crew. I can't think of a better place to play.

Being with the White Sox was a tremendous thrill. I was on a cruise in Germany when the Sox won it in 2005, so I didn't even get to call the White Sox for tickets. I was thrilled to death, not only for the players, but for trainer Herman Schneider, because he was with me in the minor leagues when I was coaching at Rochester and managing at Fort Lauderdale. He's done a great job, and it shows you what you can do if you have desire.

64

Third baseman Pete Ward was acquired by the White Sox from Baltimore on January 14, 1963, along with Ron Hansen, Dave Nicholson, and Hoyt Wilhelm, with the Sox sending Luis Aparicio and Al Smith to Baltimore. Ward had a stand-out rookie season with 22 homers, 84 RBIs, and a .295 batting average, finishing second to teammate Gary Peters in the voting for American League Rookie of the Year. He followed up with 23 homers and 94 RBIs the following season. In April 1965 Ward was a passenger in a car that was rear-ended and was never the same player after suffering a neck injury in the accident. He was traded to the Yankees on December 18, 1969, for Mickey Scott and cash and retired following the 1970 season.

TOMMY JOHN

PITCHER

1965–1971

WHEN I WAS TRADED TO THE WHITE SOX, the Indians called my home, and I was at school. They wanted to tell me before it was out on the news wire. My dad put a call into my college and got me between classes. He said, "How would you like to play in that Miami golf classic they have every spring?" I asked, "Why? Are the Indians going to train in Florida?" He said, "No, you've been traded to the White Sox so you won't be training in Tucson, you'll be training in Florida."

Ray Berres, Al Lopez, Don Gutteridge, and Tony Cuccinello all worked with me. That's where I learned how to pitch. Ray and Al had the patience of Job working with me, because I just couldn't comprehend what they were trying to get me to learn. They just kept at it and kept at it, then after a while, a light came on.

They wanted you to be a sinkerball and curveball pitcher. I was a curve-ball pitcher and had a tendency to drop my elbow and get under the ball. When you are in high school or American Legion, you throw the ball by guys. When you get to the big leagues, you don't do that. We didn't have a throwing program like they do now. We just played catch. Every time I threw the ball in the outfield, if my arm dropped, I would hear this whistle and I'd turn around to see Ray Berres. He would have his elbow up in the air. He told me, "If you aren't going to throw it right, then don't play catch. All you are doing is practicing mistakes. That's not going to help you a bit."

The desire was to have you sink the ball, because we didn't have hard throwers. Probably the hardest thrower on our staff at that time was Gary Peters, and Pete sank the ball and had great movement to go along with a great hard slider. Comiskey was a big ballpark, and they wanted us to sink the ball. Once I found out what they wanted me to do and how to do it, then it was much easier for me to repeat it time and time again.

In 1965 we were second to the Twins. We floundered a bit in '66, but in 1967 we were in it until the final weekend of the season. Four teams went at it all year, and we had a doubleheader with Kansas City on Wednesday after being rained out Tuesday. Catfish Hunter and Chuck Dobson beat us in that doubleheader, and we went from first to fourth place.

Our manager, Eddie Stanky, offered the pitchers a new suit of clothes if you threw 20 ground balls and pitched a complete game. Back in those days, we didn't score a lot of runs. You would be pinch-hit for a lot of times in the seventh or eighth as we tried to get an extra run or maybe back into a game. I think I got him for a couple suits and especially remember when I had something like 23 groundballs in nine innings once at Boston. The grounders could be base hits—he just wanted us to pitch down in the zone. Remember that the grass at Comiskey Park was really long. Gene Bossard and his son, Roger, had a moat built in front of home plate. It made it difficult for guys to lift the ball out of the ballpark.

With our offense, you had to concentrate more, and it made you pitch, not throw. If you gave up three runs, you were probably going to lose the game. Less than three, you had a chance. I always felt that made me a better pitcher, knowing I didn't have a lot to give up, so I went out and pitched. A lot of times guys give in and throw something down the middle of the plate and think, *I'll get him next time*. For us, there was no next time with the White Sox. You pitched as if the first inning was the eighth or ninth inning.

I came within about three days of being drafted into the service and joined the Indiana Air National Guard. I would go once a month and go to my home town of Terre Haute, Indiana. If we were on the road, I would fly back on a Friday night. I'd drive to Mom and Dad's house, then have the weekend with the Guard. When it was over on Sunday, I would jump in my car, drive back to Chicago, and meet the ballclub wherever it was. The Sox accommodated me and would move me up or back a day if needed.

When the Guard had the two-week summer camp, I would pitch a Sunday, go to camp, fly in on Saturday night, pitch Sunday, then rejoin my Guard

Tommy John's claim to fame occurred three years after he left the White Sox, when a doctor replaced a ligament in his pitching arm with a forearm tendon. The surgery now bears his name and has revolutionized sports medicine.

67

unit wherever they were training. I'd play catch while I was there. We had Tom and Dick Van Arsdale, two pretty good NBA players, and Tom McCraw, who was a major leaguer like me. I'd play catch with him every night if I could. Then I'd head out and pitch on my Sunday off, then come back and throw when I could. It was what you had to do when you were in a Guard unit during Vietnam.

I got off to a good start, and my ERA in 1968 was 1.98. That was the year that Bob Gibson's was 1.12 and Carl Yastrzemski led the American League in hitting with a .301 average. The next year the owners had their meeting and cut the height of the mound down from 15 to 10 inches.

I was pitching in Detroit that year and went 3–0 on Dick McAuliffe. On the next pitch, he ran up like he was going to bunt, and I threw a strike.

I threw several more pitches and then out of nowhere I threw a ball over his head that was not at him, but ended up hitting the backstop, it was that wild. He looked at me and charged the mound. I tried to tackle into him, figuring that if I tackled him, the fight would be over before anyone got hurt. When I hit him, he drove his knee into my shoulder and separated it, so I didn't pitch much after that.

The 1969 decision to put Astroturf in the infield at Comiskey Park really hurt me. I remember calling our general manager, Ed Short, and asking him why. He said, "It will help us." I told him we didn't have anyone to catch the ball on that surface. It's one thing to put in Astroturf when you have an infield like Whitey Herzog had in St. Louis with Ozzie Smith and others. We didn't have anybody like that. We had a slow batch of infielders, but for whatever reason, they decided to put it in. My ERA went up past three right away. They said I'd have the chance to get more double plays, and I agreed, but only because I knew there would be more runners on base. Putting the Astroturf in was not the best move the Sox ever made. It was a bad decision.

The team started floundering about then, and we made some bad trades. In 1970 I was starting every five days no matter what, and I don't think I won a game in April. I was pitching in Baltimore and looking at finishing the month 0–5 or 0–6. Somebody said to me that it must be terrible, but I looked at it as I was supposed to be the ace of the staff. I led our team in innings pitched even though I missed a couple of weeks after getting an injection in my elbow that missed and hit my ulnar nerve.

When they traded me to the Dodgers for Dick Allen, it was probably one of the best trades in baseball history in terms of helping both teams. During my last year, the Sox's radio station was nonexistent and when Dick came in and had that great year in 1972, they got a big new deal on a real station. Dick Allen helped the Sox get out of the doldrums, and I went to the Dodgers and played for championship teams there.

I beat Steve Carlton to win the pennant in a rainstorm in 1977, and we had a party afterward at a restaurant. Roland Hemond was there and offered a toast that he helped the Dodgers win more than anybody because he had traded me to them for Dick Allen. That was great, and I always admired Roland for his sense of humor.

If I ever had a chance to do anything in the White Sox organization, I would jump at it because that's where I learned how to pitch only 160 miles from my hometown in Terre Haute. Chicago is a second home for me. I loved

68

playing there, and if I could ever do anything to help the White Sox, I'd do it in a heartbeat. I have a special place in my heart for the White Sox and follow them all the time.

Left-hander Tommy John was acquired by the Sox on January 20, 1965, along with Tommie Agee and Johnny Romano from Cleveland in a three-team deal that also included the A's. John blossomed in his first two seasons with the Sox, going 14–7 and 14–11. His record dipped to 10–13 in 1967, but his ERA was a measly 2.47 that year. He earned a berth on the American League All-Star team in 1968, but his season was cut short by a shoulder injury suffered in a scuffle with the Detroit Tigers. The 1969 arrival of the Astroturf infield to Comiskey Park coincided with John's losing record the next three years, but his ERA never climbed above 3.61. On December 2, 1971, the Sox traded John and Steve Huntz to the Dodgers for Dick Allen.

Tommy John's greatest claim to fame came in 1974, when he injured the ulnar collateral ligament in his pitching arm. Dr. Frank Jobe replaced the ligament with a tendon from John's right forearm. John returned to the Dodgers' rotation in 1976, and the revolutionary surgery that bears his name has saved countless pitching careers since. He went on to pitch for the Yankees, Angels, A's, and back to the Yankees in his 26 seasons and finished with 288 wins, the most in history by a pitcher not in the Hall of Fame.

ROGER BOSSARD
GROUNDSKEEPER
1967–Present

I WAS RAISED AT OLD COMISKEY PARK, and my dad was the groundskeeper. When I was 10 years old, I used to go on the field and shag balls. We had uniforms as kids, and I played with the sons of Billy Pierce, Earl Torgeson, Ray Berres, and Sherm Lollar. It was very much about family back then. I'll never forget those days.

I went to Purdue University and studied agronomy, but I actually think I knew what I was going to do when I was nine or 10 years old. My dad grew up like I did under his father, who was the groundskeeper with the Indians. At nine years old, you don't really know what you're going to do, but when you come here all the time, it is just passed on that way. My dad never forced me into it. It just fell that way. I went to school and then came back, and now here I am.

My first year here was in 1967, and it really was a special year. My dad was here, and people came up with the ludicrous idea that balls were being frozen. What they thought was that my dad was putting them in a room with a humidifier. I've heard through the grapevine that, after you have the balls in there for a few days, they can gain anywhere from a quarter to a half ounce. Well, everybody knows that was done that year with Eddie Stanky as our manager. Hawk Harrelson and I have had many laughs, because he remembers coming in here as a player, and we used to wet the ground in front of home plate until it was like mud. We had Tommy John, Joel Horlen, and Gary

Peters—all low-ball pitchers. That, along with the heavy baseballs, certainly indicated there weren't going to be a lot of balls hit out of the old stadium. Believe it or not, our leading hitter among the regulars that year was Ken Berry, and he hit about .240, but somehow we were still in first place with six games to go. The groundskeepers helped a little bit that year.

Disco Demolition was a nightmare. [On July 12, 1979, the Sox were forced to forfeit the second game of a doubleheader against the Tigers after a radio promotion to blow up a pile of disco records between games led to a riot on the field at Comiskey Park.] That was the only night in 43 years when I said I didn't want to be involved in baseball. I knew how Custer felt at the Battle of Little Bighorn when he saw everyone coming at him. It was amazing to see all the potholes that were made. They took benches from the picnic area and built a bonfire in center field. There's nothing more depressing than being a groundskeeper and seeing a bonfire in the middle of your field. Bill Veeck's secretary told me later that he got thousands of letters in the three weeks after that from people who said they would never come back to Comiskey Park. I always felt bad for Bill after that. It was a horrible incident.

Leaving that stadium was not difficult, though, because it had seen its time. I'm proud to say that I am the inventor of the drainage system that most fields use now, and I was able to incorporate that here at the new park. This is the new house, it's the new car. Some of the old-timers have asked me if I miss being over there, and actually, I don't miss it at all. We're in the new house. You couldn't work for a better person than Jerry Reinsdorf. Before we moved over here, he asked all the department heads, "What do you want?" It was a great move.

There were some heart-tugging moments, though. When we moved over here, I brought the infield clay over from the old field. It was that important, not only to me, but to our infielders. I got a call that first year from a lady who was probably in her mid-fifties. She said, "Is it true that you brought the old clay over?" and I assured her we had. She started crying, and I didn't understand why until she told me that years before, my father had allowed her family to spread her father's ashes on the infield. She said, "Now I still know where my dad is." That was very touching to me, and I was happy for her.

We were state of the art in 1991 when this place was built, but over time, things change and they get better. Jerry made sure we kept up with the times. When we got U.S. Cellular on board for naming rights, Jerry put that money

Head groundskeeper Roger Bossard works on his masterpiece—the infield at U.S. Cellular Field. *Photo courtesy of Bob Vorwald*

back into the park. I don't think you can say enough about a person who does that. I'm in charge of the cleanup crew as well as the grounds crew, and he wants to make this place like Disney, and it is. He has kept all the amenities up to the level of the newer stadiums. It doesn't get any better.

My daily routine for a 1:05 day game starts around 6:15 in the morning. My crew gets in around 7:00 AM. The first thing we'll do is start matting the warning track and wetting the infield portion of the field. The infield for the ballplayers and then for the groundskeeper is the most important part of the field. About 70 percent occurs in the infield. A lot of fans don't understand that each infielder has his own space or spot, and each guy likes it differently. When Robin Ventura was here, he used to like the area around third base extremely soft. When Ozzie played, he always wanted the back six feet of the infield on the firm side so when he took his first two steps, he could get good footing. However, he wanted the area in front of that to remain soft to cushion the ball so it would stay down. When Eric Soderholm was here in the late '70s, he had two bad knees. My dad was here, and Eric asked us to keep it like mud to protect his knees. I go back to the days of the late Bill Veeck when he said, "A good groundskeeper is the 10th man on the field and can be worth three or four games a year." The Bossards, of which I am the third generation, like to feel that we've done our part.

I'm down at spring training with the players almost the whole time. When we get a new player, we meet, and I ask them how they like the field—firm, soft, whatever. They are all very genuine, and I try to achieve the goal of giving them what they want. I work for them. I have a conversation with Ozzie and Kenny probably a half-dozen times a year to discuss what they want. You hear the old adage called "home-field advantage," and that's what we do, whether it's tilting the foul lines, adjusting the mounds, adjusting the grass or batter's box, even keeping the bases 90 feet. Obviously, there's things that I wouldn't do, but I hear could be done!

I've probably got the rake at home that my dad used in the '40s. I still have a hose handle my dad used that he made himself in 1940. I still use it. It's special after all these years because it has been so refined from the pressure of the water that it gives out a perfect spray. I only use it one time a day. Most of the other times, I just use my finger. I was raised the old way and I guess I've been fooling them for 43 years. I'm not going to complain.

When bad weather comes, I do get a lot of guff. I have a Doppler radar here, and feel sorry for the weathermen in town, because it's difficult being on the lake. Fronts will be coming in, and then, all of a sudden, they will back off. I work closely with Kenny [Williams], Ozzie [Guillen], and the umpiring crew chief, and it can be trying at times, deciding what the weather will be. There was one time two years ago where we called a game. Jerry Reinsdorf was involved in it, and the weather was what we call "training," meaning there was just storm after storm lined up for hours coming our way out of Iowa. Well, that train split up after about the fourth car, and we had called that night game at around 3:30 or 4:00 in the afternoon because we didn't want to inconvenience our fans. At around 5:30, the sun came out and was shining brightly, so that's one mistake I remember when trying to call our weather. I've also called some good ones, but it's always challenging.

73

I've built the fields for 11 of the last 14 stadiums, and I've got 'em fooled, I guess. In 1984 the Saudi royal family contacted Major League Baseball and got to me. I went over to Saudi Arabia and actually designed and built the first four natural grass soccer fields for the royal family. I'm still in touch with them, and Prince Abdullah and I became very close friends. He's been very good to me and my family. It was quite an experience, and I made some good friends over there. It was the experience of a lifetime. We flew three 747s full of sod from California over there, and he had to pay quite a large price for that project. Prince Abdullah was the George Steinbrenner of soccer. They had artificial turf, but at that time they didn't have any grass things at all. I worked for a year and a half on that system. In Riyadh, they get sandstorms every day, so I put two irrigation systems in to make sure that I could flush the sand down through the field because of the salinity level of the sand that flies through there.

The Cubs asked me to rebuild their playing field in 2007. I enjoy a challenge, and that was the ultimate one for me. Yes, I have caught some grief from some White Sox diehards over that, but that's no surprise!

I am just like the players, because all you really want is that World Series ring. It's something that you can't buy. Dad was here for 51 years and got an American League championship ring in 1959. I was fortunate enough in 2005 that we won it. Things need to click, and everybody in sports will tell you in a championship year, everything just works. The ball hops the right way, the blooper just falls over a first baseman's glove, and that was our year. It was the most exciting year I had here. I'm happy our field held up so we could play the two World Series games here in bad weather. The players won it, they got me my ring, and I was very happy for that.

My nickname "the Sodfather" started on the radio, I think, a few years ago. I think it fits me, and it's cute, I guess. We did a commercial for the team last spring, and that was really fun. It was shot in Arizona to look like we were in Chicago, and the shoot lasted around three and a half hours because we were laughing so much. It went great, but I wish I could see the blooper reel from that shoot.

I could have never imagined all this when I was nine years old. One thing I will say: I do strive for perfection. I think everybody can appreciate wanting to be the best, and that's the way I was raised. A lot of pressure comes along with that, and sometimes you pay the price by not sleeping at night and worrying. To be good, that's what you have to do.

The name "Bossard" is synonymous with outstanding groundskeepers. Grandfather Emil was head groundskeeper with the Indians from 1932 through 1968, and Roger's father, Gene, filled that role for the White Sox from 1940 through 1983. Roger joined the Sox organization in 1967 and took over from his father as head groundskeeper after Gene's retirement. Nineteen of the 30 major league teams use his patented drainage system, and he continues as a consultant to the royal family of Saudi Arabia, for whom he built natural grass soccer fields in 1984 and 1985. He is a consultant for 14 MLB and four NFL teams.

The
SEVENTIES

ED HERRMANN
CATCHER
1967 ★ 1969–1974

MY GRANDFATHER PLAYED IN THE MAJOR LEAGUES. He lived in Cincinnati, and we were in San Diego. But we went back, and I saw my grandpa several times before he passed away. The first time, he gave me a catcher's glove, which at the time I really didn't care if I had one since I wanted a mitt with fingers in it. As it turned out, he knew something I didn't. I had the opportunity to talk with him in depth about sports when I was about 10, and the one thing I'll always remember is that he told me to do it because you love it. Don't do it for any other reason. That's one of the reasons I got involved in sports—I love them. Sports was something I worked on day and night—baseball, basketball, and football. I had a whole group of guys who got together all the time. We played baseball in the street and in our backyards.

I played high school baseball with Dave Duncan, Bob Boone, Tim Blackwell, and other great players. The year I graduated, everybody but one player on the team signed a pro contract.

I signed professionally with the Braves and went to the Florida State League. I signed as a pitcher, and when we got down there, we had no catchers. They asked if anybody had ever caught before, and I had caught maybe five games in high school, so they asked me if I would catch one game until they brought in some catchers. I said I'd be happy to, anything to play. I never saw the mound again. My life was behind the plate.

I really did it enjoy it because I was more of a football-type baseball player. I enjoyed the contact—that's why I liked pitching, because it was one-on-one like a runner and a linebacker. That was my mentality. Catching gave me the opportunity to stop runners coming from third to home and the opportunity to lead a group of guys kind of like a quarterback would.

Hollis Thurston had scouted me with the White Sox. He went to the their winter meetings later on, and when my name came up in the winter meetings, they had me as a right-handed hitter. I was a switch-hitter, but the Braves were hiding me, I guess, and didn't let me hit lefty. The Sox went out and got me in Rule 5 draft and put me on the major league roster. In 1965 I hurt my ankle and couldn't hit from the right side anymore and became strictly a left-handed hitter.

My first game in the majors was at Boston in 1967. Ed Runge was behind the plate, and my first time up I got a double off the Green Monster to drive in a run. Heck, I was ready to quit right then with a 1.000 batting average.

Those first years were a great experience for me because I got to learn along with the pitchers. When I would be catching bullpen sessions, our pitching coaches would be there teaching the young kids how to throw different pitches and how to hit different areas. I got to know the pitchers, so I knew how balls moved. When we got to the big leagues, it was easy for me to catch them.

The football mentality served me well when I was catching our knuckleballers. It was the challenge of a lifetime to never let one ball by me. It was impossible, but it was something to strive for. Even as many innings as I caught Wilbur Wood and got to know his ball better than most, there were still times he handcuffed me.

Every knuckleball has a different way of doing things, depending on who is throwing it. Eddie Fisher's broke down and away from right-handers on a very consistent basis. We could throw Wilbur's ball in and out because he had much better control than Hoyt [Wilhelm] or Eddie. When we needed the ball in, it went down and in to right-handers and floated out and away when he went outside. When Hoyt threw the ball, there wasn't a person on the face of the earth who knew where the ball was going. He was just phenomenal. He threw the ball, and everybody just waited to see what it was going to do.

When I first started, they had the great big glove to catch a knuckler, then they made it quite a bit smaller, so it was just bigger than a first baseman's glove but not anywhere near as big as it was when I first got there. As the years went by, guys couldn't handle the big gloves, so they started catching knucklers with their regular gloves with the breaks in them.

The way I learned to catch it, thanks to pitching coach Ray Berres, was to not look at the release point on the knuckleball, but to look at the bottom of the mound and hope to catch it on the last break as it's coming in. The ball will come through that sight zone, and you want to pick up that last break, rather than watch it leave the hand and try to go with each break. That's what helped me a lot—not following the ball, but picking it up late.

Les Moss encouraged me to put as much abuse on the opposition trying to score as I possibly could, which meant to me, don't give any ground. In high school I was that middle linebacker who loved to hit and hit some more. Les used that same mentality on me to become the person who would deny runners home plate if I ever got the opportunity. That's basically what I did. Everybody who came in from third base was a running back to me, and I did all I could to stop them from getting by me.

Chuck Tanner came in 1971 and was the probably the best manager I ever played for. He was a players' manager and a person who was quite the motivator and was probably before his time. He was very knowledgeable and was ideal to be a manager with the DH. That year I had an appendix problem, and it really affected me for about half the year because I never really got my strength back. Gangrene set in after I had it out, and I came back way too early. I wanted to get back, and that was my biggest fault.

Nineteen seventy-two was unbelievable. We had Bill Melton, who I thought was a phenomenal athlete. He hit for power and did a fantastic job coming from the outfield and playing third base. It was nice to have somebody who was consistent on both throwing and catching. To watch Richie [Dick] Allen play the way he did was something because he was in a class all by himself. He was a man playing with a bunch of boys as far as the White Sox were concerned. I've never seen a guy put a team on his back and hold them there for almost the whole year.

It was a very enjoyable year. There were a few of us who went through the years where there were only about 500 people at the stadium. To go and have the stands filled with thousands and thousands of people on a daily basis not only energized the ballplayers, but the whole South Side. Richie was a phenomenal person. I don't think there was ever a ballplayer who played for Chicago when Richie was there who wouldn't have wanted him on the team. He got along with everybody.

Ed Herrmann was a power threat at the plate and on July 4, 1972, tied a major league record by helping to turn three double plays as a catcher. *Photo courtesy of Richard Lindberg*

In 1974 I hurt my ankle really bad, and we brought Brian Downing in to do some catching. He was doing a good job for a guy who was new to catching, but he got hurt in about the third game he caught when he dove for a foul ball and hurt his knee on the dugout's old wood steps. It bothered him trying to get up and down. I was in the trainer's room, trying to get my ankle healed, and when I saw him in there, I thought I could wrap my ankle and play because I could get up and down. I was selected to the All-Star Game, but I didn't play because I wasn't ready. I wanted those three days off to get myself better and help the team.

I went out with Wilbur Wood quite a bit. We'd sit at dinner and talk about the game over a beverage or two. That's something ballplayers used to do quite a bit instead of taking steroids or the other things that have come into the game. After the game, we would sit in the clubhouse for two or three hours, drinking our beers and talking about that game. If we were leaving or had to get out of the clubhouse, it wasn't unusual to see 10 or 12 of us at a restaurant eating, drinking, and talking about baseball.

Comiskey Park was a park of the old days. It had a spacious outfield, and the grass on the infield was always very thick. The Bossards built the ballpark for the team that was there that year. Harmon Killebrew once said he could take a .30-06 rifle, lay it on home plate, fire it, and the bullet would never reach the shortstop. Pete Ward and Ron Hansen on that side weren't fleet of foot, so the Bossards would do that to offset our lack of speed. The same thing happened at first base, where it was very soggy every time a fast team came in.

Fanwise, I loved it. They were close enough that you could hear them and far enough away that if you made a mistake, you could close your eyes to them. I really liked it. I know there were some areas where there were poles and people couldn't see well, but I really enjoyed it.

There was a girl out in left field who started "the SuperHerrmanns." It was quite unique, because they went to my family first about the concept of "SuperHerrmann." A lot of it came from me blocking home plate, and that's where it originated. It was a great thing. A lot of people don't have fan clubs. They had a pretty good group of people out there. I'd go out and get on them and say, "Hey, spend a few bucks and get some seats behind home plate. You can yell at me a bit more." They enjoyed being regular people and sitting out in the bleachers.

The "Big White Machine" came about when I went to the front office in 1970 because we weren't winning, and I thought maybe we could cause some sort of stir in the media. They didn't have a clue. I had a friend, Tom Buffo, who was the general manager of Hawkinson Ford out in Oak Lawn, and he was giving cars to the ballplayers who lived in that area to use during the season. He came up with the idea because of the "Big Red Machine" in Cincinnati and said, "Why don't we come up with the 'Big White Machine'?" It had to be white, and he got a friend of his to put together an old Model A with a wooden frame. They put it on a chassis with a seat and an old flathead engine, and that became the "Big White Machine." It caused a stir. We lost more than 100 games that year, so it wasn't run a lot, but when we did win, it was fired up, and Roger Bossard drove it around. I used to build race cars, so it was fun for me to get involved in it. We were trying to do anything we could to offset the Cubs, and there were a lot of articles written about it.

It was tough to leave when I went to the Yankees. I loved the town and was there a long time. I had very good friends there. To this day, the people I was friends with from my playing days come down to the Sox Fantasy Camp. It was tough to leave, but the players in New York welcomed me with open arms.

The White Sox organization is phenomenal. Jerry Reinsdorf is a great person and one of the few owners who speaks the truth. He's always trying to do something nice for the team and the ticket holders. He comes to the Fantasy Camp every year on Thursday night and talks to those people every year, answering questions, and he does his best to tell them the straight and narrow.

From 1969 to 1974, Ed Herrmann crouched behind the plate and blocked opposing runners as the White Sox's catcher. His best offensive season came in 1970, when he hit .283 with 19 homers and 52 RBIs. He was selected to the 1974 All-Star team, but did not play due to injury. After the '74 season, the Sox were unwilling to meet his salary demands and sent him to the New York Yankees for cash and several minor leaguers.

WILBUR WOOD
PITCHER
1967–1978

WHEN I CAME TO THE WHITE SOX IN 1967, I was at the point in my career where you either have to do something or change. I thought it was an opportunity—I had been traded from the Pirates and had been with the Red Sox, and my record just wasn't that good.

I had thrown a knuckleball since I was a kid. My dad had a pretty good palm ball that acted a lot like a knuckleball since it didn't have any rotation on it. When you're a kid, you want to try to do what your dad can do, so I came up with throwing the ball on my fingertips and came up with my knuckleball.

When I got to the White Sox, my record was poor, and my fastball was a few yards too short. I told myself if I was going to do anything, I needed to change. Being with Hoyt Wilhelm, it was pretty simple—if I'm going to do anything, I have to do it with the knuckleball because my fastball isn't good enough. I just made my mind up that, *Hey, I'm going to go out there and throw knuckleballs and then I'm going to throw more knuckleballs.* I had a really good curveball, but you can only throw so many curveballs before the hitters catch on. I made my mind up that I was going with the knuckleball, and it was going to be make or break. It worked out pretty well. Hoyt told me, "If you're going to be a knuckleball pitcher, you have to throw the knuckleball. You can't being throwing sliders, then the curveball, fastball, and everything else. It takes away from the knuckleball."

The White Sox were looking for a left-hander who could be a mop-up man—I guess today they call him a long man—who could throw strikes, and I had a reputation for being able to throw strikes, so I was what they wanted. I just wanted to make myself more successful. I could throw strikes with my knuckleball, and that's what I did. Eddie Fisher was also with the Sox, so at one point we had three knuckleballers on the team. He was very, very successful, as was Hoyt, and I had a few good years myself.

The catchers had the big glove, but Jerry McNertney would use a small glove because he thought he could move it more quickly. J.C. Martin was there, later Ed Herrmann and Brian Downing, and they had seen the knuckleball. To them, it was not a new pitch. With Hoyt and Eddie there, it was no big deal to them: "Look, we have another knuckleball pitcher." It wasn't a big mystery. All the catchers I threw to in Chicago had caught it a lot, so it was no big deal.

My first year, there was a great four-team pennant race. That was the year Yaz [Carl Yastrzemski] had a fabulous year and carried the Red Sox from day one to the end. We were in it up until the last few games of the season. If we had just won one or two games in our last five, we'd have been right there, but we lost our last five games of the year.

The following year, Hoyt had a bad arm, and Bob Locker was hurt, too. I ended up becoming the short man and won the Fireman of the Year award. From my point of view, it was great for me because I got to pitch quite often.

In 1971 they made me a starter and, to be honest, I really didn't have much of a choice. Chuck Tanner had come on to manage the ballclub and he didn't want a knuckleball pitcher coming out of the bullpen because of passed balls and wild pitches. He wanted the hard throwers like Terry Forster and Rich Gossage. I held out that year because I wanted some more money, which in those days was another $500 a month or so. They had a trade set up for me to Washington for Darold Knowles, but with me holding out and holding out, it didn't happen because I wasn't signed. So I ended up signing, became a starting pitcher, and things worked out very well.

There were no adjustments for me. When we pitched relief, it wasn't for just one inning. You'd go out for three or four innings all the time, so starting wasn't a big adjustment. My biggest asset was that I could throw the ball over the plate—and I was always able to with all my pitches. When I watch some of the pitchers today, even though I love watching baseball, I can't stand to watch them nibble. It's like watching paint dry. Ball one, strike one, ball

85

two, strike two, every batter a full count—I'd rather shut the TV off and watch a cooking show. Here's the ball, make 'em hit it.

In 1972 we added Dick Allen, and he was one of the all-time greatest hitters in baseball. He could handle the bat like no one else and was a super, super person in the clubhouse. I know a lot of things have been written, but he was just a super guy. I pitched a lot because I was able to come back quicker than some, but I always looked at it as wanting to go out and pitch. I wanted to be able to participate. You're not going to win every time you go out, but I couldn't pitch like they do today once every five or six days. You've got to have rhythm and be in that rotation at least every four days, at least I would. I don't think they pitch enough. You look at a starter today, and if they go five or six innings, it's a quality start. If we only went five or six innings, we'd be looking at a pay cut.

The next year, I started both a suspended and regular game the same day, but it was no big deal. You didn't figure the first game would go too long, and I was already pitching twice a week, so I didn't look at it as any big thing. If you're throwing strikes, you're not throwing a lot of pitches. They didn't start pitch counts 'til near the end of my career. The manager who is running the ballclub, whether it be Chuck Tanner, Al Lopez, Earl Weaver, whoever, they can tell when the pitcher is starting to lose it. They didn't have to say, "He threw 85 pitches, so we knew he was tired." They could look at you and know you were tired even if you only threw 60 pitches or leave you in a lot longer.

I was in the All-Star Game three times. I wish I could've pitched in those games more than I did, but that's the way the ball bounces. You had to save some pitchers for extra innings, and the starters went longer than they do now. It was impossible to get all the pitchers in. I remember the home run Reggie Jackson hit off the light tower in Tiger Stadium. There was an awful lot of pride taken in those games.

Comiskey Park was a big ballpark, and it helped me a great deal, especially because it didn't have a short porch in either right or left. If I was in Detroit, you had that short porch in right field, or in Boston, there was the wall so close in left field, but Comiskey gave you an advantage by being a bigger park. We always had a good outfield, and they could run the balls down. I couldn't pitch any different at those parks, but I was glad to be throwing in Comiskey.

The hitters who gave me trouble were the ones who had great bat control. Rod Carew was tops, and so was Tony Oliva. People like that, you would

Wilbur Wood, seen here throwing a pitch during a 1972 game at Comiskey Park, was an American League All-Star in 1971, 1972, and 1974.

throw them a really good pitch, and they had such good bat control that they would foul it off. If you made a bad pitch, they'd jump all over it. The home-run hitters would get me, and Jim Rice, for example, got me several times, but when you go back and look at the home runs hit off you, how many of them really made a big difference? A lot of them cut a lead from four runs to three, but I wasn't walking guys, so I kept throwing strikes. I gave up a lot, but if you don't walk that guy in front, then give one up, that's the way you want to pitch.

Carlton Fisk was a pain in the ass with the Red Sox. He'd step out of the box and be throwing dirt all over his hands and legs, dirt here, dirt there, and I'd holler, "Get in the box! I'm throwing a knuckleball. Here it is! Hit it or don't hit it, but Jesus Christ, let's go!" Ed Herrmann was behind the plate, and he was laughing right along with the umpire. Give me the ball and let's go. It's either a good game or a bad game, but give me the ball and come on.

When Ron LeFlore hit a drive off my kneecap, I really think I got a little gun shy after that. I came back and pitched a few more years, but I was gun shy. You start getting that way, and it takes away from being able to throw well, and that was the end of it, that's all. You're trying to keep the ball in on everybody so they don't hit it back up the middle, and that ended my career.

In 1977 I wanted to be able to do what I did in the past, but I wasn't throwing the ball as well as I had been. I wasn't as successful as I wanted to be. We were a different ballclub, and I was on the DL a bit. The other fellows took the load over, and I wasn't as big a part as I was in 1972.

To be on the Sox Team of the Century is great. I've got a lot of great memories about Chicago and had some great years there. It sure was a lot of fun.

The White Sox acquired knuckleballer Wilbur Wood from the Pittsburgh Pirates on October 12, 1966, in exchange for Juan Pizarro. He spent his first four seasons in the bullpen and was the American League Fireman of the Year in 1968 before joining the starting rotation in 1971, a move that paid immediate dividends when he went 22–13 with a 1.91 ERA and 22 complete games in 334 innings. In 1972 Wood threw a mind-boggling 377 innings while winning 24 games with a 2.51 ERA. He won 24 more for the team in 1973 and 20 in 1974 to complete a string of four straight years with 20 or more wins and complete games along with more than 300 innings. Wood's record fell to 16–20 in 1975 when he threw *only* 291 innings.

In 1976 Ron LeFlore's line drive shattered Wood's kneecap, and he missed the rest of the season. He returned to the Sox and went 7–8 as a spot starter in 1977, 10–10 the following year, and retired after the 1978 season.

In 2000 Wood was named to the White Sox Team of the Century.

BILL MELTON
THIRD BASEMAN
1968–1975

I WAS FIRST INTRODUCED TO THE WHITE SOX when I went with my dad to the 1959 World Series in Los Angeles. We were part of more than 90,000 people at the Coliseum. My heroes turned out to be two guys I watched a lot—Nellie Fox and Luis Aparicio. I was a 12-year-old kid, and I remember thinking I wanted to be just like those guys. I got to play alongside Luis when I first came up.

The way I came to the White Sox was really simple. I used to play on the weekends, but I didn't play any high school baseball. A friend of mine decided to take me up to Brookside Park in Pasadena, California, just to play pickup games on the weekends. He loved the sport of baseball, and I had nothing to do. I was living by myself then, because my parents were in San Diego. There was a lot of A, B, and C teams with some major league guys playing in these pickup games. The Los Angeles area had lots of scouts because everybody played 12 months a year.

This was 1964, before there was a draft. I was out there playing one Sunday, and Hollis Thurston, the old White Sox scout, saw me. The first time up, I hit a long home run that went about 400 feet. The next time up, I hit another home run, and my third time up, I homered again. I guess he figured that with three homers in a game he should sign this kid and he wouldn't have to give me any money to sign, so he did. That was it.

I was scared to death when I walked into the clubhouse for my the first time in 1968. Guys like Gary Peters, Joel Horlen, and Tommy John were there, and I thought they were like old men. They looked older than my father to me! I was intimidated and had never been to a major league camp. I wasn't a bonus baby and didn't have any fanfare. It was an eventful day for me. I didn't sleep—you never sleep—and I didn't know where my locker was. I'll never forget it. I didn't eat for a week!

I came up as an outfielder, and that was a difficult position for me because I had problems with depth perception. The only reason they put me in right field was because I had a strong arm. Al Lopez told me if I was going to make it to the big leagues, it would be as an infielder, so they sent me back down. I only played about 30 games, then they called me back up. My learning experience was getting beat up for a year and learning the position.

If the attendance at your park was a million people, that was a lot in those days. A lot of teams were drawing 500,000 to 800,000 fans, and they were getting on the White Sox because we were drawing only 450,000. I didn't pay any attention when I was young to who was in the stands. I couldn't have cared less. Would it have been fun going out there in front of 55,000 people? Absolutely, but it's a different game now. When I was at home plate and there was a guy 60'6" away, I didn't care who was in the stands booing me.

I was the first real home-run hitter the Sox had, and we started to build with Carlos May, then we got Dick Allen. Those home-run records I set that should have lasted 80 years, Dick Allen blew them away in one year! We were a young team that built from within, because that's how you did it when there was no free agency. Bucky Dent, Ed Herrmann, me, then Chuck Tanner came over—you built from within and made a trade or two as well.

Fans came to the ballpark and followed you. They followed your career. They knew your average. It was an atmosphere of supporting players that came through the team system.

When I won the home-run title in 1971 with one on the last day, I also had to hit two in the next-to-last game. At that time, I had 30 homers, Reggie Jackson and Norm Cash had 32. My teammates, like Pat Kelly, made sure that I knew how many the other guys had, and I was like, "What do you want me to do? Hit three home runs in two games? I'm doing the best I can, fellas." I was the first White Sox player to ever hit 30. The toughest part was getting those two home runs I hit that night. I'll never forget the last game of that year. It was September 30, and it must have been 90 degrees for a noon game

Bill Melton hits his 33rd home run off the Brewers to win the 1971 American League home-run championship. *Photo courtesy of AP Images*

on Astroturf. I had celebrated the night before on Rush Street, which was a fair thing to do. I wasn't sure what a home-run title would mean to me. We had no free agency and didn't really care about statistics. I know it was important to Reggie Jackson, but to us, we were happier that we hadn't lost 100 games and had gotten better.

Chuck Tanner led me off and said he'd get me out of there early. I said, "Fine. What do you want me to do? Go up there and hit a home run my first time up?" He said, "That would be the easy way, then you could leave the game." I hit a home run off Bill Parsons of the Milwaukee Brewers in my second time up, and Chuck made me go out to my position at third base and tip my hat to the crowd. Then I left on a 5:00 flight. It was important to me that a White Sox player had never done it. We were in a fight to get some newspaper headlines, and the exposure was important to me. The fan who got the ball brought it to me, and I remember I signed his helmet, then gave the ball to the trainer.

To be on the NBC *Game of the Week* with Curt Gowdy and Tony Kubek was a big deal. The big teams in the East got most of it like they do now, but when we were on, you would go blow dry your hair and try to be pretty for the day. It was huge. We didn't get it that often, maybe one time a year.

I was on the cover of *Sports Illustrated*, and that was pretty cool. C'mon, it was in every airport! I think I have only four pictures, and that is one of them. One is with Michael Jordan, and I can't remember the other two. I still have that, though, and when I come to SoxFest and other things, people always bring it out. It's really nice to see, and that is still a big hit with me.

We put together a nice club in 1972. The problem for us was the Oakland A's—they won the World Series three straight years at that time. I fell off my roof and ruptured a disc in my back. That affected Dick Allen more than anyone, because he told me, with a guy like me in the lineup, he could get something to hit. When he was in Philly, they pitched around him because there wasn't another power hitter.

It was frustrating to be that close, but we didn't realize what a juggernaut Oakland would become. In 1973 Dick Allen broke his leg when I was having a big year. Injuries will derail any team, but we were a really good team for three years.

It's true that I had issues with Harry Caray. I always thought he was a Hall of Fame broadcaster, but when he was with the White Sox, he got a little tired of us in 1974 and 1975. What happened in Milwaukee was that there were guys coming to me because I was a veteran, guys like Bucky Dent, Goose Gossage, and Terry Forster, wanting to know why Harry was getting all over the young players. I was sitting in my room with Ed Herrmann, my roommate, as they were telling me the stories, and I said I would talk to him. I didn't care if he got on us, the older guys. He got on me in Milwaukee because I was on first base and going to third. I realized I was going to get thrown out at third, so I stopped halfway and headed back to second. Bucky Dent didn't see me and continued on to second. Harry annihilated me, which was fine, though he shouldn't have. I was just frustrated that he was getting on all the young guys, when it was all of us who were the problem. We weren't hitting and weren't winning. That started it between Harry and I, but I've never said he was not a Hall of Famer.

The most impressive thing when we won the World Series in 2005 was the way we won it. When people say we were lucky, so be it. But remember, that team was 11–1 in the playoffs. The domination, especially how spectacular the pitching was, is what I remember. The way the guys did it with clutch hitting, too. You just always knew it was going to happen.

I am very fortunate to be with the White Sox organization. Jerry Reinsdorf and Jeff Torborg were nice enough to bring me back after I had been out of the game for 10 years. I'm from California, but I've always liked Chicago. As a player, I never got to enjoy it. This gave me an opportunity to get back in the game, and I had always been told I should be in broadcasting. I signed with the Sox when I was 17 years old and am still with them now. I have a great feeling being with this organization through John Allyn, Bill Veeck, and Jerry Reinsdorf. To be with this organization more than 30 years is really important to me.

"Beltin'" Bill Melton was signed as an amateur free agent by the White Sox in 1964. He became the Sox's regular third baseman in 1969 and immediately established himself as the team's power source with 23 home runs. Melton followed with back-to-back 33-home-run seasons and won the American League home-run title on the last day of the 1971 season. He was selected to the American League All-Star team that year.

A fall off his garage caused a back injury in 1972 and limited Melton to 57 games. Melton hit 20, 21, and 15 home runs in his next three years with the White Sox before being traded to the California Angels on December 11, 1975, along with Steve Dunning for Jim Spencer and Morris Nettles.

In 2000 Melton was selected to the White Sox Team of the Century. He works as a community relations representative for the Sox and as a broadcaster on the pre- and postgame shows for Comcast SportsNet Chicago.

CARLOS MAY

OUTFIELDER/FIRST BASEMAN
1968–1976

I USED TO LISTEN TO THE WHITE SOX ON THE RADIO all the time when I was growing up in Birmingham, Alabama. I knew a good bit about them when they drafted me.

When I got called up, I remember we were playing Baltimore, and I had to face Dave McNally. I didn't do too well. He sawed me off a couple of times, but it was a learning experience. That was the first big league game I ever saw in person. I went to Birmingham Barons games when they played in the Negro Leagues. Oakland had a minor league team, and I saw Campy Campaneris and some other guys, but that was about it.

We opened up in Oakland in 1969, and I maybe went 1-for-4, but I hit a couple of homers after that off Jim Nash. Then on Opening Day in Chicago I hit two home runs, and they thought I was a home-run hitter. I led the league for about two days that year! It was a great start. It was a fun year, even though we weren't drawing a lot of people. Sometimes there were about 200 people in the stands, but it didn't make any difference to me. I was 21 years old, in the big leagues, and I was just thrilled. Sparse crowds didn't bother me, and I just played the way I needed to play. It was a big thrill for me just to be in the big leagues.

I made the All-Star team that year, and my brother Lee made it, too. I didn't have him show me around, because he was a National Leaguer, and we didn't get along with those guys! We had a pretty good time. The first day we got rained out, then we played the next day, so I got to spend a little bit of time with him. I pinch-hit against Phil Niekro, but I didn't do too well. I swung at one of his knuckleballs, and it hit me in the knee! I struck out, but I was happy to be there. To see Frank Robinson and so many other guys, I was excited I was there.

For my [military] service, I had to go in one weekend a month, then there was a two-week summer camp. That year, I was at Camp Pendleton. It was August 11, and we were out on the range. The night before, everybody had been drinking beer. We had some hot Budweiser, and I'll never forget it. I couldn't sleep because they had tarantulas running around there. There were spiders, and there was no way I was going to sleep, so I stayed up all night. The next morning, we had a six-round volley, which means six mortars all fire at the same time. I was the assistant ammo guy, so I was loading. The guys up on top of the hill had been drinking the night before and didn't spot my round and didn't say if it hit. We had to go back, and the order came down to clean the guns. As the assistant gunner, it was my job to clean them. I had a big, long iron rod with oil and swabbing rags on it to clean the barrel. My round was still in there and hadn't gone all the way down, so when I got the swab, I forced it in there, and my round pushed down to the firing pin and went off. I think it was the rod that shot back up and took off part of my thumb. I was lucky, though. God was with me.

I thought about baseball and didn't know if I would ever play again. They told me if an infection set in, they might have to take my whole thumb off. God was with me, and they didn't have to. I kept my thumb and rehabbed all I could out there. They did a great job for me. I must have had four or five operations, but I came back and played the next year. It was a humbling experience.

When I got to home plate my first game back, the people gave me a standing ovation, and I cried at home plate. It was awesome. It was a thrill just to be back in the big leagues. I think I got a hit that day, but the big thing was to be back. I wasn't sure I'd ever play again, but it worked out. I was honored to be Comeback Player of the Year, and I earned it. They didn't give me anything. I hit .285 and had a pretty good year.

On Opening Day in '71 I had a home run taken away. When you hit a homer, everybody wants to come out and congratulate you out in front of home plate. I couldn't see the plate. They mobbed me, and Gene Tenace, the A's catcher, was watching and then came over with the ball. I thought, *What*

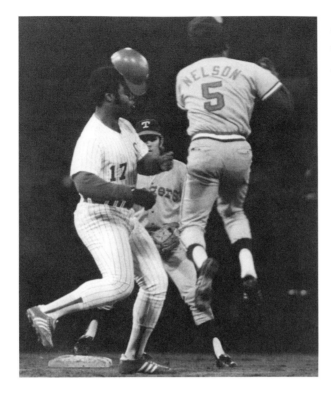

Carlos May, caught in the base paths between a couple of Texas Rangers in a game at Comiskey Park, had his most productive season in 1973, when he hit 20 homers and drove in 96 runs. *Photo courtesy of Richard Lindberg*

is this guy doing? He tagged me, and the umpire called me out. I didn't know I had missed home plate. I cursed all my teammates out after that and said I was leading the league in triples.

One time that year, I had an inside-the-park grand slam at Comiskey when Ken Berry knocked himself out. I hit a ball to left field, and he jumped for it. At the old park in front of the picnic area was a wire fence, and there was an overhang that was brick. When he jumped, he hit his head on the over-hang, and the ball hit the fence and just kept rolling. I kept running, and he was knocked out. One of the other outfielders got the ball, but I didn't know because I was still running the bases.

When Chuck Tanner came, he was a breath of fresh air and a players' man-ager. He stuck up for his players and was a good baseball man with good strategy. He taught us a lot of stuff. I learned how to get jumps and steal bases from Chuck, and he taught us a lot. He was a great manager and a great guy.

I wore No. 17 on my jersey for my birthday [May 17], but I don't know how I got it. When I got to big-league camp, they gave me 29. The next year on Opening Day, I had No. 17, but I don't know how it happened. I carried it on throughout my career.

Old Comiskey was a great, great old ballpark. The fans were right up on you. You could interact with them. After the game, we'd go out to our parking lot on Shields Street, and Walt Williams, my roommate, and I would sign autographs for the people. I enjoyed doing it. It was a fun ballpark and a good place to hit. In the summertime the ball carried well. There were times that the wind blew in, but you take the bitter with the sweet. Overall, it was a great ballpark to play in.

I was hurt and disappointed when I was traded to the Yankees in '76. I was losing all my friends, but I went to a great organization. That was awesome. They were a great bunch of guys over there with Thurman Munson, Catfish Hunter, and all the rest. They treated me well, and we got to the World Series that year.

I will always be a Chicago White Sox fan. You never know which way life is going to turn. Stuff happens. After I left the Angels, I played in Japan for four years. I could've come back and played here, but I think Roland Hemond wanted to send me to the minors, then bring me back up. I went with the money, because I had to feed my family. I played over there for four years, then I hurt my knee and was done.

Outfielder Carlos May was drafted by the White Sox in the first round of the 1966 amateur draft on June 7, 1966. He had an outstanding rookie season in 1969, with 18 homers and 62 RBIs in just 100 games. On August 11, 1969, while serving in the Marine Corps Reserve at Camp Pendleton, California, a mortar accident cost May part of his thumb. He missed the rest of the season and underwent several surgeries, yet managed to rejoin the Sox in time for Opening Day 1970 and played in 150 games that season. May was an American League All-Star in 1969 and 1972 and spent seven full seasons with the Sox before being traded to the Yankees on May 18, 1976, for Ken Brett and Rich Coggins. He played with New York in the World Series that year, split 1977 with the Yankees and Angels, then played four seasons in Japan before retiring. He currently serves as a community relations representative for the White Sox.

NANCY FAUST

ORGANIST

1970–Present

WHEN I WAS ABOUT FOUR YEARS OLD, my parents bought an organ, and it captured my fancy. My mother had been a professional musician from the time she was a teenager, so I always had her around to help me. I picked up everything mostly by ear, but she was there to guide me. She wasn't a piano or organ teacher, but she helped me. Since then, I rely heavily on my ear, and if I know a melody, I can play it, but with sheet music in front of me, I fall apart!

When I was going to college, I had friends who were sports enthusiasts. They knew just what it was I could do and figured I'd be good at a ballgame, even though I had never attended a ballgame. They encouraged me to write letters to the teams to express interest that, should an opening occur, I would be the right woman for the job because I could play anything for anybody. I actually was a psychology major at North Park College in Chicago, but when I graduated in 1970, I got a call from Stu Holcomb, who at the time was the White Sox's general manager. He said, "The job is yours." I came in and learned fast.

The first day at the game, I got to Comiskey Park about an hour early, and Stu gave me a list of the players and the states that they were from. He told me if I wanted to play a state song for each player, that would be great to give them a little encouragement. My first day at the park, I was nervous, the PA system was bad, and I was way out in the center-field bleachers, which is where the organ was then. I took advantage of being out there with the fans, which was great. That day, the fans were asked to stand for a moment of silence before the game, but I couldn't hear the PA system, so I launched into the national anthem. Well, I felt lucky to be able to come back for a second day after that one.

I played out in center field for two years. My second year was when Harry Caray was hired. I would listen to his broadcast and sometimes pick up on something he said and play along. Harry would say, "Hey, how about that! I'm talking about carry me back home and she's playing 'Carry Me Back to Old Virginia.'" He became aware of me and built up the music aspect of the game. That got people's interest. My third year, Stu brought me in behind home plate, where there were more fans and more activity.

For the seventh-inning stretch, Bill Veeck realized Harry was up in the booth, waving his hands and always looking down at me. It was so great because the position of the organ allowed us to have visual contact with each other. I'd look up and wave to him, and he'd look down and wave back. Bill told Harry as long as he was up there getting all the attention by waving his arms, he should get a microphone. Bill said, "The fact that you don't sing well is a plus. The fans will all identify with you." That's how it got started. Every day before singing it, Harry would always say, "Let me hear ya, Nancy!" That made people wonder who the heck Nancy was, so I have to credit Harry with giving a name to the sound from the organ.

The beauty of me being placed out with the fans was that it enhanced my baseball knowledge, of which I had very little, but I was surrounded by those who did. I still am with the fans, and I still get wonderful ideas from them. I still love the idea of that interaction.

"Na Na Hey Hey Kiss Him Good-bye" was a song that I had been playing regularly, but until all the ingredients were there for tremendous fan response, nobody noticed. It was a hot summer evening in 1977, and we were vying for first place, playing the team we were fighting with for first, the Kansas City Royals. I just happened to play the song after we knocked their pitcher out of the game, and everybody suddenly sang along. After that game, I was bombarded with, "What was that you played, Nancy?" I thought the name of the song was "Sha Na Na"—I didn't know the real name, I just knew it was a good song. Sometimes, I play things and I don't even know who sings them or what the name is. So I said, "Oh, that's 'Sha Na Na.'" It created such a wonderful impact, and we just never let it go. I could have never managed how big it got. Those were days when there was a lot less fan participation, so to hear to everybody sing something other than "Take Me Out to the Ballgame" was quite a phenomenon.

Nancy Faust plays the organ at a Chicago pub on October 26, 2005, while the White Sox play the Houston Astros in Game 4 of the World Series in Houston. The White Sox won the game 1–0 to sweep the Astros for the World Series win. *Photo courtesy of AP Images*

It is true that Jimmy Piersall asked me to stop playing while he was trying to read commercials on TV. I was doing my job, and he yelled down at me to cut it because I was bothering him. I received a phone call from Bill Veeck, who said, "Nancy, I want music at the park." Then Jimmy yelled at me again, so the next time Bill called, I told him Jimmy didn't want me to play because he was doing a commercial in the TV booth. Bill said, "Who pays your salary, young lady?" With that, I had to disregard Jimmy's request.

Leaving old Comiskey Park probably hit me the most on the last weekend before it closed, realizing we would never have quite the same camaraderie with the people who sat around me. They were season-ticket holders and my extended family. We spent many years together, and I realized we were going to scatter in the new park. That was the toughest thing, knowing that things were going to change forever in the new scenery. I remember playing "You Are the Wind Beneath My Wings" and I know I played "This Used to Be a Playground" before we left.

On a normal day I start playing about an hour before game time, hopefully setting a mood that conveys baseball as people are coming into the park. I like that time because I can play and complete a whole song and not be interrupted by the game. It's a favorite time for me—I can incorporate some new material. I see a lot of people as they pass my booth, and my door is always open. One thing I truly love about my job is having that interaction with the fans. It's a continuum, so year after year I see the same people. Sometimes I hear sad stories about what happened over the winter, and I take those personally and hard, and sometimes I get to share good news. It's a renewal of those friendships every spring.

During the game, I play in between some of the innings, depending on what's going on with the scoreboard, which has created so much entertainment itself. The scoreboard director lets me know if there is a window of opportunity to fill in during some down time. I play as each visiting player comes to bat, and I try to play something appropriate for them. I handle rain delays and always try to reflect whatever is happening on the field when I can.

If I hear a song at home that I know everybody is familiar with, I'll try to incorporate it and play it at the right time at the park. I want to use songs that most people are familiar with, and that's how I decide. I listen to the radio, and sometimes I hear a song that's old, but I never learned, and I'll think that brings out good feelings for me and maybe our fans will feel the same way. I write the words down, then that helps me think of the melody so I can play it.

It's hard to say I have favorite players, but let me say that it is a privilege to play for the likes of Jim Thome, Dick Allen, and Carlton Fisk. I always welcome a player who has a name I can do a lot with. Tim Salmon of the Angels, for example, was fun. I'd play "Charlie the Tuna" for him or "Under the Sea" or "Jaws." His name lent itself to so many songs, and I do think in terms of what songs I can play for players.

I make lists of songs, because if I don't I'm afraid I might forget certain songs I like. In addition to the organ, I have added a sequencer and a drum machine, and I coordinate them with my playing, so I use numbers for that and write those numbers down, as well. It's a little more complex than it used to be, but I think the end result is worth it.

To do this for 40 seasons, I couldn't have imagined it when I started. I couldn't have imagined even 20, to be truthful. I thought maybe this was a youth-oriented thing and when I was 30, maybe somebody else would come along and take my place. I'm glad it didn't happen. For a long period of time, I had only missed five games in my whole career.

"Nothing But Nancy Day" was quite an honor, and it happened in 2005, which is when we won the World Series. I was asked to throw out the first pitch, and that was a real thrill, especially because I got it over the plate. It was a special honor by the organization and something I'll always remember. I had a No. 88 jersey that day because the fellow who made the jersey for me asked me what number I wanted, and I told him to pick something. He told me since there are 88 keys on a piano, he would give me No. 88. Coincidentally, it had been 88 seasons since we had won our last World Series, so that turned out to be an appropriate number.

The World Series was an unbelievable feeling. I think what struck me most was the behavior of the Chicagoans during the rally. We brought the organ down to the rally that day to set up and play by the stage. We were coming downtown in a van and thought we were getting there nice and early, but it was streaming with people who were yelling and ready to go. I don't know how they all came out of the woodwork. It was like the world had ended with all the confetti raining down. I was so proud to be associated with the team and so proud to be a Chicagoan. It was awesome to be part of that scene; it was a very proud time for me. I was struck by the outpouring from our fans, remembering their family and friends who couldn't be there or had passed on before the Sox won the Series. I was so touched by that.

I couldn't have imagined what this has become, and maybe because I have been here so long, I guess I'm part of the tradition. I'm happy to have that on my side and lucky to have some visibility. I could never have imagined my whole career would be here. I do regret a little bit that I have become a one-trick pony, because if you ask me to do anything else other than play the organ, I'm not sure I could. I've met so many fans over the years who are such avid fans. It's in their genes. It's been a wonderful life!

Baseball treasure Nancy Faust was hired as the White Sox's organist for the 1970 season. Forty seasons later, she still entertains the U.S. Cellular Field crowds with her catchy tunes and humorous snippets from her perch on the main concourse behind home plate. In addition to her work with the White Sox, Nancy has spent time as the organist for the Chicago Bulls, Blackhawks, Sting, and DePaul University.

CHUCK TANNER

MANAGER

1970–1975

IMANAGED IN THE MINOR LEAGUES FOR THE ANGELS for eight years, from the lowest league to the highest at Triple A. My last year managing at Hawaii in Triple A, I had 98 wins and 48 losses. It was the best record in all of baseball, and we had started out that year 18–18. Juan Pizarro was with me rehabbing, and the Cubs wanted him. He was being interviewed on TV, and Stu Holcomb, who was president of the White Sox at that time, was watching when Pizzaro said, "Chuck Tanner is the best young manager in all of baseball. We played together with the Milwaukee Braves, and he changed my whole career. He can communicate with the young guys and also the veterans." Holcomb heard that interview, and at the end of that season in Triple A, we were in Tucson, and Glen Miller, who was the Sox's farm director, came up to me and said, "Chuck, we want to talk to you after the game." They took me to a hotel and offered me a two-year contract. I wanted three, and they said they would only give two. I said that I'd take two, but I knew I was going to manage as long as I wanted to in the big leagues, and two years was going to cost them more! We laughed about it, and then I agreed to manage the White Sox. Roland Hemond, who was the Angels' farm director at the time, was there, and they hired him, as well.

I was ready, because I had put my time in the minor leagues and had two years of Triple A experience with Hawaii. We were very successful there with both veteran and young players in the Angels organization. I had great success with my pitching with Double A in El Paso. I think that lay the groundwork, and I really thought I was ready. I remember telling the Sox I was going to manage the same way in the major leagues as I did in the minors. I had the confidence, and that was a goal I had set.

I went to the Sox at the end of 1970 to finish out the season, and I think we were 3–13. I told them, "I'm here to observe and analyze. I'll change the pitchers and not worry about trying to manage." I could see when we had a guy on second and nobody out, if the hitter was trying to drive him in instead of getting him over, I knew he was a guy I didn't want on my team. I watched how that team played and knew there was no way we could win playing that style of baseball. We needed to play as a team, and I learned that by watching those last games of the year. I wasn't worried about the record, I was worried about the start of the next year and how we were going to put it together. That was the best thing that could have happened to me was to be with that team and see how they finished the season. I really learned a lot about the personnel and was determined to put my type of team on the field the next year.

The first winter we were there, Roland Hemond and I went to the base-ball meetings, and I think we traded 16 players in 24 hours. We got a couple ballplayers to add to the good ones we had to mold it together. I added five or six guys from A ball to the big leagues, because I said we were going to take the best 25 players, no matter what level. I had Johnny Sain as my pitching coach, which was fabulous because I think he was the greatest pitching coach who ever lived. He took care of our staff, and he and I worked really well together. We didn't have much money to work with, but the fans loved us.

We made it work. We took over the worst team in baseball, a team that was 56–106. After my first year there, we were the most improved team in the major leagues and finished third. As I said, I went in there and told them we were taking the best 25 guys north. We molded that team with a lot of young guys. We traded Luis Aparicio and Ken Berry and, because they were good players, people were all over us for things like that. The girls in the office were in mourning when Luis left, but I said, "We finished last with him, we can finish last without him." We were getting multiple players for those guys, and I could use each one to his strength. Pitching was the key with Wilbur Wood and Joel Horlen, until he got hurt. People don't realize I put Goose Gossage and Terry Forster in the bullpen.

They were 19 and 20 at the time. We made Wilbur Wood a starter. Later, it was easy for everyone to say, well, of course you would do that, but when I was doing it, all the wags were up in the Bard's Room [dining room] saying I wouldn't last very long.

I was going to do it my way. I had worked way too hard to get there to do it otherwise. I had the reins, and I took charge. If I wanted a player brought up, they did it. That's the way I was. Maybe I was so dumb, I was smart. I just felt it would work, and it did.

We changed our colors to red and white pinstripes at home. Hemond and I designed the uniforms because we wanted something exciting. We changed everything around, and it worked.

In 1972 we acquired Dick Allen and almost beat that great Oakland A's team. John Allyn, the owner, presented me with a ring. He said, "Chuck, I had this made specially for you because you saved our franchise." When we got there, they were drawing around 400,000, and I think we increased the attendance by more than 700,000 fans.

They loved Allen—he was like the Pied Piper. For me, he was also a manager on the field. He helped the young players. He and I went up together to see Goose Gossage when Goose went into the Hall of Fame because Goose was one of those guys. Dick was instrumental in keeping our team together. He was no problem. I knew him when he was a little kid. I used to talk to his mother. He was my leader, and I made him made my leader. He ended up being the Most Valuable Player in the league that year. I never had a problem with him. All he did was lead my young kids from A ball, and they listened to him. He taught them during the games and throughout the season. For me, he goes down as one of the greatest White Sox players who ever played.

We finished five and a half games behind the A's that year. It was really satisfying that the trades we made worked out. I think that was the start of success for the White Sox from then on. The franchise was uprighted, and the fans came back to the ballpark.

Allen got hurt in 1973. He was the best player in baseball, and we couldn't afford losing him. You can't replace a guy like that, and that really hurt us.

I think we had a good part in turning around a lot of careers. I had good coaches in Al Monchak, Joe Lonnett, and Johnny Sain. Those guys were always with me. It was putting together what I learned in the minor leagues

White Sox manager
Chuck Tanner was never
afraid to speak his mind.
*Photo courtesy of Richard
Lindberg*

and deciding how we were going to play the game. Everybody hustled and gave it their all every game. Consequently, we were a very aggressive team on both offense and defense. I liked to say when we were on offense, we were offensive-minded and when we were on defense, we were offensive-minded. We didn't have any qualms about anything. If we lost a tough game, that was yesterday, and let's go today. I learned that even if we lost four straight, we could find something in those losses that could help us win the next two. It was a case of never quitting. I never quit, and my players never quit. They knew that every day they came into our clubhouse, it was a new day. Every day, we had a chance to do one of two things, either beat the best team in the world or get beat by the best team in the world, because in the major leagues, the talent is that good. If you get beat by a great team, which they all are, that's not a bad deal. And if you beat a great team, that's not a bad deal, either.

I loved managing at Comiskey. I loved the people there. One time after a game, there was a church near there having a party. They were cooking a lamb and had closed off the street. There were some girls who worked in our office who had invited my wife and me to the church. Babs and I went, and I remember having lamb on newspapers—it was like a family there. Those White Sox fans not only appreciated the fact that we went there and won, but they treated us great as people. We didn't think we were any better than anyone else. Those fans knew that, and they took to our ballclub.

We had Bill Melton at third and Ed Herrmann behind the plate. Wilbur Wood and Jim Kaat were our pitchers. Heck, nobody wanted Kaat, but he won 20 games for us twice. I give Sain all the credit in the world for working with those guys. We weren't afraid to move players around. Hemond said when I got there, "Chuck Tanner has the knack of making a slow team look fast." They said, "What do you mean by that?" He said, "You watch him manage and you'll find out." I believed in movement. I played a run-and-hit game and had guys moving on the bases all the time. We stole 190 bases or something like that one year. Our aggressiveness on offense contributed to all our victories.

I remember one day at Comiskey we were playing the Yankees, and Ralph Houk was managing them. Mike Andrews was playing second base for us, and we won the first game of a doubleheader against them. So here's the little old White Sox taking down the big, bad Yankees. We were losing in the second game, and I was resting Dick Allen. He had played every game so far that year. He was in the clubhouse resting, and I heard Harry Caray saying, "There's an off-day tomorrow, and Dick Allen is not playing in the second game," so he was kind of second-guessing me. I told John Allyn, "Don't worry, he's got tonight off and tomorrow off, and it will be a good rest for him, but if we have to win this game, he'll win it for us." John was always in my corner, and anything I needed to do, he let me.

It was the last inning, and we were losing something like 2–1 with two outs, and Andrews came up. He always had a good eye, and he worked a walk. Now I brought up Allen to hit, and the place was going crazy. Ralph Houk came out and brought in his star reliever, Sparky Lyle. Mike and Lyle played together in Boston, and as he was walking by first, Mike told me later he saw Sparky walking in with his big chew as slowly as if he were plowing a field. He yelled at Lyle, "Hey, Sparky, you're in deep shit now!" I think Dick Allen hit the second pitch in the upper deck, and it must've hit a seat while it was still going up, or that ball would still be going. We swept that doubleheader, and after that game we could hear that nobody had left the stadium. They were cheering, and you could hear it all down in the clubhouse. I had chills when that happened. Old Dick just took off that 100 percent wool shirt and his underwear and all the other stuff he was wearing, even though it was about 110 degrees out there. Our young kids like Bucky

Dent, Terry Forster, and Jorge Orta were just looking at him with awe. Those people didn't want to leave Comiskey that night, and that's one of the greatest thrills I ever had in baseball. That's when I knew that this is the big leagues, baby, and this is where I want to be as a manager.

When I left in 1975, Bill Veeck had bought the club and wanted to bring back Paul Richards. They wanted me to stay and said I could be a vice president and, after a year, I'd be back managing again. I thought, *I don't want to do that and go off the field.* Then Richards told them I was one of the best managers he knew, so Paul asked me to be the third-base coach and he'd get me more money than I was making to manage. I was thinking, *Geez, oh mackerel, what in the world am I going to do here?* Then Charlie Finley was talking to Dick Dozer, the writer, to find out what was going on, and Dick told him I was getting pushed aside for Paul Richards. Charlie told Dick to have me call him, and then Charlie told me he wanted to sign me. So I met him at a club, and Jerome Holtzman was there. I told Finley I wasn't going to negotiate and I needed a three-year deal. He wrote the deal on a napkin, and I took it.

I went out there to Oakland, and we set the all-time record for stolen bases. I had Bando and Garner, you name it, everybody was running. If Finley hadn't traded Vida Blue, Rollie Fingers, and Joe Rudi during the year, and the commissioner hadn't disallowed it, we'd have won it that year. While those guys were in limbo, we played a lot of games with just a 22-man roster.

Then Charlie traded me to the Pittsburgh Pirates for Manny Sanguillen and $100,000, and that really turned out well for me. I ended up with eight years in the big leagues as a player and 19 more as a manager.

The White Sox were great. If it hadn't been for John Allyn, the owner of the White Sox, giving me that opportunity, who knows? When you get an opportunity, you have to take advantage of it. I was so fortunate, because not only did I have the backing of John, but Roland Hemond and I had been together working for the Angels' minor league system, and we worked together really well.

It was a thrill to be in Chicago—it's the greatest big city in the country. We got the fans to come back, and the ballpark was explosive, so it was really something.

After an eight-year major league career and eight seasons managing in the minors, Chuck Tanner was hired as the White Sox's manager in September 1970. In his first full season, his 1971 club went 79–83, and in 1972 the Sox improved to 87–67 and finished second in the American League West behind the World Champion Oakland A's. The Sox slipped to 77–85 in 1973, rebounded to .500 at 80–80 in 1974, then went 75–86 in Tanner's final year at the helm. After the 1975 season, Tanner left for Oakland, where he managed for one year before being traded to the Pittsburgh Pirates.

Tanner managed Pittsburgh for nine seasons, and his "We Are Family" Pirates team rebounded from a 3–1 deficit to defeat the Baltimore Orioles and win the 1979 World Series. He managed the Pirates until 1985, then spent three seasons as skipper of the Atlanta Braves. Tanner is currently a senior adviser with the Pirates.

ROLAND HEMOND

General Manager

1971–1985

Executive Advisor to the General Manager

2000–2007

In 1970 Glen Miller, the farm and scouting director for the White Sox, recommended Chuck Tanner for the managing job and me to come here as the director of player personnel. He convinced John Allyn, the owner, and Stu Holcomb, the executive vice president, that we would be welcome additions to the White Sox. It turned my career around to have an opportunity to come to Chicago, and I was really happy about that.

I remember as my plane was approaching Chicago, I was looking down on this great city and got a little bit nervous. It was great to be here, and I spent 15 great years here that I remember with pleasure.

Chuck and I were hired simultaneously. They knew how I felt about Chuck since we had both worked for the Angels. I had been with them for eight years and was their farm and scouting director when I left. We were a duo, and we brought Johnny Sain as our pitching coach, which was a big hit because of Johnny's background as one of the greatest pitching coaches of all time.

It was hectic when we started. We went to our first winter meetings in Los Angeles, and in the first 18 hours there were 16 players coming or going from the White Sox. We were having press conferences repeatedly. Everybody in baseball was shocked and wondering what was going on. Trading Luis Aparicio to the Red Sox for Mike Andrews and Luis Alvarado took some courage. That trade was not well-received at the time, but we improved by 23 games in 1971 from the previous year, so it worked out well.

In 1972 we traded Tommy John to the Dodgers for Dick Allen. Al Campanis, the Dodgers' general manager, let me know he might trade Allen. He said it would take Tommy John and Terry Forster. I said, "You may get Tommy John, but you're not going to get Terry Forster in the deal." I conversed with Chuck Tanner and John Allyn, and we decided we could give them a utility infielder named Steve Huntz. The deal was done the next day and kind of shocked the baseball world. Dick came on and had an MVP year in 1972. He was a tremendous athlete who did remarkable things. He had great power and ran the bases really well. That club made a run at Oakland that year. We were right there until the latter part of September, and Dick Allen was named the MVP. That turned out to be a fantastic trade.

In 1975 Bill Veeck had bought the club, and the winter meetings were at the Diplomat Hotel in Miami. We were in the lobby and had an "Open for Business" sign, and everybody was kind of startled at how we were going about it. It drew a lot of attention. I noticed there was a place we could connect a telephone, so I told the switchboard operator that would be the White Sox hotline for the day. Lo and behold, before the day was over, from 10:15 PM to midnight, which was then the trading deadline for the winter meetings, we made four more trades. We made six trades in three days after Bill acquired the club.

Going down to Florida for that meeting, it looked like I might not have a job, Bill might not get the club, and the team might be in Seattle, Milwaukee, or Toronto. Instead, when we came back, Mayor [Richard M.] Daley sent a couple of the bands from the "Saturday Morning Parade" to greet us at the airport. What a difference a week makes.

Working for Bill Veeck was fantastic. Every day was an adventure. I would never ask him exactly what he had in mind. I knew that great mind of his and his sense of planning would lead to some sort of production. He would come up with ideas, and then we would try to execute them as best we could.

They would make for great copy, and the fans enjoyed many of the productions and various promotions that he put on at the ballpark. It was a daily adventure, and he always taught you about life. He had 36 operations in his lifetime and never complained. He remained positive about everything, which helped me in the ensuing years when I was not working for Bill. He left his mark with me and so many people.

We had a bad team and finished last in 1976. Free agency had come about. We had two promising young pitchers in Terry Forster and Rich Gossage, but they were going to be free agents after 1977. Bill couldn't compete with some of the clubs on the monetary issues because he wasn't financed for the demands of free agency. So he said, "White Sox fans haven't been accustomed to seeing home-run hitters since Dick Allen left. Let's give some action to power hitters." We traded Gossage to Pittsburgh, which brought Richie Zisk in. The Bucky Dent trade on the last day of spring training brought Oscar Gamble from the Yankees. One hit 31 home runs, the other hit 30. Eric Soderholm was signed as a free agent. He had recovered from a knee injury and was the Comeback Player of the Year with 25 home runs. Chet Lemon had a very fine year, as did Lamar Johnson.

We were called the "South Side Hitmen" and weren't all that good defensively, but we scored a lot of runs. We had some great, late dramatic victories, and that's where the "Na Na Hey Hey Kiss Him Good-bye" song was started by Nancy Faust. Standing ovations came about so that players had to come out of the dugout and tip their caps after a home run. Those curtain calls started here at Comiskey Park, and now it's a regular ritual at games. All that started right here, and Bill really created it when he signed those home-run hitters. The South Side Hitmen of '77 will always be remembered.

Comiskey Park was an active place and sometimes was considered America's biggest saloon, according to Bill. People had fun coming to the park. Bill would say, "You can't promise victories, but you should make people have a good time." He did that with the various promotions he put on, and fans would leave the ballpark thinking, *We didn't win tonight, but we had a ball. We'll come back.* Or we would win, and then it was so much the better.

We were handicapped financially, but we still competed and gave some of the top clubs all they could handle. Our clubs hustled and played hard. Bill made it entertaining, and the players loved playing for him and in Chicago. It wasn't easy, but we had a lot of fun.

Roland Hemond talks with Tommy Lasorda of the Los Angeles Dodgers before a 2006 meeting. The two teams share spring-training facilities in Glendale, Arizona.
Photo courtesy of AP Images

113

I stayed on when Jerry [Reinsdorf] and Eddie [Einhorn] bought the team. That's part of being a general manager, and I enjoyed the changes. Each time ownership changed, I had to prove myself and adjust my approaches because of the new leadership. On the other hand, you keep your principles and keep your word as your bond so you have good relationships with the other general managers, and it was still a lot of fun to be a part of. I'm very grateful to Jerry and Eddie for the role they played in helping us build a winning ballclub.

It was quite a spring when we got Carlton Fisk. He became a free agent on a technicality, and it took quite a bit of time for the negotiations. It was a coup to get that done, and Jerry and Eddie supported it to get that done. That was a start in 1981 to get the building blocks for the club that won in '83. I purchased Greg Luzinski from the Phillies. He was a hometown boy coming back to Chicago and gave us big thrills hitting balls up on the roof. Floyd Bannister was one of our free agents who had 16 victories on the '83 ballclub.

In '83 we had young pitching. LaMarr Hoyt came from the Yankees in the Gamble trade. Britt Burns and Richard Dotson came. Harold Baines had been a fixture here for a few years. We traded for Julio Cruz at the deadline, and he played a major role for us in the second half. He was going to become a free agent, so we really got him for that half-season. Tony La Russa had him batting ninth and Rudy Law leading off, and they could both fly. If either one was on base, they could steal a base or score from first on an extra-base hit. Law stole 77 bases, and Cruz had about 25 more. Unfortunately, he had a turf-toe injury after that and was never the same after we had signed him to a long-term contract.

We clinched the division early in September, and I didn't know what the reaction would be. It was pretty evident we were going to win it, because we had a lead that was around 20 games. When Harold Baines hit the fly ball to center field and Cruz scored the winning run, it was sheer bedlam, and the celebration was as intense as if we'd have won it on the final day of the season. It was a great night. I wore a suit knowing that there was a good possibility it would be drenched—it certainly was.

That was a great club that had great cohesion. It was really fun to watch them perform and reward the White Sox fans with that division championship. The whole town was happy. That was a magical year.

Losing to the Orioles was a tough break. Greg Luzinski got hit by a Mike Boddicker pitch on the left elbow during the second game. Usually when Bull got hit, it was like him flicking off a fly, but when he threw the bat down, I could see it hurt him. He didn't have the same ability to drive the ball after that. When Ron Kittle got hit in the knee in the next-to-last game, I saw him walking in the next day and said, "Ron, is that the best you can do with that leg?" and he said it was and missed that last game. We missed his bat for sure. You have to be lucky, and we got a couple tough breaks that might have made the difference. Hoyt was ready to pitch a fifth game, and Britt Burns threw a superb ballgame in Game 4, but he lost it in the tenth inning.

When I left after 1985, I kind of left my heart in Chicago. We had won 85 games, which isn't easy to do in the big leagues. We lost Bob James, our closer, in Baltimore with about a month to go, and I knew we were in trouble. Rudy Law got hurt in that same game sliding into second base. If the two of them had stayed healthy, I might have remained the GM. You march on with great memories, and I knew Jerry and Eddie had been good to me.

Harold Baines ranks very high on my list because of his character and his approach. He gave his best at all times. I was with Hank Aaron way back when I was with the Boston Braves and remember when he was signed from the Indianapolis Clowns of the Negro Leagues. I was a youngster breaking into the game, and I typed up the scouting report from Dewey Griggs, our scout. To see Henry go to Milwaukee and become the home-run king is high on my list as well.

One of my favorite deals was when we claimed Jim Kaat on waivers for $20,000. John Allyn, our owner, was having financial problems and asked me where we were going to get the money. We were out of the race, but I told him I thought Kaat could still pitch. He came over and won 20 games twice, so when you get that many victories for $20,000, it's a little bit like Bobby Jenks being claimed by Ken Williams and helping the Sox win the championship. People don't recognize little things like a waiver claim, but the one on Kaat, my job was really on the line for that one deal. He turned out to be John Allyn's favorite player!

The Chicago White Sox are still part of me. I came back recently to help Ken Williams when he was named general manager. He did a remarkable job of putting that championship club together in 2005. To be fortunate enough to be here to enjoy that with all the White Sox fans was one of the highlights of my career. When Geoff Blum hit that home run in the extra-inning World Series game, my wife turned to me in the stadium and said, "Happy Birthday, Lovie." And I said, "That's right. It's after midnight." We embraced, and the next day I was getting calls from all over asking who that woman was that I was hugging! My children were calling me on the cell phone and told me we could win two games on my birthday. The Sox did, and it was my greatest birthday of all time.

I still love coming to any event for the White Sox, because it's like coming home to family. We reunite at things like fantasy camps and SoxFest, and I love it.

Baseball lifer Roland Hemond joined the White Sox as director of player personnel in 1970. He was promoted to general manager in July 1973 and was the architect of the 1977 South Side Hitmen and the 1983 Western Division champions. His champagne-soaked suit from the 1983 clincher hangs on display outside the Bard's Room dining room at U.S. Cellular Field. He returned to the White Sox as an advisor to general manager Kenny Williams from 2000 to 2007.

In 2003 the Sox created the Roland Hemond Award, given each year to those who better the lives of others through extraordinary personal sacrifice.

JIM KAAT

PITCHER

1973–1975

I GREW UP IN SOUTHWESTERN MICHIGAN and probably listened to more White Sox games than any other team. I listened to "the Commander," Bob Elson, a lot. Every Sunday, because of the doubleheaders, I could listen to eight games. I could listen to the Cubs with Burt Wilson and Jack Brickhouse. I had the Tigers with Harry Heilmann. Later on, I had Blaine Walsh and Earl Gillespie with the Braves, and then I had Bob Elson. I listened to him from 1945 or '46 on into the 1950s. A big thrill for me in the big leagues came after my first shutout and home run took place in Comiskey Park, and I did a radio interview with him. I thought that was awfully cool to have a guy I listened to as a kid all of a sudden interviewing me about a game I pitched.

When I was released by the Twins in 1973, I was sad because I really wanted to play my entire career in Minnesota. The only time I was on the disabled list in my career had happened the year before, when I slid into second base and broke my wrist at Comiskey Park. At the time, I was hitting .290, leading the league in pitching, and of all things, that was the last year before they went to the DH. I was out the rest of the year and the following year. I was just a little slow in coming back because I had missed half a season. I kept telling our bullpen coach, "I know they're going to dump me, but they're going to be sorry because I was just getting my groove back." So I was sad on one hand, because I loved playing in Minnesota, but by the same token, the teams that were interested in me were the Yankees and Royals, who were in a pennant race and wanted a veteran pitcher. But the White Sox were lower in the standings, so they had the first claim.

I was playing golf at Minnetonka Country Club, and I'll never forget it. I was on the sixth green, and a kid drove out on a golf cart and said Roland Hemond was on the phone. I knew Roland was with the White Sox, and I went to the phone, where he told me they had just claimed me off waivers. He said, "You are the first player to fall under the new rule, the 10 and five rule. You have at least 10 years in the big leagues and five consecutive years with the same team, so you have a right to turn the deal down." I said, "Why are you interested in me? You're 15 games out of first place." He told me they were looking ahead to next year, they felt I still had some good years left in me, and Johnny Sain and Chuck Tanner liked me. That made big points right there because it's always nice to be wanted.

I was making $60,000 and fought taking a cut every year. Roland said, "We're prepared to sign you to a contract for next year at $70,000." I thought, *Wow! A $10,000 raise? Could he send the pen over the phone line?!* Obviously I said it was terrific and that I was looking forward to playing there, so it turned out to be a great move for both of us. Roland went out on a limb, because there I was, going on 35 years old, and he had a lot of young pitchers. So to put me on the roster and use me instead of some of them was a bold move. It worked out well for both of us. It was a career resurgence for me.

I'm sure Johnny Sain had a certain amount of influence on getting me over there, because we had been together in 1965 and 1966, when I had my best years. If you took the four years I had when Johnny Sain was my coach, and I could have had those stats over my career, I'd have set all the records. They were 18–11 and 25–13 with the Twins and 21–13 and 20–14 with the White Sox with good ERAs and throwing lots of innings. He was a great influence on me.

As soon as they got me there, Chuck Tanner told me they were going to send me to the bullpen to work with Johnny for about 10 days. I started about 12 days later against Detroit, a team that always killed me. I was thinking that here was my first start and it had to come against the Tigers, who could usually hit me blindfolded. I went down every day and worked with John. My arm strength was coming back, and I pitched nine innings and only gave up one run on a Frank Howard home run.

Without Chuck, my career would have ended in 1974. I got off to a bad start. My record was 4–1, but it had no business being that good, just that everything was falling into place. Then it caught up with me, and I was getting hammered. I wasn't hurting, there was nothing wrong with me, I just stunk. Harry Caray was murdering me on the air with, "Well, when your slow curve and your fastball are the same speed, it's time to call it a career. I don't know why they keep running this guy out there. He's 36 years old, and we've got young kids in the bullpen." He went on and on.

We got off a road trip, and I was going to put my luggage in my truck, and Chuck Tanner happened to be there right by me. He walked toward me, and I thought I knew what that was going to be about, but he said, "Come in and see me tomorrow when you get to the park." I figured I was going to get my release the way I was going. He called me in and said, "You've been averaging 15 wins a year in this league for 15 years. There's no reason why you can't continue. I'm going to put you in the bullpen. I'm going to use you. I'm going to get you as much work as I can, then I'm going to start you a week from Monday against Cleveland." I went to the bullpen and actually picked up a win on one of those games where you come in, then your team gets a few runs, and you get the win.

I was 5–6 when I started that Monday, and Johnny had worked with me on a quick release that became a trademark for me—a quick pitch and quick motion. I said to Brian Downing, "We're not even going to use signs tonight. I'm going to throw batting practice. I'm going to get the ball, throw it over the plate, get it again, and throw it over the plate. I don't care if I give up 12 runs. This is what we're going to do." George Hendrick hit two home runs off me, but Dick Allen hit two home runs for us, and we won the game 7–3. I went nine innings that game and then went from 5–6 to finish that season at 21–13.

The quick pitch was unusual because pitchers tended to take a lot of time, and I would get the ball and be ready to throw again. I didn't know it at the time, but hitters like to have a lot of time to get ready. Brooks Robinson told me later that he never got a chance to get comfortable because I was working so fast. I was finding out some of the advantages of it as I went along. My defense loved it, and umpires loved it. Dick Allen, who was one of my closest friends on the team said, "You and Bob Gibson are my favorite pitchers to play behind. You're not going to waste any time, and we're just going to get after it." In old Comiskey Park, the umpires had to walk through the

Jim Kaat posted back-to-back 20-win seasons for the White Sox after being released by the Twins.

dugout to get to the home-plate area. They'd say, "Are you pitching tonight? Good. We'll be out of here in about an hour and 40 minutes."

You know how a catcher will run down to first base on a ground ball and back up the throw? When Brian was running back, he would run three fingers or one finger across his chest protector. I only had two pitches—a fastball and a breaking ball—and he didn't care if I threw a big breaking ball or a fast one. We just had two signs, and he would flash one of them across his chest protector. If I didn't like it, I would rub my glove down my pant leg, which meant it was the other sign. By the time he got back behind the plate and the hitter stepped in, I already knew the sign, and boom! I could go. It became quite frustrating for hitters because they wanted more time to get ready.

I went into September 14–13, then I won seven straight in September. Every day we would go to the bullpen, and Johnny would say, "You can get quicker. You can get quicker." I imagined in my mind that the bases were loaded and the hitter had just hit a ground ball back to me, and I was throwing it back home for a forceout. That was my mental picture of what my pitching motion was. It was step and throw. I called my fastball "Peggy Lee," which I got from Tug McGraw with "Is that all there is?"

It was so neat to be pitching at Comiskey Park because I had listened to so many games from there. In the late '40s my dad took me to a game there to see my hero, Bobby Shantz, pitch. I tried out there in 1957, and Cookie Lavagetto said if I signed there, I'd be on the staff in three years. I had my first start there, but it wasn't very successful. I had my first shutout there. I hit my first home run there. We had an awfully good team with Minnesota with some thumpers, and I pitched on the right day a lot, so I had a very good record in Comiskey Park and felt very comfortable there. It was a pitchers' park, with 350 feet down the lines, and the ball wasn't as lively. You didn't have home-run hitters up and down every lineup, and the White Sox were usually more about pitching, speed, and defense. All those things made it more conducive to me pitching well in Comiskey.

The DH rule in 1973 worked both ways for me. If I was 1–1 in the eighth inning, I didn't have to be lifted for a pinch-hitter. It probably added three to four wins a year to my record, but I always took a lot of pride in the fact that if I was a better hitter and better fielder than my mound opponent, it gave me a chance to win the game. If I could be responsible for one run a game by a bunt, hit, sacrifice, sac fly, or whatever it might be, and then make a fielding play to save a run, all those things would factor into me winning the game. I liked the fact that pitchers could hit, and I wish they still could.

As I said, my hero was Bobby Shantz, and I would listen to his games as a kid. I had a picture in my head of what his motion looked like from Bob

Elson's descriptions—he comes off the mound, lands on the balls of his feet, jumps toward the plate, is square to the hitter, and is in position to field the ball. I practiced that ad nauseum when I was a kid off the garage wall of my parents' house. When I went to my first spring training in 1958 and we were doing pitchers' drills, we were about five minutes in when Walter Beck said, "Kid, you're just like Bobby Shantz." It was the classic case of mimicking your hero. Even with my new motion with the White Sox, my getting into position to field the ball had been ingrained.

After 1975, the White Sox were very good to me. Roland called me and said there were three teams in the National League looking for a veteran pitcher—the Phillies, the Pirates, and the Mets. He told me they were looking to make a deal for me because I had just had two very successful seasons, then asked me where I would prefer to go, if they could accommodate me. I told him I'd love to go to the Phillies. I had seen them the past few years, and they were a team that was getting better and better. They did me a favor when they traded me to Philadelphia.

I enjoyed my time in Chicago. Oakland was just so good then, and although we had a good team, we just weren't good enough. Mr. Allyn was losing money, so I knew financially it was in their best interest to trade me. This was something that was better for all of us.

It's kind of humbling to run into and get letters from the Chicago fans. I had two great seasons there, and we didn't draw a lot of people, so the people who were there were ardent and avid fans. I loved my time in Chicago and always appreciated the fans' support.

The White Sox acquired left-hander Jim Kaat via waivers on August 15, 1973, after he was released by the Minnesota Twins. Kaat went 4–1 to close the season and, after a stint in the bullpen in early 1974, he posted a 21–13 record and 2.92 ERA. He followed up with a 20–14 mark in 1975 and was chosen for the American League All-Star team. Kaat won a Gold Glove after all three of his seasons with the Sox as part of his career collection of 16. The White Sox were in rebuilding mode and traded Kaat and Mike Buskey to Philadelphia on December 10, 1975, for Alan Bannister, Dick Ruthven, and Roy Thomas. Kaat moved into the broadcasting booth after his retirement and is currently with the MLB Network.

STEVE STONE

PITCHER

1973 ★ 1977–1978

BROADCASTER

2008–Present

I DIDN'T KNOW MUCH ABOUT THE WHITE SOX when I was sent here before the 1972 season. I knew the Giants had tried to trade me the year before, but it didn't go through. They tried to trade me again the next year in a deal for Andy Messersmith, but that didn't work out because the Dodgers asked for one more day and made a big deal out of it. Apparently, Roland Hemond knew I was available. He went after Kenny Henderson, and they responded by asking for Tom Bradley. Then Roland wanted to give them Stan Bahnsen, and asked, "How about Stone?" to be part of the deal. The Giants thought about it for three or four seconds and said the deal was done. I was a member of the White Sox.

Rick Reichardt told me to live downtown, and it was the best advice he gave me as a member of the White Sox. In 1973 we had a pretty good team. Dick Allen was on that team, and for a while we were okay. I love the city of Chicago and fell in love with it in 1973. A lot of people view me just with the Chicago Cubs, but I originally came to Chicago as a member of the White Sox. It wasn't until 1974 that I went to the Cubs.

The old Comiskey Park was a good park to pitch in because you had to really hit it hard to get it out. As far as the team was concerned, we had a good center fielder in Kenny Henderson, who came over with me. Dick Allen was a guy who probably could have made the Hall of Fame, had he played the game with a little less of the night life. I had a good time. It was a team of veterans, and I was a young player in only my third year in the major leagues. Johnny Sain was my pitching coach, and I went 6–11 that year.

That was a year that I learned a lot about pitching, and I also saw two of the best bookend relievers come to the major leagues at the same time. I saw Goose Gossage and Terry Forster, and both of those guys went on to have pretty good careers. Unfortunately, Terry hurt himself, but Goose went on to the Hall of Fame. Both of them came up through the White Sox system when the team was owned by John Allyn.

What happened to get me back to the Sox was I didn't throw very much in 1976 because I had a rotator cuff injury. I was the first Cubs player to play a full season without a contract, so I was a reluctant free agent. I didn't want to leave the Cubs at that point, but they didn't want to sign me to a contract. I became a free agent, and they pitched me one game in September when Roland Hemond happened to be in the stands. My arm looked pretty good. I gave up one run on four hits in five innings. He called me up. In those days, several teams actually drafted you. It didn't cost you anything, and they could negotiate with you. He said, "Everybody says you have a bad arm." I said, "Roland, my arm is not bad. In fact, it's 100 percent healed. All I want is an opportunity." That was the year Bill Veeck brought 27 injured players to spring training for the 1977 season. He guaranteed me a contract and treated Eric Soderholm the same way. We were the two out of those 27 who had good seasons. I won 15 games to lead the staff, and Soderholm hit 25 home runs. The "South Side Hitmen" were one of the most exciting teams the White Sox ever had until the world championship of 2005.

I think it was as much fun as I had ever had, until I got to Baltimore in 1979 and played with a really good baseball team. We were okay. We could certainly hit the baseball. We had 10 guys who hit 10 home runs or more, and in those days that was a lot. That was before the steroid era, and it was a whole lot of fun. Bill Veeck made it so every day was a party at the ballpark. I remember a doubleheader with the Yankees that drew something like 55,000 people, an amazing number. It was a day where everything seemed to be exciting in the city of Chicago. That year played out, unfortunately Kansas

City caught us. 'Til the day he died, Bill Veeck said that if he had had the money, he could have bought a shortstop. Alan Bannister, God bless him, hit very well, but made something like 40 errors at shortstop and wouldn't have been in the equation. That was the biggest problem with the South Side Hitmen. We could hit, but we couldn't field. Other than that, it was a whole lot of fun to be there.

I believe in '78 we were just an adequate baseball team. I didn't think we were real good. I thought that team in '77 had done pretty well with the rental players, like Richie Zisk and Oscar Gamble. By the time '77 ended, Veeck was looking to unload some of those players, and we just weren't all that good. I had a contractual situation with Bill Veeck where I got my free agency after the '77 season. I elected not to take it and told him that he gave me one year when nobody else would, so I would give him back one year in '78. I didn't declare my free agency, although he encouraged me to do that. I said, "I'll give you one year, because your young pitchers aren't ready yet." In '78 I was 12–12 and led the staff in victories again, so we were even. I went into free agency, and Baltimore offered me a four-year deal. They were a very good team with Earl Weaver as manager and had great pitching with Jim Palmer, Mike Flanagan, Scott McGregor, and Dennis Martinez. I decided to take that offer at the insistence of Bill Veeck. He told me it was four years of security, and he couldn't offer me that. He told me to go there and seek my baseball destiny and wrote about that incident in his second book.

One of the amazing things that happened to me was in the 1982 season when I was working as an analyst for *Monday Night Baseball* on ABC. We did a game in Chicago and we used to get in the day before. I was sitting with Jerry Reinsdorf watching the game, and he offered me the pitching coach job after we talked about pitching the whole game. I told him that I wanted to sit back, because I had just left the field when I retired on June 2. I said, "Realistically, I have a chief's mentality and I'd like to see how that plays out for a few years. Maybe in a few years, but right now I want to follow this television deal."

Years later I was working for a radio station that was the flagship station of the White Sox radio network. In order to give them something else to sell so they could amortize my contract, I said, "Why don't you have me do Friday night games. I could do 13 Friday night home games. You could sell that as a package, and I could be the third man in the booth with Chris Singleton and Ed Farmer." They said it was okay, and that would be the deal. Then I got a call while I was at dinner, and they asked me if I wanted to get back to doing

Steve Stone (left) and pitcher Ken Kravec take a three-mile run on the first day of training at the team's "early bird camp" in Sarasota, Florida, in February 1978.
Photo courtesy of AP Images

baseball with just one team. I had been with ESPN for a couple of years doing national games again. I said I would love to do it, then I got a phone call from Brooks Boyer of the White Sox, saying, "I know you're doing 13 games for us. How would you like to do them all? Singleton wants to go to ESPN, and we will let him go if you agree to come back." I talked with my wife, and she told me to go do it because doing baseball games is what I love to do.

I came and worked with Ed Farmer for a year. It was a very good year, and I really enjoyed it. I wasn't sure I wanted to do baseball every day again because I was a bit older and it really was a grind, but I found the White Sox to be a wonderful organization and Jerry Reinsdorf exactly the same man as he was when he offered me the pitching coach job in 1982. It worked out really well.

The next season they asked me what it would take for me to come over to the television side. I told them they would just have to ask and we'd have to work out a deal. Other than that, I thought that's where I belonged, because television is an analyst's medium. Radio is a play-by-play medium. Analyzing replays is something that I do, and predictions go much better when you can see them on television as opposed to saying something on the radio and telling everybody you were right when they can't see it!

Steve Stone had two stints with the White Sox as a player. He was acquired on November 29, 1972, along with Ken Henderson from the San Francisco Giants for Tom Bradley. He went 6–11 with a 4.24 ERA in 1973. After that season, Stone was traded to the Cubs along with Steve Swisher, Ken Frailing, and a player to be named later for Ron Santo.

Stone signed with the Sox as a free agent on November 24, 1976, and went 15–12 with a 4.51 ERA to lead the Sox's staff that next season. He followed with a 12–12 mark in 1978 and signed with the Baltimore Orioles on November 29, 1978. Two years later, Stone won the American League Cy Young Award with a 25–7 mark.

After a lengthy career as the Cubs' television analyst, Stone joined WSCR-AM as baseball contributor while working for ESPN television as an analyst on their Major League Baseball coverage. He joined Ed Farmer on the White Sox radio team for the 2008 season and, a year later moved back to the TV booth alongside Hawk Harrelson.

MIKE SQUIRES

FIRST BASEMAN/CATCHER

1975 ★ 1977–1985

I HONESTLY KNEW NOTHING ABOUT THE WHITE SOX. I grew up in Kalamazoo, Michigan, so I was always a Tigers fan. I had an idea that I was going to get drafted by the Sox, but I didn't know if I'd be worthy of it or not. When I got drafted, I signed, and the first thing you do is start looking to see who is ahead of you in the organization. I was figuring out what I had to do to take the next step.

I signed as a first baseman/outfielder, and they sent us to Sarasota for the rookie league. Joe Jones was the manager, and I asked him where he wanted us to go, and he told me, "You can go anywhere you want." I went to right field with a bunch of other guys, then I looked, and there was nobody at first base. So I got my glove and went to first base, even though I hadn't played there very much at all. I just wanted to be where there weren't as many guys to have a better opportunity. About three days later, they called me and a couple of other guys up to Appleton, and on the way up they asked me if I'd played first base. I said sure I had, even though I hadn't much, and they put me there. It's history from there.

Basically, I learned first base on the fly. I ended up taking a lot of ground balls. In Michigan in the winters I played a lot of hockey. I couldn't skate, so I was always the goalie. I think my hand-eye coordination had a lot to do with that. I made a lot of plays that were just reaction plays that surprised even me. My manager told me at the end of the year that I needed to hit for a bit of power, but defensively I could play at the major league level right then—he had said so on the reports he sent in. The next year, I went to Knoxville and won the Silver Glove Award there. It was a step-by-step thing for me, and I had to adjust to every situation and step forward.

When I got the call to come up, I was in Knoxville, Tennessee, and they told me two or three days beforehand that I was going to be called up. It was definitely a dream come true. I had always wanted to play big-league baseball—it's every little kid's dream—and fortunately it came true. I remember my very first big-league at-bat very well, because I came up against Nelson Briles and hit into a double play. I ended up going 2-for-3, but my first at-bat didn't go so well. I didn't know how long I'd be there. When I went up for the first time in September of '75, I wasn't really ready and didn't do very well. Just getting the opportunity and walking through the tunnel and into the dugout, then seeing everything that was so big and so green is a memory I will never forget.

Once you get to the majors, it's about having the confidence and belief in yourself that you can stay there. I remember a couple times after striking out, saying to myself, *What am I doing here? I don't belong here.* After a while, my wife and dad were big confidence-builders, telling me I could play here and that I was as good as the other guys up there. That helped. Then you start playing well and you know you can compete with those guys.

I always wanted to be a catcher, and my dad was a catcher. When we played sandlot baseball, I was always the catcher because the other kids didn't want me to pitch since I threw so hard, even at a young age. I learned to catch that way. One day in 1980 my family was sitting by the pool before spring training, and Roland Hemond came over. We started talking, and another player walked by who was a left-handed-hitting catcher. Roland said, "That's the quickest way to the big leagues is be a left-handed-hitting catcher." All I said to Roland was, "I always wanted to be a catcher." He looked at me with a glimmer in his eye and asked me if I would be willing to try it. At first I thought he was kidding. Then, when I realized he wasn't, I said I would, and he told me he'd talk to Bill Veeck. He talked to Bill, and they decided to give it a try. Tony La Russa was always willing to try anything, and they called Wilson and had a left-handed mitt sent down the next day. They threw me behind the plate during batting practice to see if I would blink, and I didn't, so I kept at it. There were two games that year during blowouts when they put me back there, just in case, so I could be the third catcher.

All I asked was for an incentive in my contract that if I got hurt catching, I would be taken care of, and Bill and Roland took care of me. I almost had to catch late in a tie game a few years later, but we didn't score, so it didn't happen. I had the gear on and was ready to go. I didn't do any practice during the season, because I was ready for an emergency situation and knew I could get back there and catch. I couldn't have thrown anybody out without working at it, though.

When I caught against Milwaukee, Ed Farmer was the pitcher, there was a runner on second, two outs, and Robin Yount was up. Yount was good buddies with Farmer because they had played together. The count went 3–2, and Ed took the ball, stepped off the mound, and was looking to center field, thinking, *Spanky, just call a curveball, please.* Being a hitter, I'm not as stupid as I look, so I called for the curve. Robin waved at it for strike three, then started hollering at Ed, "There's no way you call for a 3–2 curveball with Squires catching! No way!" I called it since it was his best pitch.

Playing third base was Tony's idea. He called me during the winter before the 1984 season and asked me if I would have a problem playing third base. They had been looking for a left-handed-hitting third baseman and couldn't find one. He said, "I'm tinkering with this idea, and would you be willing to give it a try? Do you think you could do it?" I told him, "Tony, I'm not worried about it. I know I can do it. I'd have to adjust to the throw, but I'm more worried about swinging the bat." He told me, "That's just exactly what I wanted to hear." I went to spring training and took ground balls with about four or five coaches watching me to determine if I could do it, and they saw that I could. I played some third and didn't make any errors. There are a couple of plays that are tough to do, and I don't think a left-hander could play there every day. In a pinch, maybe to give a third baseman a day off against a tough righty, you can go. I remember being in against the Tigers one night for five innings when LaMarr Hoyt threw a one-hitter. I moved to first in the sixth, and we won the game. I think I played 13 games there that year and started four. Of those games I started, we won three and lost one.

When I first got to the big leagues, I was more or less of a platoon player. That way you still get eight or 10 at-bats a week. Later I became more of a defensive replacement and got only two or three at-bats a week, and it was tough. Tony told me a few years ago, "If I had been an older manager at the time, you would have gotten a lot more playing time." I could have played

Mike Squires (left) congratulates LaMarr Hoyt after Hoyt won the first game of the 1983 American League playoffs against the Baltimore Orioles. The White Sox won 2–1 but ultimately lost the series. *Photo courtesy of AP Images*

the outfield, too, but he didn't use me there. I think he tried to get me a few more at-bats with the third-base thing. The last two or three years, I didn't get much of an opportunity to swing the bat.

When people say you can't wait to get to the ballpark, that's what it was like in 1983. I couldn't wait to get to the park every day, especially the closer we got to clinching it. We all wanted to clinch it at home. It was like being in a fantasy land. Everything was going our way, we were making our own breaks, and nothing was going wrong. We couldn't get beat. Somebody stepped up every game.

I can't remember if they told me about raising the banner the night we clinched. They might have, but everything was a blur that night because we were having such a good time. I do remember getting to the park and being in the lineup. Tony had chosen me to raise the championship banner because I had the most seniority. Standing on the right-field roof overlooking the crowd was unreal. The whole team got introduced, and I was waiting up there. It still gives me tingles when I think about it. Then I had to fight my way through the crowd to get back down because I was playing first. I must have had a ton of assists behind [Richard] Dotson, and Seattle had a ton of left-handers in the lineup. We were all playing on only about four hours of sleep, but it didn't matter. We were having too good a time.

You can't let losing to Baltimore diminish what we did during the season, but it was a big letdown. We had our opportunities to win the fourth game in Chicago when we lost in 10. We all felt that with Hoyt going the next day, if we could win that game, we were going to the World Series. Who knows? We had a great year, had the best record in baseball, but we didn't win. We all felt like next year we're going back, we're going to do it again, and we'll see what happens. We fell short.

It never worked out again. I hate to say this, but we went to spring training in '84, and I don't think that we worked as hard as we should have. I think we took for granted that we were good, we were the same team, and we were going to go through it again. But it didn't work out that way. You just hope and pray you can get back to the playoffs, and it's a big letdown when you have a terrible year. At the All-Star break, we did get back to first place, but then everything was downhill in the second half.

I pitched that year in Detroit in Tiger Stadium against the team I grew up pulling for. I loved it. We were getting killed on a freezing Sunday afternoon, and I was playing third base. Tony had gone through the bullpen, and we had to play in New York the next day. There was one guy left in the pen, and Tony walked out to the mound, then pointed to me at third base. I turned around and looked at the bullpen down the left-field line, but that was Detroit's bullpen. So he called me in, and all he said was, "I always wanted to see you pitch in the big leagues." He gave me the ball and walked away. Carlton Fisk was standing there looking down at me and said, "Spank, what do you want to throw?" I told him, "One is a fastball, two a curve, three a slider, and four is a change-up." He said, "Yeah, right." I had almost signed as a pitcher, but most people don't know that. I threw two pitches, and Tom Brookens popped the second one up, and that was it. I led the league in ERA that year!

I'm pretty proud I played my whole career for the White Sox. People ask me if I played anywhere else, and I say I wasn't good enough to be traded. Hopefully, I'm kidding, because I know there was some other interest from other teams at one time. To this day, I still really, really like the organization. Jerry Reinsdorf is a great guy who's done wonders. I pull for the White Sox to win all the time.

Mike Squires was drafted by the White Sox in the 18th round of the 1973 amateur draft. The left-handed-hitting first baseman had brief stints with the Sox in 1975 and 1977, then arrived to stay the following year. His best offensive season was in 1980, when he got a career-high 343 at-bats and hit .283. Squires won the American League Gold Glove at first base in 1981. In 1983, the day after the White Sox clinched the AL West title, Squires was selected to mount the Comiskey Park rooftop and raise the team's championship banner.

"Spanky" was an outstanding first baseman who spent the latter part of his career as a defensive specialist. In 1980 he went behind the plate twice for an inning and became the first left-handed catcher to appear behind the plate in the majors since Dale Long caught two innings for the Cubs in 1958. Squires also played an inning at third base in 1983 before playing 13 games at the hot corner in 1984. On April 22,1984, he made his lone pitching appearance in the majors and retired the only batter he faced.

Squires was a White Sox for his entire 10-year playing career. He currently works in scouting as a special assistant to the general manager for the Cincinnati Reds.

ERIC SODERHOLM
THIRD BASEMAN
1977–1979

I WAS COMING OFF KNEE SURGERY when I came to the White Sox. I had been with the Twins, and Calvin Griffith, the owner, had a reputation for being tight with a buck. I had played four years in the big leagues and was still making less than $25,000 a year. In 1974 I hit .276 and went in to see him for a $10,000 raise, and you would have thought I shot him! He pulled a piece of paper and started telling me things like I had popped up on April 10 with the bases loaded, hit into a double play on April 28, made an error in May—he had a whole list of things. I held out for two weeks in spring training and got a $2,000 raise. He told me if I didn't want it, I could go sell fish in Miami. It wasn't a hard decision to leave that kind of mentality.

The free-agent draft had just started, and I was taken by four teams after the '76 season. My agent suggested I give it a shot, and Bill Veeck must have had a soft spot in his heart for rejects or people with injuries because of what he went through in his lifetime with all his ailments and injuries. He always gave people a second chance, and that was certainly my case, coming off a bad knee operation. He doubled the salary I had been making with the Twins. It was a no-brainer.

I came to Chicago, and Roland Hemond signed me. I said, "Hey, where's Bill Veeck? I'd like to meet him." Roland told me Bill was in the hospital with emphysema. I said that was too bad because I would have loved to meet him. Roland called the hospital, and Bill said I should just come over. I went to Illinois Masonic Hospital, and there he was in his hospital bed with his wooden leg propped up on a pillow and an ashtray built into it! I said to myself, "That's my kind of guy!" He told me they needed a solid utility guy who could help out at several positions, and I said, "Mr. Veeck, I've worked very hard training in the off-season. I'm in great physical shape, and my leg feels great. I'm going to be your everyday third baseman." He said, "Son, if you do that, you come see me at the end of the year, and I'll take good care of you." Sure enough, the last day of the year after I hit .280 with 25 home runs and won the Comeback Player of the Year award, there was a note in my locker to go see him. I went up there, and he had a two-year contract for me for $150,000 per year. He remembered what he had told me in the hospital. I respected him immensely. He was like a second father to me. Anytime, somebody gives you a chance when most people have given up on you, there's a soft spot in your heart for them. I have that for Bill Veeck.

It's not a bad idea to pick up players like Bill Veeck did, because they have something to prove. I needed to prove to Calvin Griffith that I could come back from a knee operation and that I was good enough to make more money than he was offering. I had that kind of motivation going for me. Richie Zisk was given the boot by the Pirates. Bill brought together a bunch of rejects from other teams. We kind of blended because we all had that same energy of something to prove. That's a big motivational factor.

I'm a big believer in energy and understanding it. There is no question that at Comiskey Park, when we were behind and came back to win so many games, it started to snowball and gain energy when the fans got behind it. Pretty soon there were 25,000, 30,000, 40,000, 50,000 people in the stands feeling it. Everybody expected us to beat people 10–9, so there was a big entertainment value to that '77 club. Plus Bill Veeck tried to give the people more than their money's worth with trapeze artists, belly dancers, and who knows what else before each game. You can honestly say that at that time in baseball you were really getting your money's worth—a family could afford to come to a game and really enjoy it. It's cold and businesslike today at a lot of places. There was a different energy then, and the fans got behind us. They were rocking and rolling in the stands, and there's no question that the energy in the stands helped us maintain the belief system that we could beat anybody, even if we were behind late in the game.

It was spontaneous joy. There were many people on the team who were uncomfortable with things like the curtain calls, but the fans kept shouting

Eric Soderholm displays his old uniform and a photograph showing him as a member of the 1977 White Sox, dubbed the "South Side Hitmen," in August 2000.
Photo courtesy of AP Images

and shouting. It was really the fans who got it going, not any player with a huge ego who wanted to jump out and tip his hat. The fans kept shouting, "Curtain call, curtain call!" Once it broke and one of our guys did it, it was like Roger Bannister breaking the four-minute mile. Once he broke through something that wasn't supposed to be able to be done, then everybody did it. Our fans loved it—it was contagious, even though we felt as players a little uncomfortable doing that. Then it spread to different teams, though Kansas City really took offense to it and thought it was bush league. There was a big controversy over that with Hal McRae and the guys over there. Now you see everyone doing it, but we were the start of the whole thing due to the demand of the fans.

I think my signature moment that year came in spring training. In my mind, it was still questionable as to whether I was going to be able to come back from a very serious knee operation. I remember hitting a ground ball in spring training deep and to the right of the shortstop. I really had to push it. It was the defining moment for me. I beat the throw to first base and hit the bag with the my injured knee. It held up, and it was then I knew I was going to make it back.

During the season, we were playing Kansas City in a big four-game series, and I hit a three-run homer off Doug Bird in the bottom of the seventh to give us a lead. There were something like 55,000 people at that game, and they just went bananas. I remember going around the bases and feeling like my feet just weren't touching the ground. It was that much of an energetic high. After the season, being awarded the Comeback Player of the Year was a very special thing for me.

I don't think people think we choked. If you look at the last 30 games of the season, we went something like 15–15. We weren't on a hot streak and were playing decent ball, but Kansas City went 26–6 to finish the year. They went by us like we were standing still. I guess you could say they had a better ballclub, and they certainly had better pitching than we did.

We were just like the "Bad News Bears" that had a great run. We were 100–1 in Vegas before the season, and nobody could believe we were in it. We were riding the momentum factor, and it was a great season. More than 30 years later, people still come up to me and tell me, "Oh man, I was a kid, and my dad took me to a game that year. It was so exciting." I can't tell you how many people come up to me to say what a great season that was. For a team that didn't win the pennant, it might have been one of the most memorable seasons in White Sox history.

It was brutal to go from that fun and enjoyment in '77 to '78, where Bill Veeck did the best he could to try and make up for the loss of Richie Zisk and Oscar Gamble. He signed Bobby Bonds, who was done, and Ron Blomberg, who turned out to be kind of a bust. To go from the excitement to being 10 games under .500 to where everybody knew we weren't going anywhere and didn't have the ballclub to compete was awful. The days were long, and the drives to the park were long, no question about it. Going from that winning feeling to a feeling of despair was difficult, both in life and in baseball.

Nineteen seventy-nine was more of the same, so they decided to make some moves. I remember Bill Veeck told me they had an opportunity to trade me for Ed Farmer and they needed pitching. They took votes—he said it was a close vote—but they decided they had to make that move, even though he didn't want to get rid of me. Bill liked my work ethic and my charisma with the fans, because I wrote poetry and things like that. There were some people who were saddened, but it's baseball and it's a business. You do what you have to do. I hated to leave, because even though I was on a bad team, I loved Chicago. That's why I still live here. It's just a city that I've felt close to, and people here have taken me under their wings. I was only here three years, but they made me feel good, and it opened up a lot of doors for me in the business world. I was able to be very successful largely due to the popularity I had when I was with the White Sox. I'll forever be grateful.

The fans claim you forever. I'm shocked that some of the current athletes who could own this city don't live here. I enjoy the four seasons—even winter is pretty tolerable. It's a beautiful place and a place my wife and I love. It's been a great ride for us. I've had a fabulous life largely due to the benefits of having played for the White Sox.

After missing the 1976 season due to a knee injury, third baseman Eric Soderholm signed as a free agent with the White Sox on November 26, 1976. He smacked 25 homers, hit .280, and drove in 67 runs for the South Side Hitmen and was named the 1977 American League Comeback Player of the Year by the *Sporting News* as the White Sox finished third in the AL West with a 90–72 record. In 1978 Soderholm followed up with 20 home runs and 67 RBIs.

On June 15, 1979, he was traded to the Rangers for Ed Farmer and Gary Holle. He retired after the 1981 season and started the Front Row Ticket Service in Chicago. Soderholm currently owns and operates the Soderwold Healing Arts Center & Spa in Hinsdale, Illinois.

JIM ANGIO
TELEVISION DIRECTOR
1978–Present

Iwas a young kid with a crazy dream. I went to Southern Illinois University because they said they had a good alumni program, and in 1974 that helped me. WSNS, Channel 44 in Chicago, called down looking for a young guy who wanted to work in sports. On May 23, 1974, I started at Channel 44 in the production department. We were doing sports and lots of other things, and I learned the basics of television. In the spring of 1978 I started doing White Sox baseball. It was a dream to spend a summer at the ballpark, and I was one of two guys directing, so we split the road trips and the games.

We were a bunch of young guys, and Hughes Television Sports really helped us with the road stadiums, so we didn't get the wool pulled over our eyes the first time we were in a city. Bill Veeck was one of our biggest supporters, and he brought us into his office one afternoon for a meeting. I was a nervous wreck, but he talked to us about the beauty of baseball on a summer night, being with friends and family, throwing your legs over the railing, and having a beer and enjoying life the way it was meant to be.

Harry Caray and Jimmy Piersall were the first two announcers I worked with. Harry was wonderful in imparting his love of the game to us. We all looked up to him. Jimmy was always willing to teach, and we went out and taped clinics with him before the game. We didn't have all the portable equipment we have now, but we would haul the clunky cameras and cables out to the field for Jimmy to show us how to slide into second base or field a ground ball. It probably looked like a movie set out there with all the equipment.

I'll never forget when we were in Boston and Jimmy told me to get to Fenway Park early. He had a bat and ball, and after I borrowed Richard Dotson's glove, he put me out in left field. Jimmy taught me how to field balls that were hit off the Green Monster. I had no idea the wall was made out of corrugated tin at the time, and I was chasing balls all over out there. I had to direct a game in Kansas City with ice on my legs to cover the strawberries I got while Jimmy taught me how to slide on the Astroturf there. You couldn't do that stuff now.

In 1981 the ownership of the White Sox changed to Jerry Reinsdorf and Eddie Einhorn, who wanted to set up a regional sports network. They did a pay-TV deal with ON-TV, where you had to use a converter box and helped start a company in 1982 called SportsVision. We did the Bulls, Sting, and Hawks, and that's when we started doing all the White Sox games, home and road. That changed to SportsChannel, then Comcast SportsNet, and I've seen over-the-air TV go between WFLD and WGN-TV. I've been fortunate enough to have some staying power, work well with others, and keep going.

Nineteen eighty-three was great. It was the summer of the 50th All-Star Game at Comiskey Park. For SportsVision, we televised the Old-Timers' Game that preceded it and used NBC's production truck. I had Harry Coyle, their legendary director who practically invented televised baseball, standing over my shoulder the whole time. I was pretty nervous.

The Sox team that year was great to us. After the break, Hoyt [Wilhelm], Dotson, [Floyd] Bannister, [Greg] Luzinski, [Ron] Kittle—it seemed like everyone got hot. The old ballpark was rocking, and that was the first year of the Super Suites and the new color DiamondVision scoreboard. It was a fun year on all counts.

That was the last year local stations were allowed to televise the playoffs, so I directed the series against the Orioles. I still get goosebumps thinking about that series and still cringe when I think of the home run Tito Landrum hit off Britt Burns in Game 4. He had pitched a whale of a game.

I've been fortunate to do some great games in my 31 years. Most recently, Mark Buehrle's no-hitter against the Texas Rangers and his perfect game against the Tampa Bay Rays stand out. He's one quality guy, and I was happy for him. All the no-hitters stick out, even the improbable ones like Joe Cowley's.

Tom Seaver's 300th win was important. Seaver was a wonderful guy to be with. He was destined for a career in television after his baseball days were

Jim Angio has directed White Sox television broadcasts for more than 30 years. *Photo courtesy of Bob Vorwald*

done. He would come into the TV truck to chart pitches on the day before he pitched. He'd have his tobacco, little spit cup, be nice and preppy in his alligator shirt, and watch the game with us, paying special attention to the center-field camera so he could watch the pitcher/batter shot, then he'd cut out after about the eighth inning. We developed a bond with him, so when he won his 300th game in Yankee Stadium, that was a big one for me.

My typical day starts around 10:00 in the morning, when I read all about the White Sox online from a variety of places. All the information on the Internet is great for getting ready for the game, knowing who was called up, and who is or isn't playing. I make a headshot sheet with photos that aids our cameramen so they know what to look for if I ask them for a shot of a visiting coach or player. That takes about an hour, then I head to the ballpark by 1:30 and start with a chat with our game producer to discuss show elements we are using in that night's game. We check out and test the cameras around 3:00 PM, then give a meal break. After that it's time to finish up all preproduction, get scenic shots from around the ballpark, and tape our opening around 6:30 PM after the batting cage is moved. We assemble pieces for that in the truck and then hit the air at 7:00. At that point we go until the fat lady sings!

I operate by using five main cameras. I've done games with up to 12 cameras, but the extra ones are specialty ones that can give us some unique or different looks. Camera 1 is at the end of the third-base dugout, or low third. Camera 2 is the coverage camera, or high home, that is set up high above home plate. Camera 3 is high first or mid-first, set up even with first base for a higher shot. Camera 4 is in center field for the pitcher/batter shot, and

Camera 5 is our low first at the end of the first-base dugout. Adding cameras after that adds an important dimension to the game and allows us to show much more, especially for specific situations or if you get blocked by the walls in a certain stadium or a coach walking in front of a low camera.

Once the play stops, your focus shifts from the camera monitors over to the replay monitors. The producer picks the replays, but you want to make sure the machine is cued, it's the right picture with no technical issue, and it's the one you want. There are 80 monitors on the wall in the TV truck, so I'll also be checking the ones with our graphics, our scorebox line, and any other effects we might be using.

I'm really proud to be part of the White Sox. In 1983 they gave me an All-Star ring, and that was really important. Being able to share in the successes and get invited to many of their events over the years show they recognize and trust me. I'm always trying to show the club in the best possible light and want our broadcasts to be positive. That's one great thing about working with Hawk Harrelson—he can make a bad game good.

I take pride in all that has changed in my time and all that we've done. Sometimes I will be out and hear, "Aren't you Jim Angio?" It's not that I'm a big celebrity, but to hear a fan say he's watched you all his life is very special. You bring some of your personality and your sense of direction to put your signature on each telecast. I don't care how many people the game goes out to, whether it's one or 1 million, we just want to walk out of the truck and know we did the best job we could. It's always been a pleasure to do a good game. Have I ever done a perfect one? Maybe once or twice, I felt like we really had it, but I can always find something to nitpick about. I may be too hard on myself, but I always want to do a better job. I take pride in 31 years of this. It's my legacy.

141

Jim Angio has been directing White Sox telecasts since 1978 and currently covers the games for both WGN-TV and Comcast SportsNet Chicago. He is a legend in the television industry and has received multiple Emmy Awards for his outstanding coverage of the Sox and other Chicago sports.

ED FARMER

PITCHER

1979–1981

BROADCASTER

1991–Present

I HAVE BEEN A SOX FAN MY WHOLE LIFE. My mother brought me, my two brothers, and some of our friends to Opening Day for my first game. She knew nothing about it and asked us where we wanted to sit. One of my friends, John Esposito, said we should ask for the third-base side, five or six rows from the field. She said that to the guy at the ticket window, and the guy said, "Sure, you and 50,000 others." Someone had just turned in some tickets, and he had four box seats near the field and two by the walkway at old Comiskey. That was my first time at the ballpark and, when we walked in, I couldn't believe it. It was a big cement area, and there was a nut and bolt factory across the street where the new park is now. I couldn't believe there was a baseball field in the middle of all of it. I said to my mom, "I have to play here someday. This is great. This is it!"

We'd go to Sox games whenever we could. My brothers, Tom and Dan, and I talked my dad into buying a box. We had Box 54 and would come early and trade the tickets in, because if you were a child under 14, they'd give you back ticket money, since children would pay less than an adult. When Dad found out and asked what was going on, I told him we got three or four bucks back per ticket, and that's how we were able to eat at the games!

My favorite players were Luis Aparicio and Billy Pierce. Aparicio was the fast guy on the team, but Billy was a pitcher who lived in my neighborhood. I was born in Evergreen Park but grew up in Chicago on Francisco, and Billy lived a few blocks away. I would go see him and get his autograph. When I signed and got my second year's contract mailed to me for $550 a month, I took it over and asked him what I should do. He told me to sign it and send it back to them before they changed their minds!

When I came to the White Sox years later, I was with a first-place team in the Texas Rangers and was traded for Eric Soderholm. I was coming to a team that wasn't in first and had flown home to California to get my wife and daughter. Roland Hemond called me in California and asked if I could get there by tomorrow, and I told him, "Absolutely." I had had arm surgery and was on my way back. I have fond memories of being able to come here and play. They started me my first three games, and I pitched a total of nine innings and gave up 13 earned runs, so it wasn't hard to figure out my earned-run average.

It was great to come home. They moved me to the bullpen, though they probably would have liked to move me to Siberia. I told our manager, Don Kessinger, that I could pitch short relief, and he looked at me kind of funny and said, "I don't think that's gonna happen." They worked me in the bullpen, and in my next 27 innings, I only gave up three hits. Kessinger resigned not long afterward and said, "I have to tell you something before I go. I thought you'd snapped your cap when you told me you wanted the ball in short relief, but you know what? You can do that job."

Tony La Russa got here and challenged me every single day to do a better job than I did the night before. He'd say, "You know, what you did last night is history. You're only as good as your performance today." He was right. I've been lucky.

In 1980 I pitched even better than I did in '79. I set the club record for saves in 1980, even though I spent the better part of three weeks in the hospital not long after the All-Star Game. I was ready to go every day. In 1981 my kidney function was starting to decrease, and I couldn't do the things I used to do. When I signed with the Phillies in 1983, I was in renal failure.

With Bill Veeck in charge, I don't think anybody knew what was coming each day. We had those uniforms. I never wore the shorts—I think they were only worn one day. We had that collared uniform shirt, and I remember telling Richie Zisk with the Rangers that it was the worst-looking uniform I had ever seen. He told me it was the most comfortable he had ever put on, and I told him I would take his word for it because I didn't ever want to wear it. Two weeks later, I was traded and standing in the Sox clubhouse going, "Hey, do you tuck this in or what?"

It was always something. We always had guest batboys. We had Hervé Villechaize from *Fantasy Island*, then we had Frankenstein one night. I was here for Disco Demolition and got to pitch the last two and two-thirds innings. What was interesting about that was that there must have been 54,000 people in Comiskey Park, but they were well-behaved, except when everybody was throwing a disco record onto the field during the first game. They were like Frisbees. I would get the sign, and all of a sudden something would go past my head, and it was a 45 disco record.

When I got into radio, I was scouting for the Baltimore Orioles. I was their head major league scout and the national cross-checker of high school and college players. I would be in Tampa one day during the spring and could be in Seattle the next day seeing a high school or college player. Wayne Hagin was doing the Sox's games during the regular season at the time with John Rooney. Wayne would come in and ask me questions, "What do you know about this team?" Well, I had already seen them and was writing reports on them. I'd tell him some things, and he'd say, "You should come over and do the game with me." I said, "Well, sometime if I had a day off." He said, "John Rooney is gone on Sundays, and I'm up here by myself." Not long after, I was watching Toronto on a Sunday, and they had a Sunday night game at Comiskey. I was stopping here to see my brother Tom, then I was flying into Los Angeles. Tommy came with me, and I went up and did the game on the radio. Jerry Reinsdorf talked to me afterward about joining them. They made me an offer the Orioles couldn't match, and the next year I was scouting and doing Sunday games on the radio. After that year, Jerry wanted me to go up and do the radio full-time. Kenny Williams has come and asked me a few questions here or there from time to time, but I have no duties whatsoever in the scouting department anymore. I never want to make it sound like I do, but he will certainly ask my opinion on things, and then as soon as I tell him, I'm sure he forgets it!

I learned from John Rooney, and if you can get a better teacher than that, I don't know who it could be. He was a great partner, told me the parameters

144

Aaron Rowand, Geoff Blum, Joe Crede, and Ed Farmer (right) wave to the crowd at the White Sox victory parade and rally on October 28, 2005.

of the broadcast booth, and I learned straight from those. Now I get to have a conversation every night with D.J. [Darrin Jackson], and we may have certain things that we miss during a broadcast, but not many. As far as what I am going to say each night, it comes from the heart as a White Sox fan. I wouldn't want it any other way. We're all White Sox fans, and I've had a chance to do something that everybody has dreamed about doing. I'm a very lucky person to work for the team I grew up loving and still love. When they don't play well on the field, I never lambaste them for not making the right play on the field, but I will say something like, "This isn't White Sox baseball." I know how difficult it is out there for everybody and how difficult it is for us White Sox fans to get a loss here or there and not like it. Sometimes I have to turn the microphone off. As far as starting a ballgame, I sit down and start talking—what comes out of my mouth is right there. I want it to be spontaneous.

Calling the World Series was as good as it gets. I've had a good seat the last 19½ years and cherish being a White Sox broadcaster, but the World Series was for everybody. My mom and dad never saw the Sox win. I gave one of my friends a World Series cap I got in the winning locker room, and I'm pretty sure he put it on his dad's grave because his dad never saw the Sox win. I'm getting goosebumps talking about it now. I can't thank the team enough. As a White Sox fan, that was pretty good.

We didn't beat the Astros' four starters in those games, we beat their bullpen. When we left Houston, I got to go up front in the plane as we were taxiing out. The guy pulling us out waving the orange batons had his Astros jersey on because he knew he was taking the world champions out, but he wanted us to know he was still a Houston fan, and I like that. That goes with our territory here as Sox fans. You know the Cubs' fans are passionate about their team. As Sox fans, we demand this team to win.

I did both Mark Buehrle's perfect game and his no-hitter. I also had a game in Cleveland where he faced 27 guys. People forget that one. The no-hitter, he retired the first 13 Texas Rangers on April 18, walked Sammy Sosa, picked him off first base, then retired everybody else. Thirteen out, walk, pickoff, 13 more. In the perfect game, I wouldn't say, "He's got a no-hitter." I wouldn't say, "He's got a perfect game." After two innings, I said, "He's retired everybody. To the bottom of the second." Then the third and the fourth I said, "The Rangers go off in order for the fourth time." In the seventh, Darrin Jackson, my partner, said to me, "My hands are sweating." I said, "My back is soaking wet!" When Buehrle got through the top of the seventh, I think I said something like, "Buehrle is perfect through seven. To the bottom of the seventh, the Sox need to score some more runs." Then we went to the eighth, and he got them out in order again. I said, "Folks, to the bottom of the eighth. He's perfect through eight. Come back and stay with us for the ninth, because this could be something special."

When [Dewayne] Wise made the catch in the ninth, I thought the ball was gone. It was a 2–2 pitch to Gabe Kapler, he hit it, and I said, "Wise will race to the track, he's at the wall" and usually I would say, "That ball is gone." Then I was surprised. I took it to the crescendo of, "This ball could be gone." I was very excited about the catch. The last batter was Jason Bartlett, who has killed the Sox in Minnesota and with Tampa Bay. When Buehrle got him to ground to [Alexei] Ramirez, he had a perfect game. There I was—I had to come up with something to say, this isn't happening! I think I called him "Mr. Perfecto" or something like that. The strangest thing I did about that game was put down April 18, 2007, the date of his no-hitter, on top of my scorecard before the game, and I've never done that. I thought he was going to throw another perfect game in Minnesota in his next start. It's a strange game, but it's the greatest game I've ever played.

I've always been a White Sox fan. I've always been connected in some way. I thought it was a great place to come and play. It's been a great place to live. With the Reinsdorf family and Jerry taking over like that, it's just been a tremendous life for me. I had boyhood dreams of playing here with the Sox. C'mon, I'm little Eddie from Francisco on the South Side and I'm proud of Chicago. Whether you are a Cubs fan or a Sox fan, I think it's great, and I'm proud of my ballclub here on the South Side, too. When I was a kid, I was actually making my way from Francisco toward Comiskey Park and really didn't know it. I played in my neighborhood, then wound up at 51st and California, and then at McKinley Park at 39th and Western. My next stop was at Comiskey Park. That's all I've ever wanted to be was little Eddie from the South Side of Chicago, and I'm doing a job that I thank God I have. I thank the White Sox for giving me the opportunity. It's been a great time here. It really has. I've seen some great things here and enjoyed some great people.

147

Lifelong Sox fan Ed Farmer was traded to his favorite club from the Texas Rangers on June 15, 1979, along with Gary Holle for Eric Soderholm. He went 3–7 with a 2.43 ERA and 14 saves for the Sox that season. In 1980 he saved 30 games for the Sox and pitched a scoreless inning as an American League All-Star. Farmer went 3–3 with 10 saves in 1981, then signed with the Phillies as a free agent. He pitched 11 seasons in the major leagues.

Farmer joined the White Sox's radio team as a Sunday fill-in in 1991 and moved into the booth full-time the next season, where he currently teams with Darrin Jackson. Farmer underwent a kidney transplant donated by his brother Tom in 1991 and is a tireless advocate for organ donation and kidney-related causes.

HERM SCHNEIDER
HEAD ATHLETIC TRAINER
1979–Present

I GREW UP IN ROCHESTER, NEW YORK, and as a youngster, started hanging out at our minor league ballpark. I was persistent or made a nuisance of myself, I'm not sure, but I got an opportunity to move up and do things like be clubhouse attendant, then became the assistant trainer. I went to school for training and started off in the Orioles organization in the Instructional League, then went over to the Yankees organization for 10 years before coming here in 1979.

I worked in winter ball in Puerto Rico for nine years for a team that had a working agreement with the Yankees and White Sox. I took care of many Sox players, and Roland Hemond came down many times to check on his players. I guess I took good care of them, and it made a statement to him so that when the Sox's head trainer job became available, I was on his mind.

The facilities at old Comiskey were a bit worse than what we had in New York. I came from a world championship team in New York in 1977 and 1978, and some people thought I was a bit crazy for leaving that team to come to the White Sox, but I've always been the type of guy who believes sometimes you have to take two steps back to take 10 steps forward. It's really worked out well.

The core of each day is pretty much the same. We get here pretty early, around 11:30 AM for a 7:00 night game. The players start showing up around 1:00, and we start treatment. The guys who need the most work come the earliest. The guys who are playing and might need the least amount of work

Herm Schneider checks out Alexei Ramirez after he was hit by a pitch from Cleveland Indians relief pitcher Chris Perez in the ninth inning of a game on June 29, 2009, in Cleveland. Ramirez had to leave the game, won by the White Sox 6–3.

Photo courtesy of AP Images

go next—we don't want to punish them by having them come in too early. We get them taken care of just before batting practice starts and go from there. It's a pretty full day.

You try to be a positive force in the players' lives. Sometimes they need a pat on the back and sometimes you have to be firm with them, whatever it takes. It's a feel, not something you can read about or be taught. A lot of it is timing, as well. When a player gets injured, the first thing you want to do is explain to him what's going on. It's hard for them to get to this point without having had some sort of injury, but a lot of times, it's a problem they've never had before, so that can be uncharted waters for them. You have to take them through their day a little bit, tell them what's going on, and how we're going to get through this.

Ozzie and Kenny call me the "Grim Reaper," because when they see me, it's usually not, "How are you, how are you doing, and how's the family?" When they see me, there's usually a problem. I try to keep myself distanced from them as much as I can, because every time they see me, they cringe! I try to keep them apprised of situations that could turn into a problem but not bother them with every little thing that could cloud their minds.

We spend a lot of time on what we call "pre-hab." We don't want to get to a rehab situation if we can ever help it, and we hold guys accountable to do their work so they don't get hurt. If they do get hurt, they have a good foundation built to come back from that problem at a fairly good pace. I've always been an advocate of doing this, but it involves work. You get guys who shy away from work and would rather do things that are more fun. Working on a shoulder program, for instance, isn't fun, but I tell our fellows it's making deposits in your career. The payout is really big on the back end, and you never want to be bankrupt and have nothing there. If you get injured and you haven't made your deposits, being bankrupt is no fun. The players can relate to that.

We've had so many success stories I can't even relate them all. I've never lost anybody, and most of our guys have come back. There were a few players who made it back, but their injuries were bad enough that they were never quite the same.

Bo Jackson was an incredible person. He never held a grudge about being injured—and if anybody ever had a reason to do so, it was him. He knew those were the cards that were dealt to him, and he just played them the best he could. He went about his business and is a great man.

When Michael Jordan wanted to try baseball, we really had to start from scratch. We took the three or four months we had and tried to build a good baseball foundation. That's all we had time for. We worked on baseball-type skills, strengthening his hands, getting his coordination down with a glove and a bat, and things like that. It was the dead of winter, so it was a challenge. We got it done.

Dealing with the media when there is an injury is challenging, but I usually try to calm things down by saying, "Let's see how he is tomorrow." We need that cooling off period and then we can see how he feels the next day. Most of the time, I've seen the injury before and have a bit of a history with how long it takes on the average person, so I have a range for how long that might take. You get that with experience.

When science comes about, you have to be responsible for more and more things, like MRIs, etc. That's been a big change I've seen. When a person gets hurt, and you do an MRI, you can't expect his joint to look the same as that of an average person, when you factor in that he's played baseball his whole life. You have to do some distinguishing, and that can be a problem when a radiologist reads everything and the player worries about something being really wrong, when it's more about normal occupational hazard for what they do. You have to look at new equipment out there, but you can't buy everything, because then you become just a gimmick guy. There's a fine line you have to walk.

I'm very proud of this organization and very proud of this group. We've changed the whole medical program here over the course of 30 years. We're held in high regard by our peers and other teams, and that makes me feel very proud.

After spending nine seasons in the Yankees organization, Herm Schneider was hired as the White Sox's head athletic trainer prior to the 1979 season. Under his direction, the White Sox have consistently been near the top of baseball with the fewest number of player days spent on the disabled list. Schneider has supervised the major rehabilitation programs for a countless number of Sox players, including Bo Jackson, Ozzie Guillen, and Robin Ventura, and his tireless commitment to the well-being of Sox players makes him one of the most popular members of the organization.

The
EIGHTIES

BRITT BURNS

PITCHER

1978–1985

IFOUND OUT SECONDHAND THE STORY about being discovered by a *Tribune* book critic. [Bob Cromie, the *Chicago Tribune*'s book editor, was passing through Birmingham when Burns threw a no-hitter and sent a clipping on the game to Bill Veeck.] I honestly couldn't tell you if that happened. What I do know is that the scout that came to see me was Ken Silvestri, and he saw me my senior year. The critic's story has stood up over the years, so there must be something to it.

I knew absolutely nothing about the White Sox. We were made aware that the Yankees were scouting me, as were some men from the Scouting Bureau, but we had not heard the White Sox's name at all until draft day. It was kind of a surprise to end up being drafted by someone we weren't even aware had seen me play. It turned out to be a tremendous opportunity, but I had no idea who they were or anything about them.

It certainly was a good thing for me at the time to be on the fast track. I had some talent and was too naïve to know that I wasn't supposed to be able to do that. It worked out pretty good, and I did figure out that I could contribute. I am of the opinion that if kids can handle the workload, we should go ahead and let them get the experience. For me, all of that turned out to be the right thing to do.

My first major league start came when I was 19 in 1978. Gordie Lund called me in the hotel lobby somewhere in Iowa, where we were on the road.

I was somewhat aware I was doing well in the Midwest League six months after signing, but I didn't know how that measured up to anything else. They told me I was going up, and I thought it was great that I'd be moving to the Knoxville Double A team, which was around four hours from my home. He said, "No, you're going to Chicago." That was a shock. I started against Detroit, and I didn't really know what to think. I did what I knew how to do, which was compete and throw strikes. I was a one-and-a-half-pitch pitcher with my fastball and high breaking ball. I didn't get out of the fifth inning, then pitched against them 10 days later and didn't get out of the third.

I don't recall being scared or nervous. It was so surreal at the time that I don't know how seriously I took it, because it was such a shock. I didn't really know what to think other than to say to myself, *Okay, I'm here. Let's go do what I do.* It wasn't until later on I realized that I'd have to make some adjustments and do some things. That turned out to be a learning experience for me that I might not have gotten otherwise somewhere else. It worked out well.

When I was a rookie, I was allowed to just go out and pitch. I wasn't told "You have to pitch this guy this way," or, "You have to do this to this hitter." I was told to go out and do what I do, which I took to heart. Everything starts with throwing strikes and then making adjustments to what you see. A lot of guys pitched to avoid contact, but for whatever reasons, I didn't think in those terms. I grew up with the thought that walking people was something you just didn't do. That was the worst thing you could do. The only other alternative was to throw it over the plate. You can't get upset if guys are 2–0 or 3–1 trying to be pinpoint accurate, then turn around and be ticked when they give up a bunch of hits. I threw it over the plate, and my stuff was good enough to let me get away with some pitches that were all over the plate until I learned how to make adjustments.

Really, what I learned was I didn't need to make any changes. What I needed to do was get to know hitters and how they reacted to my stuff. That all came in time over the next two or three years, and it became more of a game once I knew everybody and they knew me. That was different from the beginning when it was, Here's my stuff, and let's see what happens.

The toughest thing I ever went through was in 1981, when my father was hit by a car. It was such a shock. As close as my dad and I were and as much of a shock as that was when it happened during the strike, you never think about something like that happening because it's too horrible to think about. When things like that happen, you do the only thing you know, which is

155

keep moving and keep going. I tried to be optimistic that he might pull out of the coma, but he didn't. He ended up dying. There is a part of me that misses my dad to this day, and I always will. I went through a 30-inning scoreless streak while he was in the hospital, and it created a level of intensity and urgency, so I could go back and have good news for him. He was in a coma, so I didn't know if he could hear anything, but I wanted to pump him up. My heart was so much with him that I didn't have any anxiety when I was pitching. Playing baseball became something far different for that period of time. My talent came out, and I had success during that period of time unlike anything I had had before. I learned something from that, because, like a lot of young kids, I would stress out. While my dad was in the hospital, I didn't have thoughts like that.

I was surprised to go to the All-Star Game that year. The year before, I led the league in pitching at the break, and that's the one I had hoped to be a part of, and I thought if I didn't make it that year, I wouldn't at any time. With my dad's situation, it never even crossed my mind. When it happened, I hoped my dad could hear me. It gave us all some optimism at the time. I took a couple of high school friends, and we had a good time. The old stadium in Cleveland was packed and rocking. I've never seen so many people in a park in my life. I didn't get to pitch, but that was okay. I didn't get to soak it all in because I was worried about my father, but it was an honor to have been chosen to be there.

In 1982 I had shoulder tendinitis for the first time. I was fortunate I never had anything that was serious. The emotion and adrenaline you get from competition take care of that, and I found out later if it doesn't, you've got a problem. I'll always remember what a great guy Herm Schneider was for taking care of me. We would get through it. That stuff would come and go, and I had confidence in our training staff, and it worked out.

We had an energy and optimism in 1983 with everybody excited about the season. As the season went on, everybody started realizing we had the talent to do it. It all came together. When a team wins like that, there's a certain chemistry there. If general managers could bottle that, you could really be something. As much as you try to bring talent together, there's a camaraderie that becomes chemistry and manifests itself in two-out RBIs and well-pitched games—little things that chemistry seems to bring out. We had a group of guys who liked being around each other, and there weren't any cliques in the clubhouse.

Left-hander Britt Burns joined the White Sox's starting rotation in 1980 and went 15–13 that season. He was named to the All-Star team in 1981 and had his best year in 1985, posting an 18–11 record.

Every day was a chance to win another ballgame. I wasn't really on top of my game, but Hoyt, Dotson, and Bannister were on a roll. I got my stuff together later in the year, but they were solid start to finish. It was fun coming to the ballpark. I'd had enough experience by then to know what it meant to be on a team that didn't have a chance to win. That made for a long year. This was one of those things where you loved going to the ballpark every day. It sounds cliché, but it was true. You looked forward to seeing what was going to happen next, who was going to step up, and how we were going to do it today. It was pretty cool.

The night we clinched, there was champagne everywhere. Later on, there were several racks of babyback ribs that were sent over, and they ended up in front of me. I made as many disappear as I could. The families were there, and Jerry and Eddie were, too. I savored the moment, and nobody was in a hurry to get out of the clubhouse. It was a special time.

Going into Game 4 against the Orioles, I hadn't put anything together that would have given Tony La Russa or Dave Duncan any confidence until September. The starts I had that month were good ones, and I was back to my right stuff. Tony and Dunc had the confidence to give me the ball in the playoffs, and to this day I wouldn't have said a word if they had given the ball to LaMarr that day. Obviously, Tony's mind was focused on what we would do the next day if we won, so it was either Burnsie that day or the next. They gave me the ball, and it was one of the most anxious days I've ever had. I knew what we were up against and what it meant.

I remember going to the bathroom behind the bullpen at old Comiskey Park and just trying to settle myself. I couldn't wait to get going, and the more I thought about it, the more anxious I became. Stepping to the mound in the first inning was like my first time in the big leagues. It was a new experience for me, and I went out and just did what I knew how to do. I let it go, went after people, and hoped for the best. It just happened to be the best performance of my life given the situation.

There wasn't anything strategic about it where we weren't going to pitch to a certain guy and throw a certain pitch. I knew those guys because I had pitched against Baltimore a lot and I knew them all well. I walked Gary Roenicke three times since he was the one guy in the lineup I wasn't comfortable with. I felt pretty good about everybody else and pitched accordingly. Tito Landrum hit a home run off me in the tenth, and it was one of those things. If you keep pumping fastballs early in the count to get ahead, somebody is going to run into one, and he did.

We've talked about it individually and collectively over the years—how special winning anything is. So many things have to come together, and you don't necessarily have control over all of them. We had something cool there and have cherished it over the years. We still talk about it and maintain that with Hoyt coming back the next day, that was as close to a sure thing as you could have. If we could have gotten by Baltimore, we felt we would have beaten Philadelphia. We came up short, though. I will be forever grateful to Tony for letting me pitch Game 4. I hate losing, and that is the bottom line, but if you end up having to take a nail, at least we made it a heck of a game.

I remember the big crowds at Comiskey and, as I found out, they used to serve liquor there and not just beer! It was billed as the "World's Largest Outdoor Saloon." I remember how nuts the fans would get. They were unbelievable. I saw a guy try to climb the foul pole from the lower deck to the upper deck, then had a moment of sobriety when he realized what he was doing. He froze there, and they had to get the fire department to get him off the foul pole, which delayed the game. I remember learning we were on the South Side and that it was the tougher side of town. When we had 40,000 to 50,000 at Comiskey, that place rocked, and those people loved us.

When I hurt my hip in 1985, it was not fun. I felt like I had come full circle and had become a reliable major league pitcher. I had gone through the process of getting there, had some ups and downs, and was ready to establish myself as a front-line performer. I was 26 years old and had six years in the big leagues, so I was certainly in position to do that. It was hard to deal with, but as I reflect on it now, I'm happy I got to that point. I was able to get to the point in my career where I was a quality major league pitcher. Had my career ended before that, I wouldn't have had that same peace of mind.

I finished up that year in Minnesota and tried to pitch, but couldn't. There was something inside me, and I told Tony and Dunc that after that I was done. I said, "Y'all better get something for me while you can." I don't know how I knew that, but in my heart I knew it. The degenerative arthritis in my hip was there, and I had a weird feeling. They talked to Harrelson about it, and they had an idea it was coming. That's what it came down to.

It's my understanding that full disclosure was made to the Yankees and others before I was traded. The thought was that maybe if I rested it I could keep going, but once a joint gets to that degenerative stage, there is no going back; it's not going to heal. That was it, and there was nothing I could do about it.

I was always treated well, and the people were good to me. Midwest baseball fans love and appreciate their baseball, and that is really cool. In Chicago, we may have been the red-headed stepchild, but we were every bit as worthy as the Cubs. After those years, we solidified a solid base of White Sox fans, and that's really cool.

Britt Burns was drafted by the White Sox in the third round of the 1978 amateur draft and made his major league debut with two starts later that summer. Burns joined the rotation for good in 1980 and posted an impressive 15–13 mark. In 1981 Burns went 10–6 and was named to the American League All-Star Game, but that season was marred by the death of his father, who was struck by a car in July and lingered in a coma before passing away in September. He posted a 13–5 mark in 1982, then struggled in 1983 to a 10–11 record.

With the Sox trailing Baltimore 2–1 in the 1983 American League Championship Series, Burns took the ball and delivered the finest performance of his career. He shut out the Orioles for nine innings, only to lose when Tito Landrum hit a homer in the tenth. Burns struggled in 1984, when he went 4–12, but he bounced back to go 18–11 in 1985, despite battling arthritis in his hip. Burns was traded to the Yankees on December 12, 1985, along with two minor leaguers for Ron Hassey and Joe Cowley. He never pitched for the Yankees, and his hip injury forced him to retire shortly afterward. Burns now works with the Houston Astros as their minor league pitching coordinator.

TONY LA RUSSA

MANAGER

1979–1986

I STARTED IN THE WHITE SOX ORGANIZATION and had an opportunity to be a minor league player/coach at the end of very poor professional playing career. I was a player/coach in Denver in 1975 and then in Des Moines in 1976. I had the good fortune of working for Loren Babe at Triple A. As a player/coach, I had some communication with the front office, including Roland Hemond. I had some decent years and was invited to big-league camp as a player. There was a strike that year, so I got the chance to play and met Bill Veeck. Right away, Paul Richards said I couldn't play, that I was a bum, and they should cut me as soon as they could.

Those three years of having some contact with the Sox, I guess they thought there was a place for me somewhere else, so in '78 they gave me the Knoxville job as a manager. I was blessed and had a great team there, then I ended up coaching with the Sox. In '79 Bill and Roland gave me a chance, and there I was.

It was totally unexpected to get the managing job in the middle of the '79 season after parts of two years managing in the minors. My wife, Elaine, was pregnant with our first child, Bianca, and she was due in six weeks. It was a very tough personal decision, but I figured you never know if you'd get another chance. I took the job, and our baby was born in Chicago.

When Jerry and Eddie came in, I still don't know how I ever survived that. Bill Veeck took a real shot with me. A lot of the publicity when I was hired was that Bill was too cheap to hire a real manager! I wasn't expensive, I know that. In 1981, when Jerry and Eddie came in, they said they were going to make some resources available and they did right away. We got Greg Luzinski, and they signed Carlton Fisk and did a lot of other things. I don't know how I survived. I guess they were busy doing so many things that by January they decided, "Let's just keep this guy." I kept staying, had a little success before '83, but I really don't know how I survived the early days with them. Since then, Eddie has always been a good man, and Jerry continues to be one of the best friends I ever had.

The '83 club was very tight. We had some early adversity and were under .500 late in May. Once we got it rolling, the tightness of the team took over. We had such great veterans, like Luzinski, Fisk, and Koosman and a great group of young players who were respectful of the game, along with a great coaching staff. Once we got the bit in our teeth, we were just relentless. I think part of it was that every time we lost two in a row, all we heard about were the swoons that had hit other Chicago baseball teams. Our guys would just not back off. We clinched it by September 17. It was hard to lose games because we were so hot.

Every day was another hero. I remember one game with the Angels where there was a rain delay, and we tied it late when Marc Hill, our backup catcher, got the big hit to win it. It was a lot of fun with the mix of guys we had, like Scott Fletcher at shortstop; Julio Cruz, who replaced Tony Bernazard; and Harold Baines, who was already legendary at that point. We had a really good mix, and they got hot at the right time.

Another thing I remember—because in St. Louis I've had to hear that Dave Duncan can't coach young pitchers—is that we had Hoyt, Dotson, and Burns. They were all young pitchers, and it was our first year together with Dave as my pitching coach. He did a terrific job. Charley Lau was great. I can't speak enough about how great my coaching staff was. You'll never top that with Charley as hitting coach, Dave the pitching coach, Jim Leyland coaching third. We had Art Kusnyer, Eddie Brinkman coaching the infielders, Dave Nelson, and Loren Babe. That group was unbelievable.

You don't have a crystal ball. We had a big lead on September 1, but if you look at baseball history, there have been plenty of big leads erased and teams embarrassed. We refused to back off, and it was that healthy theory that if you turn it off, you might not be able to turn it back on. We hadn't done it. Players want to play for a championship, and as a manager and part of the

Manager Tony La Russa pauses on the dugout steps before a 1985 game at Comiskey Park. La Russa had a mark of 522–510 in his seven-plus seasons with the White Sox. *Photo courtesy of AP Images*

coaching staff, you want to be able to say you helped contribute to getting your team to the postseason. When we clinched, it was one of my happiest moments in uniform ever.

We celebrated, and that team let it loose. I was proud of how the whole organization was included. Roland Hemond came in and got drenched.

Jerry and Eddie were both part of it. David Schaefer of security, the Bertucci family—everybody felt a part of it, and they were.

I put the majority of the blame for 1984 on myself, just being inexperienced and never really challenging the team the right way. We did take a couple hits when Carlton got hurt and Bull did, too. We made a dumb move that we liked at the time, but turned out not to be very smart. It should have been helpful when we traded for Ron Reed, but we gave up Koosman, who was one of our key leaders. I guess we were enjoying our win the year before too much, and I didn't do a good job of letting our guys know that it was a brand new year. We had a run right at the end of the first half and went into the All-Star break in good shape after winning seven in a row. You had the feeling that it was all going to work, but that was baloney, because you had to make it work. It was a great learning experience for me, and ever since then, if we've made it to the postseason, the coaches and I push the club even harder than before.

When I was fired in '86, it was very demoralizing because it was a true family here. The whole organization was a family, and I felt like a big part of it. When somebody tells you they don't want you in the family anymore, it hurts. I always kid Jerry—and it's the truth—that my family took it so seriously, my wife wouldn't talk to him for years. She felt like he should have stepped in.

The reality was the team was really struggling. I made a big mistake, because Ken Harrelson came in as general manager and he had a plan. His plan got in the way of some of the things we were doing, but really and truly, Ken should have had his own manager and coaching staff there. Who knows? Then his plan might have worked. The situation was unworkable, somebody had to go, and I went.

I have no problem at all with the White Sox—I have good memories. When I was managing Oakland and we were in the same division, I had to give the Sox the Heisman effect with the big stiff-arm, but when we were in different divisions and when I went to the National League, I always pulled for the White Sox. I enjoyed their World Series win in 2005 almost as much as they did. Every time I've come back, I've always felt the closeness. Once the game is played and over, you can't lose the feelings you have, the respect and the affection. I always felt it and I've always given it back.

Tony La Russa took over the White Sox as manager on August 2, 1979, at the age of 34, one year after he earned his law degree from Florida State. After three middle-of-the-pack seasons, La Russa's Sox posted an 87–75 mark in 1982. In 1983 the Sox went 99–63 en route to the AL West title, and La Russa was named Manager of the Year in the American League. The team went 74–88 in 1984 and 85–77 in 1985. La Russa was fired by Sox general manager Hawk Harrelson 64 games into the 1986 season and finished his Sox career with a 522–510 record. He took over the Oakland A's several weeks later and led them to three straight American League pennants and the 1989 world championship during his 10-year tenure there. In 1996 La Russa was hired to manage the St. Louis Cardinals. Under his command, the Cardinals have won two National League pennants and the 2006 World Series.

RICHARD DOTSON

PITCHER

1979–1987 ★ 1989

I WAS A FIRST-ROUND DRAFT PICK OF THE ANGELS and was surprised when I was traded to the White Sox. I was at work at a lumberyard and stopped at my dad's house on the way home. He told me I had been traded, but he wouldn't tell me to whom. I grew up in Cincinnati, which was National League country, so when I went through all the possible teams, the White Sox weren't one of them. I was surprised when it was.

It was a great opportunity for me, because Gene Autry owned the Angels at the time and was spending a lot of money bringing in free agents, so the minor leagues were kind of backed up. By being able to come to the White Sox with Bill Veeck and the limited budget he had to work with, it gave me the opportunity to advance a lot quicker. At the time, I didn't know that, so I was in shock a bit. I had just signed with the Angels in June and then was traded in December. At that point in your career, though, you just want to be able to play. It didn't really matter which team I was with as long as I got the opportunity to compete.

My first big-league start in September of 1979 came against the Angels. There was a big deal about me pitching in that game, because the Angels were in a pennant race and here the White Sox were pitching this 20-year-old kid. Of course, I wanted to show the Angels they had lost out, but it didn't work out as well as I'd have liked. I gave up six runs by the second inning, but at least I didn't take the loss, because we scored some runs.

When you get into baseball and get the chance to pitch in the big leagues, you're just living in the moment. I was behind in the count a lot and just trying to throw the hell out of the ball, and the Angels were a veteran team and took advantage of me.

My next start was at Oakland, and I threw a complete-game shutout, which worked out pretty good. Oakland wasn't the team the Angels were, but it was great. My sister lived in Northern California and got to see me come and pitch. I had a nice complete game for my first win in the big leagues, then a week later I beat them again, so I finished the season 2–0. After that, I was really looking forward to the next season and competing for a job on the major league staff.

Looking back on it, just because you get to the majors doesn't mean you get to do what you want. You have to learn a lot of things. I was gifted with a lot of talent and ability, but that will only take you so far. You're used to doing what you do against inferior competition, but big-league hitters know how to look for a pitch, how to hit in situations, and it was a learning curve for me. I had to learn to be consistent day in and day out, to come out every fifth day to be ready and peak. I had some success, but it was sporadic. I'd do really well, then hit my head against the wall the next time out. A lot of that was from me because I was so competitive and because I had good stuff. I'd try harder, and that doesn't necessarily equal success. You still have to get ahead, you still have to get the ball down and do all those things.

It kept getting a little better. Nineteen eighty was a good year, and in 1981 I was dealing and was locked in. I had four shutouts by June, but then we went on strike for a month and a half. I came back to Cincinnati and was throwing batting practice when I wasn't working. By the time we came back, I'd lost that feel that I had. In 1982 I was horrible. I was something like 3–11 at the All-Star break.

One consistent thing that was great about the opportunity I had was Tony La Russa, who will be in the Hall of Fame, as a manager every year. Just the way he goes about his business was the same, and I knew what he wanted out of me and how I had to go about my business. I think that really helped me.

We had a young team, then Veeck sold the Sox, and Reinsdorf came in. We got Pudge, we got Bull, and we were going to build something. When I look back on it, I had a lot of people who helped me those years both as a pitcher and a person. Jerry Koosman and Dick Tidrow were tremendous to me. Those guys were veterans and helped me get better. In high school I was

167

only 2–2 my senior year as a pitcher. I had a great arm, but I was more of an outfielder than a pitcher. So as a pro I did a lot of on-the-job learning. I had the stuff, but I had to learn things on the field. Fortunately, I was blessed with guys who helped me.

We were competitive in 1982, but in 1983 we wanted more. That's the way it should be. We didn't get off to a very good start. When we traded Tony Bernazard to Seattle for Julio Cruz, that was right when we took off. Julio added a lot to our team because he had speed, was a great fielder, and had a great attitude. We had a bunch of different guys, and he fit right in. He was a catalyst to get us going, and like Doug Rader said, it wasn't always pretty, but we got it done. It just started snowballing, and we really got rolling.

I think LaMarr Hoyt, Floyd Bannister, and I went 42–5 in the second half. We were good. Everybody kind of clicked, and we just had a good team. Defensively, we were a lot better than we'd been before. We hit for a lot of power and had some speed. Our bullpen didn't really have a name closer, but we had a lot of guys who did really good jobs. Koosman pitched out of the pen a little bit as did Dennis Lamp, and they could both spot start. Salome Barojas and Dick Tidrow were part of the committee, and it was really special. That was what it was all about, we wanted to win.

The night we clinched was really exciting. Any time you do something like that, you are excited and also looking forward to the next step. Big leagues, minor leagues, no matter where you are, you want to win. It's more rewarding when you go out there and feel like you're accomplishing something. Being able to share that with 24 other guys, the coaching staff, the traveling secretary, the whole front office, was a blast.

I had to pitch the next day. That night I didn't do a lot of champagne popping, and I was ready to pitch on Sunday. I think I had 18 wins at the time and, personally, I wanted to get to 20. Tony instilled in me that you don't ever want to lose the edge. We won, but I still wanted to be ready to pitch the next day. They found enough guys who could go that day, and we won the game.

Baltimore was the one team that had a winning record against us during the regular season. Two of my seven losses that year were against the Orioles. I had two complete games, gave up only four hits, lost a one-hitter 1–0 in Baltimore, then lost a three-hitter in Chicago, so, personally, they were a pain in my butt. Then the playoffs came, and it was worse.

The first inning of Game 3 at Comiskey killed me with Eddie Murray's home run. It was terrible, and even to this day I remember that. First of all,

I feel like I let the team down, especially because I had pitched so well against them during the year, even though I did lose both games. I remember the buzz in the stadium, and I hadn't felt that very often. You hear the term and it's true—there was electricity in the air, and it was really good. Baltimore had a good staff, and they were awesome pitching against us. They had a good team, but if we could have won that fourth game, we might have taken it with LaMarr pitching in Game 5. We didn't, and you can't win when you only score three runs in four games.

I actually started off 1984 great and was 11–4 at the All-Star break. I don't believe our team was complacent, but we just didn't play well. The second half of that year, we weren't good at all. We all had a lot more expectations than what we did. The second half of '84 I didn't pitch as well, even though I felt pretty good. I pitched a three-hitter against Detroit right before the All-Star Game and tweaked my groin, so the second half of the year, I had my groin wrapped and bandaged on my push-off leg. I didn't do as well and finished 14–15.

In '85 we played well, but I wasn't really part of the team because I was hurt. I really think if I had been healthy that year I could have helped us win the division. There was a circulatory problem in my upper chest. I had an overdeveloped pectoral muscle that, when I raised my arms to throw, cut off the circulation in my arm. I started out and felt okay in spring training, but I'd throw for a few innings and then wouldn't feel right. I had pain in my arm in a bunch of different spots. I started the season on the DL, then came back for a while. In Minnesota went to warm up, and my elbow was killing me. I think I maybe got through a few innings and then was done. At the time, as much as I was confused, I think everybody else was confused, too. Finally, I went to California and saw Dr. Lewis Yocum, and the first thing he did was take my arm, put it above my head, and take my pulse. He told me when I did that, I didn't have a pulse. So that's how it started, and when I raised my arm up, it completely cut off the circulation to my shoulder and my arm. I elected to have the surgery to cut the muscle in two, but it didn't work out. After that, I never threw the same again, and I never felt the same. It was miserable.

I didn't miss a turn in '86, but my arm killed me. There wasn't a start I had that year where my arm wasn't killing me. It didn't matter how many days off I had, it still hurt. I still went out there and competed. I tried, but it just didn't work out. Through the course of 1987, it was better. By that time they had dismantled our team. Tony was fired and Roland Hemond was gone. It was sad. I think we really had something going there, but things just fell apart.

169

Richard Dotson had a 97–95 overall mark in his White Sox career, including a 22-win season in 1983.

The Chicago fans like winners, and we weren't doing it, so they were really hard on Tony. I feel for a manager in that situation, now that I'm into coaching. It's the players that do it, but I think they felt they had to make a change. It was like we were rebuilding again, and for me, I never did get physically close to where I was before. I could try as hard as I could, but I didn't know what was coming out of my arm from pitch to pitch. It was that bad. I threw pretty hard, in the low 90s when I was younger, and heck, I wasn't that old then, but I'd give it my all and sometimes it would be 83 mph or sometimes 87 mph. I had quite a five-year learning experience where I knew what it was like to be on top and then to be on the bottom. Now, if you're going to be on the bottom, it might as well be in the big leagues, but it definitely hurt. I can remember coming in and actually crying after a game because I was so frustrated. The competitor in me was still there, but physically I wasn't.

I thought I could still pitch even at 85, 86 mph, but the problem was, it was never consistent. That became harder, because it was almost like learning to throw again. I just didn't know what velocity I would have on a given pitch. You can't do that in the big leagues, because those guys can hit. I got my ass handed to me for a while, but I still competed, and the desire was always there. It still is.

As far as a favorite game, I don't have one that really sticks out, but I loved the games where I went out there and battled my tail off and gave my team a chance to win. One time we were in Kansas City, and I gave up a grand slam in the first inning, so right away we were down 4–0. I ended up pitching until the tenth inning and had a chance to win it because we had come back to take a 5–4 lead. It was a day game, so it felt like about 140 degrees on the field, but I stayed in. In the tenth somebody hit a ground ball to the right side of the infield, and I was late getting over to cover first. It was a bang-bang play, and they called the runner safe. So after all that, I battled back and had a chance to get a complete-game win and I didn't cover first base! I think we ended up losing the game, but those are the types of things that stay with me—things that aren't easy, but I never gave up and would always do my best to grind it out.

I was fortunate enough to be selected to play in the 1984 All-Star Game in San Francisco. I lived in Northern California at the time, so my family came to the game. It was nice to be able to go home and stay at my house, then drive in to San Francisco for the game at Candlestick Park. It was really fun, and although I wasn't a real social guy when I played, I did meet a lot of nice guys. It was a blast to take it all in. It was also a great day to pitch because the game started in twilight and there were a ton of strikeouts because none of the batters could see a pitch.

Now that I'm a pitching coach, I realize you can't pigeonhole a guy and tell him there is only one way to do it. I think sometimes people in this game

171

try to reinvent it, but I think it's too easy to say, "Well, it's different now than it was then." The one pitch I notice that people use much more now is a cutter. Guys threw sliders, and to me, it's almost like the ones that were a bit short were cutters. I do think I might have been a better pitcher with a smaller breaking ball. Being able to throw a breaking ball when you're behind in the count is huge, and I don't think I was ever able to do that consistently. When I got behind in the count, it was fastball or change-up for me. So to be able to use a cutter as a breaking ball you can throw behind in the count is definitely an advantage. It looks like a fastball, doesn't break much, but it breaks right at the end.

When I first got out of baseball, the White Sox invited me to go to their fantasy camp, but I was so closely removed from my playing days, that I pretty much told them to shove it. Now I go every year and enjoy it a ton. First of all, I get to see guys I played with—but I've met other White Sox players from other teams, like Bill Melton, Carlos May, and Ed Herrmann, who are tremendous. A lot of the campers come back every year, and it's like a family. It really is nice.

In the off-season I usually hunt with Greg Walker and Greg Luzinski, and we have a blast. My teammates are quality people, and I don't get to see enough of them. It's a special thing, and that team was a special group of guys. A bunch of us had been there for a few years, and then we added some of the veteran free agents, who were great and made it that much better. I'd still try to run through a brick wall for them.

Right-hander Richard Dotson was acquired by the White Sox along with Bobby Bonds and Thad Bosley on December 5, 1977, in exchange for Brian Downing, Dave Frost, and Chris Knapp. He made his debut with the Sox in 1979 and joined the starting rotation in 1980, going 12–10. He had his finest season in 1983, when he posted a 22–7 record with a 3.22 ERA for the AL West champions. Injuries contributed to losing records the next four years, and he was traded to the New York Yankees on November 12, 1987, along with Scott Nielsen for Dan Pasqua, Mark Salas, and Steve Rosenberg.

He has served as a pitching coach in the Sox organization for the past seven seasons.

HAROLD BAINES

DESIGNATED HITTER/ OUTFIELDER

1980–1989 ★ 1996–1997 ★ 2000–2001

I REMEMBER THE FIRST GAME I EVER PLAYED in 1980 because my father was there to see it. I'm an old, traditional guy who likes to share my so-called glory with the people I love. I'm glad my father was there to see my first game.

In 1983 I was still young, and it was just my fourth year in the league. We had a good mixture of young and old guys—well, old in baseball terms, but not in age. We had great chemistry, especially in the second half where we played so well right up until we got to the playoffs.

On the clincher, I was up and hit a sac fly at the end. I was just hoping the fly ball got out there far enough for Julio to score. I'll never forget it. It was my first time winning something—I'd been playing for five years before that happened. It was a great moment.

The fact we didn't hit in the playoffs tells you how good Baltimore's pitching was. Good pitching stops good hitting. I still remember Tito Landrum's home run crushing us in Game 4 back home. It was a good series, but when we got there, we thought we were going to get a lot more. Things don't always happen that way.

On paper, we should have won more after that. Things just didn't work out. It shows you how hard it is to repeat and win your division. We won in

Harold Baines hits his 155th career home run during the third inning against the Baltimore Orioles in Chicago on July 22, 1987. The home run set a club record, though the White Sox lost the game 10–5. *Photo courtesy of AP Images*

'05, took the whole thing, then it took us three years to get back to the play-offs. It's not easy to repeat.

The 25-inning game in 1984 was a long day. Actually, it was a long two days. A lot of things happened before my home run. The Brewers were winning by two or three runs and then threw a ball away at first base that let us tie it up. There was a curfew in those days that you couldn't go over, so we had to come back the next day and play. Fortunately, I hit a home run to win it, but we had to play another game after that. It was a long two days.

When I became a DH, I was fortunate I could still hit a little bit. That helped. I knew I couldn't go play in the National League. I had to concentrate on the pitcher I was facing, because the only way I could help my team was to provide offense. I studied as much as I could and worked as hard as I could on my game. It allowed me to play 10 extra years.

I was crushed when I got traded in 1989, but I was surprised they retired my number when I came back a month later. It showed me how special I was to the organization that nobody else can wear it. It's a great honor to have my number retired by the White Sox. I don't sit back and dwell on it, though. A lot of players have asked me how it feels, and I tell them I don't know how to feel. I'm very grateful it happened. The White Sox also dedicated a statue of me, and that was very exciting for both me and my family. As a player, you just don't know, though. I know I really can't sit back and look at those things until I'm out of the game.

When we won it all in 2005, I was in the right spot at the right time. I didn't foresee myself being a coach in the first place. Ozzie came aboard and asked me to come along with him, so I tell people I was, thankfully, in the right spot in the right time to be with the White Sox when they won the World Series.

The World Series went by so fast, it was like it happened just like that. I'll never forget the parade, because they went through so many different communities. It was a special moment I will never forget.

When I was drafted, I was hoping maybe I could play five or six years. I ended up playing 22 seasons and now I'm coaching for the organization that gave me the chance to play this wonderful game of baseball. I'm very grateful for that.

Jerry Reinsdorf is a person who I can truly call my friend. That's hard to say in this time and age, to have a friend whom you can turn to and have any sort of normal conversation with. I know he will be there for me on and off the field. It's not just Jerry, it's all the people who work for Jerry. That goes to the grounds crew, the guys in the clubhouse, everybody. They are loyal to the White Sox organization, and that's why from the minor leagues on up there are so many people who have been here over 20 years. That's the respect they show Mr. Reinsdorf.

Outfielder and designated hitter Harold Baines was selected by the White Sox with the very first pick of the 1977 amateur draft. He came to the big leagues in 1980 and, starting in 1982, averaged 21 homers and 93 RBIs per season and made the All-Star team in 1985, 1986, 1987, and 1989. On July 29, 1989, he was traded with Fred Manrique to the Texas Rangers for Wilson Alvarez, Scott Fletcher, and Sammy Sosa. Baines rejoined the Sox as a free agent on December 11, 1995, and hit .311 with 22 homers and 95 RBIs for the 1996 season. He was hitting .305 in 1997, when he was traded to the Baltimore Orioles for Juan Bautista. Baines played parts of the 2000 and 2001 seasons with the Sox before retiring. He finished his 22-season playing career with 2,866 hits, 384 home runs, 1,628 RBIs, and a .289 average.

Baines' number was retired by the White Sox on August 17, 1989, making him the only active player to ever be awarded that distinction. In 2000 he was named to the White Sox Team of the Century. On July 20, 2008, he became the seventh White Sox legend to have a statue dedicated in his honor at U.S. Cellular Field.

After spending 2003 as a special assignment instructor for the Sox, Baines joined Ozzie Guillen's staff on March 20, 2004, as the bench coach and in 2006 moved to the position of first-base coach.

GREG LUZINSKI

OUTFIELDER

1981–1984

BASICALLY, I WAS A BASEBALL FAN when I was growing up in the Chicago suburbs. My uncle was a diehard Sox fan, so I went to games at Comiskey with him. I have to say I probably went to more Cubs games because it was a lot closer for me. As far as baseball went, though, I enjoyed both teams.

At the conclusion of 1980 we had won the World Series with the Phillies, so we went to spring training as the champions. It was then that Ruly Carpenter announced that he was selling the team. They told me they were going to move me and gave me three teams—the Yankees, the Astros, and the White Sox. I said there was no doubt that I would rather go to the White Sox. They made a cash deal, and away I went.

It was a situation that was good and exciting for me, because at that time the White Sox had come under new ownership with Jerry Reinsdorf and Eddie Einhorn, so they were showing obvious signs of improving the ballclub with Fisk, LeFlore, and the good young pitchers they had. Plus Tony La Russa had only been over there two years, and I had played with Ron Schueler, who was the pitching coach at that time. It wasn't like I was going over there and didn't know anybody. Things worked out really well for me.

It was a little tough learning to DH at first. Those were years when, with regard to the umpires, they were different in each league—some of them still used the balloon protector, and the high strike was called more than the low strike in the American League. It took some time to get used to. Fortunately,

177

Greg Luzinski slides safely into second as Baltimore Oriole Cal Ripken Jr. tries for the ball during the first game of the ALCS at Baltimore's Memorial Stadium, October 5, 1983. *Photo courtesy of AP Images*

Charley Lau was the hitting coach and very good at what he did. Basically, he left me alone, but what he did help me out with was the pitchers and how they used their out pitches. He definitely helped me with his knowledge of the pitchers in the American League.

When it was cold at old Comiskey and you had the wind blowing in, it was hard to hit in a cold, damp ballpark. I played in bigger ballparks, and I would consider Comiskey to be a fairly big one. The fans came out, and you had Nancy Faust on the organ getting them going. I thought it was really fun. I didn't mind it at all.

In 1983 we had a good ballclub. I often say at banquets and the like that it was the best starting staff I ever played behind. We had Hoyt, Bannister, Dotson, and Burns, so we had good pitching and a solid bullpen. Those starters were unbelievable. Every one of them went out there and contributed big in that year.

I hit three over the roof that year—and one of them on national TV—so that whole thing was really fun. It's not something you're trying to do, you just want to make good, hard contact and hit it on the sweet spot. That's just displaying some power, I guess.

We had some young guys on our team like Greg Walker in his first year and [Ron] Kittle. Vance Law really developed at third base behind Charley Lau's help. We had a good mix of speed and power and, as I've said, you can't say enough about the starting staff. If you threw them out there today, you'd still win a lot of games.

It had been a long time since the White Sox had won anything. It was a great feeling. When we clinched, I remember Julio Cruz jumping on home plate against Seattle. It was appropriate for the White Sox franchise that Harold Baines drove in that winning run. To win is what it's all about.

I was personally really looking forward to the playoffs, because if we could have beaten Baltimore in the playoffs, we would have played Philadelphia in the World Series. That's where I was previously, and it would have been a lot of fun playing in the field at first base back in Philly. I had it all planned out already that on the first out that came to me in Philadelphia, I was going to spike the ball like Pete Rose did, and the place would have gone absolutely bananas.

I just feel bad that we didn't get there. It was a matter of inches in Baltimore with some production with the bases loaded, we could have been two games up coming back home. The baseball gods didn't have it that way. Britt Burns pitched a tremendous game the last game in Chicago, and Landrum hit the home run in extra innings to beat us. It was a thrilling series, and I don't think we hit like we were capable of hitting. Sometimes I think good pitching stops good hitting, and that's what happened there. I was really looking forward to playing the Phillies in the '83 World Series, but it didn't happen.

The next year was hard. I had a bad knee that was giving me trouble. I had the opportunity to go to Baltimore after the White Sox and I could have stayed there, but I decided that it was time to stop. When you can't perform the way you want to perform, it's time to go.

I love Chicago. I grew up there, and it couldn't have been a better experience for me. Jerry Reinsdorf and Eddie Einhorn were definitely great owners for me when I was there. They treated the players well and they tried to please the fans by bringing in winning players to the organization.

Greg Luzinski was born in Chicago and attended Notre Dame High School in Niles. After pounding National League pitchers throughout the 1970s, Luzinski was purchased by the White Sox from the Philadelphia Phillies on March 30, 1981. The burly designated hitter hit 21 homers with 62 RBIs in his first season in the American League, then followed with a big 18-homer, 102-RBI year in 1982. "The Bull" was a powerhouse in the middle of the Sox's division championship run in 1983 with 32 homers and 95 RBIs. A knee injury hampered him in 1984, when he slipped to 13 homers and 58 RBIs. He retired following the season.

Luzinski runs "Bull's BBQ" at the Phillies' Citizens Bank Ballpark and can be found there at most home games.

EDDIE EINHORN

President and COO/ Vice Chairman

1981–Present

I WAS AT NORTHWESTERN LAW SCHOOL with Jerry Reinsdorf. We started in 1957, and we've known each other more than 50 years. I actually got a job selling hot dogs at Comiskey Park during the 1959 season. The truth of the matter was I wanted to get into the games. I used to come down and do it some days, other days I'd just show my workers' card and use it to get in, then sit in a seat. I was at the World Series. Who would have believed then any of this now? I've been in the sports business now for 52 years.

I had sold my business, TVS, and after 25 years there, I was doing too good a job, because everybody was trying to get the rights to college basketball. We had made college basketball pretty big, and I wanted to get out of there before we got smothered. At the same time, Jerry was selling his company, Balcor. I was trying to figure out what to do, and I have always loved the game of baseball. I started to inquire about buying into a team. About that time, I got a call from Jerry, who came to see me in New York. I was working at CBS at the time. He told me he had a lead on getting the White Sox, while at the same time I was pursuing the San Diego Padres. Ray Kroc won that one, and I wasn't going to beat him!

The White Sox appealed to me, and I talked to him for a long time. I said I would do it, but I wouldn't come to Chicago, because I liked working in New York. Then CBS told me I couldn't work for them and have ownership

Eddie Einhorn, second from right, talks with Jerry Reinsdorf, St. Louis Cardinals manager Tony La Russa, and Ozzie Guillen before a game between the two clubs in Chicago in June 2006. *Photo courtesy of AP Images*

in a team because they were a potential bidder for rights. I had to think about that and decided ownership was something I wanted to do, and I quit CBS. About three weeks later I got a call from Jerry, and he told me we had lost the deal to the DeBartolo family. CBS took me back and gave me a new contract. A couple weeks later my friend, Carl Lindemann, called me from the baseball meetings and told me they didn't approve the DeBartolos. I asked Jerry what that meant, then came out to see him. A third person was in it with us, but baseball didn't want him.

I said, "Who's gonna help you run it if I'm in New York?" There was a long pause, and then I said, "I guess that means me." That's what happened, and I made the decision to come to Chicago. I ran the marketing, and Jerry ran the team, but when you get into a new venture, you're a little bit into everything. When I had a decision to make, I'd go to him, then he'd come to me. That's the way it kind of ran.

We had a good start. We got the team only about a month before spring training. Roland Hemond came in one day and said, "We have a chance to get Carlton Fisk. It's on the wire." I asked who his agent was, and they told me it was Jerry Kapstein. I knew that name—he had done statistics for me when I did Navy radio, even before I got into television. I called him up, and he remembered me. I said, "Listen, we just bought this team. We'd like to get Carlton. We'll come out and meet with you, but I want you to assure me one thing. Don't embarrass me. If he's gonna go back to the Red Sox or Yankees, just tell me it's off. If there's a regular bidding process, that's different. Just tell me we got a shot going in, and I'll take it from there."

Sure enough, he said we had a shot, and I took him at his word. We went out two or three times, and I remember Jerry saying to me, "You know, we're starting to bid against ourselves." He hated that. I said, "Be quiet, that means we're going home with him." We did the deal, we came home with him, and we got off to an incredible start that year. We didn't know there would be a strike that year, but that was the start of it.

We built to '83 and we won. We thought we had a great team for the future. We won the division by 20 games and thought we were geniuses in baseball, that it was a piece of cake. Little did we know that in '84 we'd finish at the bottom with the same team and Tom Seaver! We learned a little humility in those days. Nobody knows baseball. You can think you do, but you could be in it 100 years and not really know. We had some off years, then we started to build back. We had a lot of good years, not as many as I'd like, but we kept pursuing the Holy Grail, and in 2005 we finally did it. It was wonderful for the town. I think the biggest thing I'll remember is the parade. To see what you did affected so many people—not that we got any hits—but that we were involved in something that touched so many people was a great feeling.

With the pay TV, people tell me I was ahead of my time in some things. I am progressive and I knew it would happen some day. I tried to get all the teams to go with us in one big package and be our own ESPN. They didn't want to do it, maybe they didn't trust us. We were determined to do it, and our SportsVision product was as good as anything. We were doing the stuff they do on *Baseball Tonight* before anybody. Chicago wasn't wired for cable, and we weren't capitalized like some businesses. With every start-up business, you have to spend a lot of money before you make any, and we couldn't go on funding the pay TV. We lost a little, but we got a partner. Now we have the deal with Comcast, and we're moving in the right direction.

We came from a different background than Bill Veeck. Bill and I didn't get off to a good start, but I give him credit as being the first sports marketer in the history of the game. He started doing it in the '40s, and they didn't even call it "marketing." There wasn't even such a word. He was the original promoter and knew how to do some things really well. If your team wasn't playing well on the field, he knew how to divert your attention to something else in the style of an old promoter when there wasn't television or rights fees and things like that. He wasn't financed very well—nobody was back then. There were very few who were able to sign all the big stars back then. He did what he could to keep the team here, and they had a few good years. You were competing against the Yankees and Cleveland, and it was tough back then with only eight teams. It just got too big, and we decided to get in and do things a different way. Our record in 29 years here is one of the best in baseball. We haven't won enough, though. I wish we'd won more and been in more World Series. That would have been better.

I was the villain in the new ballpark drama. I had 'round-the-clock guards for a few months that stayed downstairs in my apartment. It was tough, but we had to do it. The one thing was that when I was in law school, Big Jim Thompson was my editor on the *Journal of Criminal Law*, and that didn't hurt us. He stuck up for us pretty good when we had to do it. It was tough, and times were tough. The idea was not to use public funds for sports teams, and we fought and we fought. Part of the old park actually fell down from the upper deck in right field. We tried to move to the suburbs, and that was blocked. We didn't know what to do. Finally, they approved the stadium. We thought everyone was moving their stadium downtown, and we tried to do that. I remember Mayor Harold Washington coming over to see us and saying we couldn't move downtown because the infrastructure would be $65 million alone. I said, "That means if we can't go to the suburbs and we can't go downtown, I guess we have to go across the street." He paused, then said, "That's right." That's what we did.

We haven't regretted it. We have more demanded of us than the Cubs. We have to win, they have to show up, and that's the biggest difference. They were able to develop a different marketing strategy of the community and the neighborhood and a lot of things we don't have. They have a different standard. Here, we have to really perform to get our maximum crowds. Most of our fans are not from the South Side. They're from all over, and it's a big effort to come down here at night. We started to win, and people came. When we didn't, they didn't. That pressure is tough. You have to deal with the fan base you have. We don't compete against the Cubs, in my opinion.

We compete against ourselves and we have to beat it. Since Kenny Williams came, he has done a wonderful job keeping us competitive. You can't win every year, but now that we have a good nucleus the last few years, we've won in '05, came close in '06, and won the division in '08. Now we hope to stay up there. It's not easy, but we hope that we can for our fans, and we do the best we can to do it.

There is a great feeling here. I'm not here that much anymore—I call myself semiretired. Jerry and I have a deal—when we win, it's our team. When we lose, it's his team. We've been able to get along for over 50 years, and I always have pride in this and don't want to leave it. Every time I go out there, I see people I've known for years and years. Chicago is a very loyal town. My biggest fear is that I'll come in some day and somebody will say, "Didn't you used to be Eddie Einhorn?" Then I'm in trouble!

Eddie Einhorn was the founder of TVS, a sports programming company that pioneered college basketball on television and brought the nation the landmark Houston-UCLA game from the Astrodome in 1968. After leaving TVS, Einhorn was the executive producer of the *CBS Sports Spectacular*.

In 1981 he joined with his former law school classmate, Jerry Reinsdorf, to form a limited partnership that purchased the White Sox. He served as the White Sox's president and chief operating officer for 10 years before moving into his current role as vice chairman of the team. He served on various Major League Baseball committees and in 1990 helped MLB land its first billion-dollar contract with CBS and ESPN.

In his most recent venture, Einhorn set up the National Youth Baseball Championship, a tournament that brings together eight major youth baseball organizations and crowns champions in several age brackets.

VANCE LAW
THIRD BASEMAN/SHORTSTOP
1982–1984

I SPENT A LOT OF TIME AT THE BALLPARK as a kid with my dad [Vern Law], however the clubhouse was off-limits, because my dad didn't want us in there due to the language and other things. When I was drafted by the Pirates, I had heard the reason they drafted me was because of my dad, and I misunderstood what they meant. I thought he called them and asked to give me a chance. I didn't like that because I wanted to make it on my own. I found out later that he never made any call, but the Pirates drafted me as a nod to him for all the contributions he had made to their organization during his career.

I was thrilled to be with the team I had loved growing up and to have gotten to the big leagues with them. I played with my childhood hero, Willie Stargell, who treated me like a king when I was a kid and continued to do it when I walked into the big-league clubhouse. That's the reason he is held in such high regard, not only by me, but by so many other people.

That's why, when I was traded to the White Sox, I was devastated. I didn't follow the American League at all. All I knew about the White Sox was that they had the ugliest uniforms I had ever seen, with the white shirts and blue collars and no stirrups. That's what I put on when I got traded to the Sox in spring training. It's tough to get traded, especially when you're young. You grow accustomed to how things are done in your organization. Walking into a new clubhouse is like walking into a new classroom when you change schools. You feel like all eyes are on you. It's a very uncomfortable feeling. I didn't now anything about Chicago other than it was a huge city.

I quickly learned to love the White Sox organization. Tony La Russa called me in his office the first day, but he didn't recognize me because I wore glasses on the field, but I didn't wear them off the field. When I walked in, he didn't know who I was! I had to introduce myself. He made me feel really good right at the start. He said, "You'll be on the White Sox going north with the team unless you play your way off the team in these last weeks of spring training." I didn't feel like I would do that and felt that I could stay in the role he had for me but would work toward being an everyday player, not just a backup.

I came up as a shortstop and had played a little second base along with one or two games at third base. We acquired Scott Fletcher in '83, and at third base Aurelio Rodriguez was getting older, so Tony said, "I think you're going to help us become a better club if we have Fletcher at shortstop and move you to third." I said, "Whatever will help." I didn't care. I was out on the field and I didn't care what position I played as long as I was out there. When I got to third base, I really felt at home. Aurelio was a really big help to me. Here I am, threatening to take his job, and yet he was right there beside me giving me tips. I was still playing with a shortstop's mentality, charging everything, but at third base, you are more like a hockey goalie. You're close to the action, and it's all about footwork going front or back a step or two, then side to side to get balls. Aurelio taught me that and helped me so I wouldn't run myself into bad hops. It became a comfort to me to have him helping me learn to play there. I would play some second base once in a while and a bit of center field to spell Rudy Law when we were facing a tough lefty.

The '83 team was an unbelievable group of guys. We had veterans like Koosman, Luzinski, Paciorek, and Fisk; guys who were in the middle of their careers like Dotson, Hoyt, and Baines; then younger guys like me, Fletcher, and Jerry Dybzinski. Our pitching staff was just fantastic with Burns, Dotson, Bannister, and Hoyt all coming into their own. I couldn't have asked for a better situation.

One of the great things was that Tony was such a great communicator. Everybody understood what their roles were and accepted those roles. Everyone wants to play, but at the same time, if you were on the bench, you knew you were fine with the guys who were out there. We knew that he would be consistent in establishing those roles and following through. If there was a

187

Vance Law dives to his left to snag a ground ball off the bat of the Orioles' Rich Dauer in Game 1 of the 1983 ALCS at Memorial Stadium in Baltimore. *Photo courtesy of AP Images*

pinch-hitting opportunity, Jerry Hairston would be first off the bench. If we got a lead, Mike Squires would go in and play first base and take over defensively from Greg Walker. Spanky was just awesome there. Tony stayed consistent with everything. You can't complain if you're being used the way you were told you were going to be used.

I still believe to the bottom of my heart that we were the best team in baseball that year. We had a lot of opportunities against the Orioles. Everybody points to Dybzinski going from first to third and running me off third base on that hard hit to left field where I got held up by Jim Leyland. Dybber kept coming around second base, then I got thrown out at home because I was told to run. Everybody points to that play, but we had other opportunities. There was a balk after that, and we had chance to win that game. It's the one that really stands out, but it sure would have been nice to have LaMarr on the hill the next day, because he owned the Orioles that year.

The next year I was really comfortable and felt like I belonged. Greg Luzinski said to me, "Look at the size of you. You're 6′2″, 190 pounds. Why are you only hitting three or four home runs each year? You should hit 15 or 20. Start looking for pitches instead of always going inside-out and going to right field. Look for a ball to drive." I started to think about how guys were going to pitch me and had a better understanding of how to look for a pitch in certain counts. If a guy has thrown you several sliders away, he may come inside with a fastball, and you might as well look for it, get your foot down and the barrel of the bat around, and try to hit it out of the ballpark. I think I hit 17 homers that year, and there were many times I was looking for a pitch and hit one out. I was getting comfortable with how pitchers pitched me and with my own abilities. I attribute that to the veterans we had who talked to me and showed confidence in me.

I had no idea I was being traded. I had talked to my wife about buying a home in Chicago and making that our place, because I pictured myself staying with the Sox for the next 10 years. I came home for the off-season, and the next thing I knew, I was having that conversation where they told me they needed to get some pitching. Off I went to Montreal, and that was really tough. It was exactly the same situation as when I came to Chicago. I had great teammates and great friends and all of a sudden I was going to a team with funny uniforms in a funny city that spoke a different language.

People ask me which side of town I liked playing on better, and that's a tough, tough decision. Mr. Reinsdorf was the greatest owner and, in my opinion, still is. He treated everyone with such respect, and I love that man. I was very fortunate to play for him when he and Mr. Einhorn took over the White Sox. He was always coming down and asking how your family was doing. He was a hands-on owner, which I loved. I loved having that interaction. We had a 20-year reunion with the Sox in 2003, and it was awesome to still be cheered and recognized. It builds your ego back up once you become a so-called normal citizen again!

The White Sox acquired Vance Law and Ernie Camacho from the Pittsburgh Pirates on March 21, 1982, in exchange for Ross Baumgarten and Butch Edge. After spending his first season with the Sox in a utility role, Law earned the starting spot at third in 1983, then followed with a strong offensive season in 1984, with 17 homers and 59 RBIs.

On December 7, 1984, Law was traded to the Expos for relief pitcher Bob James. He played three seasons in Montreal, two with the Chicago Cubs, spent a year in Japan with the Chunichi Dragons, then finished his career in 1991 with the Oakland A's.

Law's father, Vern, pitched for the Pirates from 1950 to 1967 and compiled a 162–147 career mark. Vance Law is currently the head baseball coach at his alma mater, Brigham Young University.

TOM PACIOREK
FIRST BASEMAN/OUTFIELDER
1982–1985

MY OLDER BROTHER, JOHN, WAS ONE OF THE BEST ATHLETES in the country when he graduated from high school and signed with the Houston Colt .45s. It's a shame he had a back problem, but he was able to play in the majors for one game—the last game of the 1963 season. He went 3-for-3, scored four runs, walked a couple times, and drove in three runs. Those were the only at-bats he ever had in the major leagues, so he retired with a 1.000 batting average. Rusty Staub, Joe Morgan, Jimmy Wynn, Sonny Jackson, and a few others made their debut in that game.

My younger brother, Jim, played one year with the Brewers in 1987, then his contract was sold to Japan, where he played for six years and did very well. He won a batting title there. My brothers were probably the best athletes in our family, but I had the most longevity, probably because I had the most breaks along the way.

I played football at the University of Houston and was drafted by the Miami Dolphins. Joe Thomas was their general manager and made me an offer that I could refuse! I think it was a $2,000 signing bonus and $3,000 more if I made the team with a $15,000 salary. I was a ninth-round draft pick with them, but a fifth-round pick of the Los Angeles Dodgers. They offered me a $20,000 bonus—it never occurred to me to play both sports, so I signed with the Dodgers. It was a good move—my hips are so bad now from playing baseball, I can't imagine what they'd be like from playing football.

Tommy Lasorda had the most influence on my baseball life of anybody I came into contact with. The first day I signed, we all went out to eat. There was Steve Garvey, Bobby Valentine, Billy Buckner, all those guys, and they all ordered steaks. I ordered double cheeseburgers, because I was more into quantity and getting filled up, so Lasorda started calling me "Wimpy." That was 1968, and that name has stuck with me now for more than 40 years.

We did a lot of things they don't do today. Tommy told us to write a letter to the guy with the Dodgers who played our position. I'd say, "Tommy, are we really supposed to do this?" He'd say, "Yeah, just write the letter." "Dear Wes Parker, dear Maury Wills (whoever played your position), I hope you enjoyed your stay with the Dodgers, because I'll be up there to take your job soon." We all sent them to those guys, then when we got to spring training the following season, we wondered why they all hated our guts! Tommy was the first guy I met in baseball, and I thought, *Good grief, is everyone like him?* Thankfully, he was the only one like that.

I was over 30 when I finally figured out how to hit. I went into a prolonged slump and I thought I had to change everything. I stood up straight and had the bat wrapped around my head, and I decided to get myself into a better hitting position by going into a crouch and bringing my bat back behind me. I could see the ball a lot better and I realized I was making it a lot easier than I had in the past. Baseball is a series of adjustments, and if you don't do them, you'll be in the unemployment line.

In 1978 I was released twice in about a month by the Atlanta Braves, which has to be some kind of record. Then I went to Seattle in the minor leagues and only got called up because I had a couple of good games. Then Ruppert Jones had an appendectomy and was out for a month. I knew I was going to get released when he came back, so I needed to have a good game. I got in as a DH, batting ninth against Mike Caldwell and the Brewers, and went 4-for-4 with a game-winning home run. I played the next day, hit another home run, and when Ruppert came back, they released another guy. That one game preserved my career another nine years.

In 1981 I went to the winter meetings in Fort Lauderdale and tried to negotiate a contract with the Mariners. George Argyros was their owner, and when he couldn't agree on a figure with my agent, he decided to get even with me and trade me, which he did the next day. When I got home, I got a phone call from a reporter telling me I'd been traded to Chicago and asking how I felt. I said, "Chicago who? Sox or Cubs?" I had just finished second in the league with a .326 average, but the Mariners didn't want to pay me.

I really enjoyed myself in Chicago. Tony La Russa was a good manager, even though he and I didn't see eye to eye on a lot of things. I got mad at him one time and told a reporter he couldn't manage a fruit stand. I sometimes think about that and still cringe today, but I really wanted to play and, at the time, I wasn't.

My first year in Chicago, 1982, we won 87 games and were a good team. In 1983 everything went right. We had a couple good rookies with Kittle and Walker. We had 20-game winners with Dotson and Hoyt. Floyd Bannister came into his own, and Jerry Koosman might have been our most valuable player because he could do anything—start, close, middle relief—he was special. Everybody had a good year. Rudy Law stole a ton of bases, Baines was a stud, Fisk and Luzinski were great leaders, and everything came together.

We couldn't lose. I think we won 17 straight home games. You get in the habit of winning, and when you finally lose a game, you're shocked. We played so well, but I wish it had been a closer race. We had something like three weeks to get ready for the playoffs and we lost a bit of our edge when we faced Baltimore. They were a really good team with an outstanding group of guys led by Eddie Murray and Cal Ripken and a great staff. They won the World Series, and I can't help but think that could have been us. That Game 4 that Britt Burns pitched was filled with opportunities, and if we could have won that one, we'd have had LaMarr throwing Game 5, which was to our advantage. Tito Landrum hit that home run, though, and broke everybody's heart.

The thing that was truly special to me that year was the fact that we had a couple of great guys we knew wouldn't survive to the next season. Charley Lau was our beloved hitting coach, and we knew he had terminal colon cancer. Loren Babe was a longtime White Sox scout and coach who traveled with us the second half of the season knowing that he was sick and his days were numbered, as well. We dedicated our season to those two. When we lost, we said our good-byes, and it was tough because you knew you wouldn't see them again. Neither one lived to spring training the next year. I really wish we could have won it for them.

The next year was unbelievable. We had added Tom Seaver to our pitching staff and thought we'd be better, but Koosman left. He was a special guy, and that took a little bit of the wind out of our sails. Chemistry is really

Tom Paciorek (No. 44) greets Harold Baines at home plate after Baines belted a solo home run to give the White Sox a 7–6 win in a 25-inning game against the Milwaukee Brewers. The game was started on May 8, suspended after 17 innings, and finished the next day. *Photo courtesy of AP Images*

important, and when you lose somebody like Koosman, it's a loss not only on the field, but in the clubhouse, too. He was really special. It left a big absence in the clubhouse and on our staff, because you could throw him any time, anywhere. He went on to pitch well for the Phillies after that. Nothing went right in '84.

I didn't start the 25-inning game against the Brewers that year. Actually, I was eating a pizza in the umpires' room in the fourth inning, which was a tradition back then. We had ordered Connie's, and it was my day to pay. We were in there eating, and somebody ran in and yelled, "Hey, Wimpy! Kitty's got a migraine, and you've gotta pinch-hit for him." I asked when he was up, and they told me I was supposed to be on-deck right then. I had a mouthful of pizza and tomato sauce all over my shirt, went running out there, and went to bat. Don Sutton was on the mound and, three pitches later, I was on my way back to the dugout, thinking, *Man, Kittle, you could have done this yourself.* I wound up getting 10 plate appearance, five hits, and drove in three runs. If you look at the box score, you see guys going 0-for-10 and ruining their whole season. Not me, though—maybe it was the boost I got from the pizza!

It was a great compliment to be called a professional hitter. To me, it was a series of trials and errors. I couldn't figure things out in my early years or get any kind of consistency. Until I started making adjustments, I wasn't a good hitter. When I did, I got to a higher level and starting hitting .300. I think one of the reasons guys don't hit for a higher average today is that their swings are too long. They all stand straight up, wrap the bat around their head, and try to hit a home run every time up. That doesn't always work. Sometimes a single is just as good, especially with a guy on third. Choke up and put the ball in play. Charley Lau would tell me to center the ball, to think about hitting the ball between left-center and right-center. That way your body will stay closed, your head will stay still, and you'll have a better swing. Charley was the best hitting instructor I ever had. You didn't have to hit just like George Brett, he would help you adapt in your own way using his fundamentals. He was always positive, too. You could have the ugliest at-bat ever, and he'd say, "Boy, you looked hitterish up there." He always had a positive thought.

Teams are always better when you have some pranksters, too. I used to smoke a little. I'd leave my pack of cigarettes in a certain spot, and Marc Hill would put exploding caps in them. I'd light up, the thing would blow up in my face, and I'd start screaming at him. I can't tell you how many times they'd tell me I had a phone call, then there was shaving cream all over the phone. I fell for that one a lot. It was always fun, regardless of how we were doing. That's one of the reasons I hated that we went downhill in '84 and afterward, because you knew then guys weren't going to be there anymore.

In the middle of '85 I was designated for assignment and eventually wound up with the Mets. It was good for me, because we weren't in the pennant race with the Sox, the Mets were. They released me after that season, and I finished up with Texas.

Eddie Einhorn was the guy who got me into broadcasting. Toward the end of the '87 season he called me up and invited me to lunch. I loved him, and he asked me if I'd be interested in announcing for the Sox the next year. I said, "Heck yeah!" I had done a couple of games on TV in 1984 when I was on the disabled list and did the same thing for the Rangers when I was there. Anyway, I had turned 40, and it wasn't like offers to keep playing were streaming in, so I thought I'd take the first baseball job offered to me, regardless of what it was. When the White Sox called me, I said yes immediately. Ironically, about 30 minutes later, I got a call from Dan Fabian at WGN Radio inquiring about my interest in the Cubs radio job, but I had already committed to the Sox and was certainly going to honor my commitment.

I tried to have fun on the air and always respect how difficult baseball is to play. I didn't want to be too critical, because I played the game and tried to understand why somebody might fail. You want to have compassion, but you have to point out mistakes. Being a color guy is about providing analysis, and when you do criticize, you don't have to butcher a guy. I did have to adjust my relationship to the guys on the field, because I wasn't on the team anymore. You can't really hang out with the players anymore.

We worked with some great people. Jim Angio and Skip Ellison, the Sox's television directors, were both the absolute best. We had so much fun, and it really wasn't work; it was an extension of my baseball career, and I was fortunate to be able to do something where I could still go to the ballpark and be around the game. It was a great experience, and I was with the White Sox as a broadcaster for 12 years. I've also done work with the Tigers, the Braves, and the Nationals.

I really loved old Comiskey. I thought it was the greatest place in the world, both to play in and announce. I really miss it. When they closed it down, we did the last game, and I had tears running down my face. I didn't anticipate that happening. Sometimes those memories of the old place supersede anything new you can build. I know we needed a new ballpark, but I just loved the old place. Going to Comiskey was always a thrill.

I go to the White Sox fantasy camp every year and really look forward to it. I love it, and our campers have a great time. I've never heard any who didn't love it. It's always, "Man, I can't wait 'til next year, because I have to do this again." It's worth it for me just to hear Art Kusnyer tell all his stories. We have guys like Harold Baines, Ron Kittle, and Rich Dotson, and we have nothing but fun all week. It really is the one week a year I look forward to, and I would never miss it. There's too many good guys there that you look forward to seeing. It's all about the camaraderie.

One thing about the White Sox is the people behind the scenes who work in the office are wonderful. There is so much continuity, and they are all just so great, I can't say enough about them. The daily communication I had with all the really good people there was a great experience. They keep their people, and I love them.

I think I had a really good relationship with the city of Chicago. It's a great city, and there are so many wonderful people there. They would do anything in the world for you. The Sox have a great organization and great people, then you add in all the people I got to know through the years, and it was really special. Chicago is a different city, and I love it.

Tom Paciorek was traded to the White Sox on December 11, 1981, for Rod Allen, Todd Cruz, and Jim Essian. He hit .312 his first year with the team and followed up with a .307 average for the 1983 Western Division Champions. Paciorek was a versatile player who spent time at first base, left field, right field, and designated hitter. On July 16, 1985, he was traded to the New York Mets for Dave Cochrane.

Paciorek brought his wit and wisdom to the White Sox's TV booth in 1988 and teamed with Ken Harrelson for the Hawk & Wimpy show until 1999. He is one of the most engaging and entertaining men in baseball and still holds court at the White Sox Fantasy Camp each year.

HAWK HARRELSON

BROADCASTER
1982–1985 ⋆ 1990–Present

GENERAL MANAGER
1986

I WAS WORKING IN BOSTON and had three years left on my contract. I got a call from Eddie Einhorn asking me if I was interested in coming to Chicago to join the Sox and work with Don Drysdale. We talked about it, and I talked about it with my wife. I was heavily connected with the Red Sox, and the White Sox were under new ownership, so I told Eddie I'd call him back in a day or two. I checked Jerry Reinsdorf and Eddie out and decided to do it. I had talked to my wife, and I didn't think she wanted to go, but all of a sudden she said, "Let's do it."

Everything came up roses. Working with Don was great because we were buddies. He had struck me out a few times in our passings during spring training games and in the All-Star Game. A lot of people have told me they thought we were the best team ever. Don was a fantastic announcer. He knew every aspect of the game. Certainly, he knew pitching, but he was a good hitter and knew all the situations. When have what we do now with Stoney [Steve Stone] coming to TV and D.J. [Darrin Jackson] going over to radio, you have a hitter and a pitcher in the booth. I've always felt like that was the proper formula.

Don and I didn't have to be introduced. We knew each other, we'd been out to play golf together, and it was one of those situations that worked. We could get on each other, and there were probably four or five times where we *really* got on each other—I'm glad nothing happened. I had to look up at him, so that would have been a bad idea! In Cleveland we went out to a restaurant, and I was driving home when we got into it over how you handle young pitchers. I called Don a "hard-headed German," and he said something back, then I pulled the car over and said, "Let's go, son!" Finally, he looked down at me and smiled, and I melted. I was relieved, but that was part of our attraction to the viewers, because there was nothing ever etched in stone. I really miss the big guy. He was a Hall of Famer in baseball, and in my opinion, as a broadcaster as well.

Nineteen eighty-three was a fantastic season. I have never seen a team to this day that had that kind of chemistry. They started off 16–24, and it didn't look like things were going to get better, but you knew this was a budding explosion if they could come together. Don and I used to get so upset at the start of the year because of the fact that we were beating ourselves. There are more games lost by teams than won. When you don't beat yourself, you're probably going to win, because the other team may beat itself. We caught a couple of breaks when a couple of the clubs, including California, had some injuries. All of a sudden we came together, and once we did, it was Katy bar the door. We won 99 games and won the division by 20 games.

We would sit in the clubhouse after some of the games, particularly the losses, with Bull, Koos, and all the guys until 3:00 or 4:00 in the morning. That was old-school, and that's what we did when I played and what Don did with the Dodgers. We were familiar with that. Sometimes Jerry and Eddie would sit in the Bard's Room with us until early in the morning just talking baseball. It was a wonderful experience.

When we got to the playoffs against Baltimore, Britt Burns pitched one of the greatest and gutsiest games I've ever seen. Tito Landrum got him for that homer in the tenth, and we got beat, but we had Hoyt going the next day. Everybody knew that if we got to that fifth game, it was all over. LaMarr was the Cy Young winner that year, and it was going to be history. I've talked to some of the Baltimore players since then, and I ask them what would have happened if we got to the fifth game, and they just smile, because everybody knew it. Whoever won that playoff was going to be the World Champions. That team had the greatest chemistry I've ever seen. Ever.

Hawk Harrelson suspended his broadcast career to become general manager of the White Sox for the 1986 season. After broadcasting for the Yankees, he returned to Chicago and the White Sox in 1990 and continues to provide televised play-by-play coverage. *Photo courtesy of WGN-TV*

After that year, it didn't work out. That's why it's the greatest game ever invented. There are no definitive formulas or answers. Anybody who says they know anything about this game is either egotistical or lying. I've been in this game for parts of seven decades now, and the one thing I've learned is the longer I'm in it, the less I know about it.

I took the GM job at a time when the organization was sputtering. Being a general manager is the worst job in the world. It's 25 hours a day, eight days a week. I can tell you that from the time I took the job until the time I left it, I played nine holes of golf, period. I was so immersed that I couldn't sleep. I was smoking at that time, and there were days I went through a whole carton of cigarettes. Not a pack, a whole carton, and there were times I had one going everywhere you looked. I'd go home at 3:00 in the morning, then something would hit me. I kept a legal pad by my bed and would wake up and write on it and try not to wake Ariss, my wife. Since I left, I was offered two other jobs, and I told them they didn't have enough money.

I can tell you, I don't know everybody in the National League from the owner to the GM to the manager, but I know almost everybody in the American League. There's not another threesome like Jerry, Kenny, and Ozzie, where you've got the owner, the GM, and the manager who have a relationship where they can go in and cuss one another out and go back to normal the next day. That's why Jerry Reinsdorf is the most misperceived and mis-understood owner in sports. When he first got here, what started this whole thing was SportsVision. Sox fans had been getting televised games free and all of a sudden they had to pay for it—you can't blame them for not liking it. Then the next thing was the possible move to a new stadium. Jerry was never going to move this ballclub, but as a businessman and the owner of the White Sox who had investors involved, he had to try to make the best deal—and he did and he acquired some leverage. Ergo we got a beautiful new ballpark. As far as those three guys go, I believe we have, without question, the best orga-nization in baseball. No doubt about it. We have more talent at the minor league level than I've ever seen in more than 25 years with the White Sox.

What Kenny Williams has done here is phenomenal. John Schuerholz of the Braves is the definitive general manager, with 14 playoff teams in a row, but what Kenny has done is phenomenal. In 10 years he has always managed to find a way to make the club better than the year before. It doesn't always work out due to injuries and performance, but he's done a great job.

Kenny, we all know what he can do and that he is not afraid to pull the trigger. I think he works too hard. I'll say, "Let's go play some golf." He will tell me he can't do it. Two springs ago they had a general managers' meeting in Orlando. He came down, and I called him, and we talked. After I hung up, it hit me that he might like to play Arnold Palmer, so I called Arnold and told him Kenny was in town. Arnold knew who Kenny was and said he could play in the Palmer group the next day. I called Kenny and asked him if he wanted to play golf with Arnold, and he really wanted to, but he had a meet-ing and wouldn't miss it. He felt bad about canceling, but he is committed. I called Arnold and told him Kenny couldn't make it. I asked Arnold, "How many times have you been turned down to play golf with?" He smiled and said, "Not many!" That's how hard Kenny works.

A lot of the things I say on the air are things I would say when I was a player. I'd be standing in right field at Fenway Park and maybe one of our guys would strike out a big hitter and I'd say, "He gone. Get somebody else up there." I didn't invent things just to say them on the air. I've said them all my life.

I hurt when we lose, I really do. I commute every day from South Bend, and when we lose a game, especially one we give away, it bothers me. I'm hav-ing even more fun now than ever. I can't answer why. The passion is just there.

You see things around there you've never seen before. I've seen 13 no-hitters, but Mark Buehrle's perfect game was my first, and it's amazing how

201

thrilling it was. I think I've called more than 5,000 games—and if you throw in all the games I've seen and played in—to see something like that, something I've never seen before was unbelievable. It was like when I was a player in the World Series and we lost to the Cardinals. It was a great thrill, but I never knew the difference it meant to win it. It's unbelievable.

When Jason Bartlett hit the ball to Alexei Ramirez in Buehrle's perfect game, as soon as he caught it, I had tears in my eyes. There's only a few times I've had that. When Bo Jackson came back and hit the home run to right field, I had tears in my eyes because he hit it for his mom. When we won the World Series in '05, I cried. Why did I cry? I cried for Jerry Reinsdorf. All he's ever done is bring seven world championship trophies to Chicago, that's all. Everybody is starting to appreciate him now. Jerry is a strong guy and he's the kind of guy that if you ever had to go to war and could have one guy in a foxhole with you, it would be Jerry Reinsdorf. He is one of a few guys who always gives you the impression that he works for you, not that you work for him. That's unusual in today's marketplace. He wants another ring. Kenny wants another ring. Ozzie wants another ring. I want another ring. That's the way it is here.

We have four broadcasters here in Stoney, [Ed] Farmer, D.J., and me who have passion about this organization and this ballclub. You don't always see that. There are a lot of broadcasters who come to the game and want one thing— a fast game so they can do it and get out. We have four guys here who don't care if we stay here, as long as we win. That comes out in the broadcast.

There are a lot of elements and issues that go into what Jerry is trying to do. Jerry has brought back a lot of former players here. Almost everybody on our coaching staff played here. That's the way to do it and that's the way to create tradition. When you see those signs that say "Pride" and "Passion" and "Tradition" on the walls, this organization defines that.

For almost three decades, White Sox fans have been entertained by one of baseball's most popular announcers, Ken "Hawk" Harrelson. "The Hawk" joined the White Sox television team in 1982, where he was teamed with Don Drysdale. After four seasons, Harrelson left the booth to become the Sox's general manager on October 2, 1985, where he spent one season before resuming his on-air career. After spending time with the Yankees' broadcast team, Harrelson rejoined the Sox as their television play-by-play man in 1990 and continues as the TV voice to this day.

RON KITTLE
OUTFIELDER
1982–1986 ★ 1989–1990 ★ 1991

I BROKE MY NECK WITH THE DODGERS organization and went home and sat out. I couldn't play anymore. I had a unique neurology surgery, where they took some hip bone and packed it into my vertebrae. They put the screws and the halo in my head. I had a dad who was tough. It was one of those things where my dad said, "You're either going to do it or you're not." He forced me to work hard so I could get back into shape and give myself a second chance. It helped.

The way Bill Veeck heard about me was that I played in a pickup game for summer ball. I hit a home run off I-294 and hit his car while he was driving by, and all I could think about was that I had to pay for some guy's window and I had no money. He heard about it, came down, and said, "Hey, do you want to try out for us in two weeks when Kansas City comes into town?" I tried out, and he said, "Don't let this man leave without signing him!" That's how it happened.

When you get an opportunity, you have to take advantage of it, in everything in life, not just in baseball. I swung and missed the first pitch because I hadn't been swinging. I was iron-working at the time. The next one, I hit a line drive, and by the time I got done, every Kansas City player and every White Sox player was standing around the cage, watching me hit balls all over the place. I think I hit 12 out that day. One went underneath the lower deck out the windows, then when Bruce Dal Canton was pitching last, I hit one

Ron Kittle, who won AL Rookie of the Year honors in 1983, went on to hit a record seven rooftop home runs at old Comiskey Park.

onto the roof. As soon as I finished, the lens fell out of my glasses. My glasses had welding burns and flecks on them from the sparks hitting me. I was more prepared for iron-working than I was anything else.

I had success in the Sox's minor leagues and I wanted to carry it to the major leagues. The neck injury that I had was very traumatic and over time it took a toll on me. My neck hurt and, when your neck bothers you, you are going to compensate. My back started hurting. I finished my career in '91, and now I've got three fused vertebrae in my neck, two ruptured in my neck, and two taken out of my lower back. It's a great career. I probably got to play at about 65 percent of my ability. People may say differently, but I'm a pretty tough cookie and I've got great pain tolerance. I enjoyed every second of playing.

The umpire played a trick on me when I got my first hit. I hit a double off Frank Tanana. I got to second base and knew it was going down the line close. He said it was a foul ball, so I started to step off the base. They would have tagged me out, but he grabbed me and pulled me back to second base and said, "Welcome to the big leagues, Ronnie."

It was a dream come true in 1983. I was a local kid from Gary, Indiana. I grew up a baseball fan. I had some great teammates, great coaches. I went to the park every single day to be the hero. I did not play any differently. I wanted to be the hero every single night—I know you can't do that, but if you take that good attitude into the game, you'll have success. It worked. I got Rookie of the Year, a division championship team, good teammates, fun guys, and I still remain friends with them.

The All-Star Game at Comiskey that year was overwhelming. I wish it wasn't so overwhelming, because with so many people, the media attention for me being a local kid was overpowering. I really didn't even rest. It was almost like for three days I didn't sleep. When the game was over, I was just zapped. It took all the energy out of me. I didn't know how to prepare for it—I wanted to make everybody happy and I wanted to do every interview that was available. That's hard to do, but I did it, and I'm glad I did.

When we clinched, I reached in for a bottle of something. One of them was broken, and I cut my thumb open, so that was about the highlight. I'm not a cheerleader. I'm not a guy who jumps on the middle of the pile. If you look back on all the pictures of the celebration, I was to the back end of everything. I was never a cheerleader. I always felt that when you have something to do, you need to do it. Accolades will come later in life. It was nice. I was happy for the city of Chicago more than anything else.

The whole thing with the rooftop homers was unique. Babe Ruth hit the first one onto the roof, and I hit the last one in 1990. I hit two in 1983 and finished with seven. Bull and I did a back-to-back one night. Carlton and I did it back to back. I think you had to hit it 500-some feet to get it to the top. It was unique, but we had a power team. I mean, we had some great hitters. It was a great team altogether.

The best team didn't win the World Series that year. That's the way I look at it. The Orioles did win, and I tip my hat to them. I had some good friends who played on that team. I broke my kneecap in the third game, so I only batted twice in Game 3. Game 4, I never played, and I didn't get to see it except as a fan. I probably wouldn't have been able to play in the World Series if we had gone on, because my knee was that damaged. It was still a thrill and a great moment for Chicago. It turned the city onto winning, then the Cubs followed, and the Bears followed after that, and then the Bulls. It was a great start for a lot of years.

I had my run-in with Nolan Ryan once. He could really pitch. He was throwing a no-hitter, and when I swung, I almost broke my thumb. The ball caromed to first base, and Rafael Palmeiro tripped over his shoelaces trying to get it. The ball spun in the dirt for a hit. Ryan wound up throwing a one-hitter and was all pumped up. The next time I faced him, he drilled me right off the bat. I caught the ball right in my bicep and I bit it like an apple and threw it back to him. I ran down the line, and Palmeiro said, "He's right behind you, so don't say nothing." He was talking through his glove. It's respect, and I hit a home run off Ryan the next time I had the chance to face him. He's a true competitor, a great pitcher, and when you can get hit by Nolan after breaking up his no-hitter, no matter how good or how bad it is, it's still a pretty good thing.

Success in major league baseball is due to staying healthy. If you've got people who don't stay healthy, you're not going to win a lot of games. Still today, it's the same way. I was disappointed when I left Chicago. I thought I'd always stay here. It was a blessing in disguise. I got to play with some other teams and some other players. We're all on the same mission. We want to play as good as we can, as long as we can, and contribute as much as we can. I've got a good stretch of friends all through Major League Baseball and the minor leagues. I keep in touch with people I coached, and I wouldn't trade one second of my life again.

A lot of us are still around. I credit the Chicago White Sox and Jerry Reinsdorf. Roland Hemond was a big part of it by starting the White Sox Alumni. I've always done stuff for the Chicago White Sox. All they have to do is ask and I'm there. It's important to have fan loyalty and also player loyalty. You don't want somebody with a bad attitude not coming out to support your team that you played for. I think it's pretty incredible.

Ron Kittle was signed by the Los Angeles Dodgers on July 5, 1977, but suffered a broken neck in a collision at home plate and was released a year later. After a tryout with the White Sox, he signed with the team on September 4, 1978.

Kittle burst onto the national scene with a monster rookie season for the Sox in 1983, when he hit 35 home runs and drove in 100 as part of the Sox's division-winning team. "Kitty" was named to the American League All-Star team for the 50th anniversary game at Comiskey Park and was also chosen as AL Rookie of the Year.

Injuries limited his effectiveness in subsequent seasons. He hit 32 homers with 74 RBIs in 1984, but his average fell to .215. In 1985 he hit 26 home runs and drove in 58. On July 30, 1986, Kittle was traded to the New York Yankees along with Joel Skinner and Wayne Tolleson for Ron Hassey, Carlos Martinez, and Bill Lindsey. He spent time with the Yankees and Indians before returning to the White Sox in 1989. Kittle hit 11 homers for the Sox in 1989 and 16 more in 1990 before being traded to the Orioles for Phil Bradley. He returned to the Sox in 1991, but played just 17 games before retiring.

Kittle remains one of the most popular members of the White Sox family and currently serves as a White Sox community relations representative and chairman of Indiana Sports Charities.

GREG WALKER

FIRST BASEMAN

1982–1990

WHEN THE SOX GOT ME FROM THE PHILLIES, I had no idea what I was in for. Dallas Green was running the minor league system for the Phillies, and they had an enormous amount of talent. They had a great system and great coaches. I feel like it was a big advantage for me to be in their organization as long as I was, but it was just as big a break to get out of it when I did. Not to disparage the White Sox of that era, but they didn't have as much talent in the system. Nobody did. The Phillies were absolutely loaded, and I had nowhere to go, really.

I came over to the White Sox in 1980 spring training, and it was the biggest break of my career. There were some opportunities at the time. I didn't know the ownership was about to change and move into a more winning, spend-more-money mode. And that worked in my favor, too, because I got to be part of that.

Tony La Russa was the manager and had one of the great coaching staffs of all time. I fell right into that, and they were a huge part of my career as a player and coach. I've used those lessons I learned from both the Phillies and White Sox days to carry me, not only when I've got the baseball uniform on, but when I've got it off, as well. I don't know if people realize what a group they had. Tony is a Hall of Fame manager, and Dave Duncan has been a great pitching coach. Charley Lau was one of the great minds in the history of hitting. Jimmy Leyland was our third-base coach. Eddie Brinkman was a great infield instructor and personally saved my career when I got off to a shaky start early on. He just took me under his wing and said, "C'mon, kid. Let's go out to the infield every day and work."

I think most people remember their first at-bat. I was facing Oakland late in September, and Billy Martin was managing the A's. He called timeout and walked right by me in the on-deck circle, and I was there floating about six inches off the ground. He called time, and whatever he told the pitcher was wrong, because he threw me a hanging breaking ball and I got a base hit. It probably should have been a double, but I was so excited I forgot to run to second base! I'll never forget my first hit.

Nineteen eighty-three was a dream year for me. It was my first full year in the big leagues, and I was surrounded by players I had grown up watching play, and all of sudden I was on the same team with them.

That team was one of the great chemistry teams ever assembled. It started with Tony and the coaching staff and carried to the veterans on the team like Koosman, Fisk, and Luzinski. Take a guy like Dick Tidrow in the bullpen, and you might ask what he had to do with a young first baseman like me, but just to be around those guys and their leadership helped. I rode into the park with Tidrow—he had pitched for the Yankees in the World Series. Jerry Koosman was one of my childhood heroes when he was pitching for the Mets. It was great just to be around them and learn from them. We call it "passing it down the line." They taught me so many lessons about how to go about your business in professional baseball, and I listened. Looking back at my career, if I did one thing well, it's that I listened to the people I should have listened to.

The veterans supported us. We had other young players like Ron Kittle and Scott Fletcher. Their leadership contributed to the great chemistry that team had. We had also had great pitching with a staff that jelled and turned out to be fantastic. That second half of the season was one of the great runs by any starting staff. Offensively, we were diverse with speed and Rudy Law at the top of the order. We had power in the middle of the lineup and, most of all, we had guys who expected to win. Guys like Fisk and Luzinski had won before, so when we walked on the field, they expected to win. As young players going with them, we felt that way, as well. It was one of the great experiences of my life and as a young player. I chalk it up as the reason I was able to survive in the big leagues and have the career I had.

Those guys are a big reason I'm coaching now. They passed it down the line to me, and I still feel obligated to pass on all those lessons they taught me.

Hopefully, I have made them proud as I tried to pass on what they taught me to the players of today.

We had such a big lead, and I think we ended up winning the division by 20 games. It was a given that we were going to win it, and we were on such a roll. It was special because the White Sox hadn't won in so long, and it's tough to turn that around. It's tough to be in a losing situation not competing for titles and then win that first one. Clinching was just a dream come true. I come from a small town in Georgia and had seen it on TV before, but to be a part of it with a group of guys you care about so much is unbelievable. I understand how precious opportunities like that are in this game, so when you get one, you have to take advantage of it.

That team kind of provided a springboard for the new ownership and for the fans to prove that we could win. Even though we didn't win the World Series—yes, I'm prejudiced, but that was one of the most special teams that didn't win it all. I really believe if we'd gotten by Baltimore, we would have won the Series. We battled them, and it was a great series, but it was little things here and there that got us. Britt Burns pitched that great game and, if we could have won that, we would have had LaMarr coming back for the fifth game. I felt like we would have won that one and gone on to the Series. No matter what, it was a very special team. I was fortunate to be a part of it.

We stayed healthy in 1983, which is difficult to do. The next year, I think we got off to a good start, but Pudge got hurt, and we lost Jerry Koosman in a trade. Koos was such a big part of that '83 team. He didn't win 20 games and wasn't a World Series hero, but he had a huge part in our clubhouse. When there's only small things separating contending teams, clubhouse chemistry is huge. When we lost him, anybody who knew how that team ticked knew that we lost a big part of it. We didn't stay healthy, and some of our old players got older. We went down the creek for a couple of years, and it wasn't pretty. I love to kid some of the guys who came after me that the reason the Sox were good after I left is that we played so poorly, it left us in a position to draft high, and that's how we got Frank Thomas, Robin Ventura, Jack McDowell, and other guys.

No matter what, we still played the game the right way and we respected the White Sox organization. The uniform meant a lot to us, as did the fans and the city of Chicago. Maybe we weren't good teams after '83, but we still had a lot of pride in our organization. We still wanted to win and expected to win, but we didn't get it done.

In 1983 Greg Walker hit 10 home runs and drove in 55 runs as a rookie for the West division–winning White Sox.

Later in the '90s it did turn around again, and the precedent had been set by the '83 team. They said at the time the Sox couldn't win, but Jerry and the ownership wanted to win so badly, they paid the price and did what they had to do to win.

When I was released by the Sox, the one thing about me that most big leaguers don't have is that I knew at that point in my career that I was pretty much physically whipped. I'd had a lot of arm surgeries at that point, gone through some other things, and I was done. It was still tough, and the toughest part wasn't leaving the baseball field, but leaving my friends, who I had been with for eight or nine years at that point. It wasn't just the players, it was the clubhouse guys. It was Roger Bossard, our groundskeeper who has gone on to be one of the most famous guys affiliated with our organization. They are all friends, and you get so attached to those people because you see them every day over that length of time. They are your family. Then all of a sudden you get called in and you're not with the White Sox anymore. It's pretty shocking.

It didn't take me long to realize I had been very fortunate to be a part of the White Sox organization, and they would be in my heart forever. The White Sox, led by Jerry Reinsdorf, did many special things for me and my family, and the lessons I learned while wearing the uniform have helped me for the rest of my life.

Jerry Reinsdorf and I have always had a great relationship. The other close relationship I had was with Charley Lau. Even though I didn't get to spend a long time with Charley, it was a very special time. I carried him with me the rest of my career and really for the rest of my life. Jerry knew that, as well, and always offered me the chance to come back as a coach. When I got out of baseball, I felt at that time that I was so beat up physically and mentally that I needed some time away from the game. I went back to my home in Georgia and raised my family. Every year, Jerry kept in touch and offered me the opportunity to come back. I never didn't want to come back, it just wasn't the right time.

Finally in 2002 they offered me a job I couldn't refuse as the hitting coach for the Charlotte Triple A team. They had some great players like Joe Crede, Willie Harris, and Joe Borchard, so there was a lot of talent on that team. I got back into it and realized how much I loved the game. I'm very fortunate to have had that opportunity, mainly because of Jerry and my history with the White Sox. I was handed that opportunity on a silver platter. If I can pat myself on the back a little bit, I didn't take it for granted and I appreciated it.

I put in the time and am still putting in the time to be the best I can to give these players and this organization their money's worth.

I take a lot of pride in what we started in '83, and that continues to this day. You won't get me to brag about how great a player I was, but I do feel I represent the game the way it should be represented. I learned my lessons from the people I should have learned them from. Hopefully, I have passed them down the line and in some small way what I learned from all my mentors has been handed down. I hope some of that was a small part of that '05 championship team. I've been fortunate enough to be part of two of the greatest teams in modern White Sox history. Those two teams had some of the greatest chemistry the White Sox have ever had, and I've been lucky enough to be in that clubhouse with them.

Continuity helps build the culture, but at the White Sox, it starts at the top. If you just brought back old players, that's not enough. The one thing that distinguishes us as an organization is our love for the owner, Jerry Reinsdorf. All of us who have come back respect him so much and want to give him the opportunity to succeed, just like he gave us. There is a burning desire to succeed for him, and I don't know that every organization has that. We're lucky we have him at the top. We're out there fighting the fight every day for him and the players we have now. I feel lucky to be a part of this era as well as the era when I played.

Greg Walker was taken by the White Sox from Philadelphia in the Rule 5 draft on December 3, 1979. He made his major league debut late in 1982 and had a stellar rookie season at first base for the Sox the next year with 10 homers and 55 RBIs. Walker hit .294 with 24 homers and 75 RBIs in 1984. In 1985 he led the American League with 163 games played while hitting 24 homers and driving in 92 runs. After injuries hampered him in 1986, he bounced back with a 27-homer, 94-RBI year in 1987. He suffered a life-threatening seizure on the field before a game in 1988 and missed the rest of that season. He returned to play 77 games for the team in 1989. Walker was released by the Sox on April 30, 1990, and played a handful of games with the Baltimore Orioles that year before retiring.

In 2002 the Sox hired Walker as their hitting coach for the Triple A Charlotte Knights, and he was promoted to the major leagues in the same role on May 19, 2003, a position he still holds.

BOBBY THIGPEN

PITCHER

1986–1993

I WAS AT MISSISSIPPI STATE FOR TWO YEARS, and everybody knew we had Rafael Palmeiro and Will Clark, who were called "Thunder and Lightning." They were destined for great things and they were great college baseball players. We had Jeff Brantley also. When I went back for the alumni game, everyone always kidded me about being surprised that I was someone who made it to the big leagues. I had no expectations whatsoever in those days.

Like most college players and guys who end up as pros, I pitched some and played shortstop at one point. It was something that I knew I could do and felt like I learned fast when I was drafted.

I remember getting called up like it was yesterday. I was at Birmingham at the time. They said I was going to Chicago, but they didn't tell me what I was going to do when I got there. I had no clue why I was being called up because I wasn't doing that well.

When I got there I was still trying to figure everything out. My first game was against the Red Sox at Fenway Park. We were down big, and so I'm sure they thought that was a good chance to get me in and see what I could do. They said, "You're in." Well, away I went. I got through the first two innings okay, but my third one they got some hits and scored two runs.

I think you do have to be able to get past the game each day to be a closer. I didn't have arm problems and I had a short memory. I think everybody has a different personal routine that you use, especially if you're pitching well, to keep going, or maybe you change things up if it's not going so well.

Pudge was great to me. It was always like having a manager on the field. I remember when I first came in I was squinting and couldn't see what fingers he put down. He came out there and pushed up his mask and said, "Hey, kid, what gives?" I said, "I can't see the signs." He laughed at me, and we got through it and went from there.

The whole 1990 season went by so fast. We were focused on trying to catch the A's the whole season and were the kind of team that played a lot of close games. I think I was in almost half our games, and that's not counting the times I got up to warm up but didn't get in the game. I thought the more work I got, the better I seemed to throw all year. We played lots and lots of close games and won more than our fair share of them. I always struggled in the spring and I didn't have a great spring that year, but when Opening Day came around, I got the save, and things really snowballed from there.

I was fortunate enough to be picked for the All-Star team that year. Back then, we didn't have interleague play, but I had been to Wrigley Field because we played an exhibition, the Crosstown Classic, against the Cubs each year. I remember looking at the schedule and, sure enough, the All-Star Game was being played at Wrigley Field. That was the only National League park I had ever played in, and I was hoping to get to see somewhere else. Don't get me wrong. It was still an honor to go. When I look back and think of all the great players on both teams, I'm amazed.

My role as a closer continued to evolve in 1990. My first couple years, we didn't have much help in the pen, and I pitched multiple innings a lot of times. That year I had a lot of help. Barry Jones came in, and I think he got 11 wins. Donn Pall, who was a guy from Chicago, was pitching well and so was Kenny Patterson. Scott Radinsky was there, too. I had a few saves where I went more than one inning, but most of the time it was just the ninth.

Breaking the saves record was nice, but I wasn't counting it down or anything. We were trying to catch Oakland. We were a surprise team. It's August, September, and we're only three or four games out and had a big series coming up with them. My teammates were great, and the bullpen was great that year as far as getting in front of me and getting the game to me. The record was great, but it wasn't a big deal then like it is now.

I felt like I got kind of a bad rap when Francisco Rodriguez was breaking my saves record in 2008. Some guy in L.A. said I wasn't happy and wouldn't

Bobby Thigpen delivers a pitch in the ninth inning on his way to setting a major leage record of 57 saves for a season during a game against the Kansas City Royals in Chicago on September 3, 1990. *Photo courtesy of AP Images*

talk about it. What happened was that I was managing at Bristol, and there are so many demands on your time as a minor league manager that I didn't have time to do all the interviews and answer all the questions people had for me. I didn't want to make it about me. It was his accomplishment, and I didn't want the spotlight to be on me. I always knew it would only be a matter of time before someone did it, and I was happy to have the record as long as I did. He deserved it. More power to him. I knew a team would come along like ours that was good and played close games, and they did.

I threw sinkers and sliders for the most part, just using two pitches. I worked on a change-up near the end of my career, but usually I was a two-pitch pitcher. The next year I had 30 saves, but it was like something was wrong with me, even though I didn't really have nearly as many chances as the year before. People sometimes don't see the whole picture.

There were a lot of different things that made my leaving in '93 come about. Some of it was my fault and some of it was out of my control. I wanted to pitch and felt the more work I could get, the better I was. Ron Schueler was the general manager, and they did what they felt they had to do. The bottom line was that I went from one winner to another and I had a blast in Philadelphia for two months.

My return to the White Sox organization was because of Jerry Reinsdorf. Jerry would ask me every time I saw him, "When are you going to come back and go to work?" Eventually, I took him up on it.

My first year managing was in Bristol, and only two of my players on that team knew I played in the majors—Frank Viola's kid and Ozzie Guillen's kid. The bottom line is these guys are so young. I don't mind that. My job is to teach them the best I can. It doesn't make a big difference to me if they know that I used to play in the majors.

After being part of a College World Series team at Mississippi State, Bobby Thigpen was selected by the White Sox in the fourth round of the 1985 amateur draft. A year later "Thiggy" was in the majors, appearing in 20 games and posting a 1.77 ERA. He earned the closer's job in 1987 with 16 saves and followed up with back-to-back 34-save years in 1988 and 1989. Nineteen ninety was a season for the ages for Thigpen as he set a major league record with 57 saves, appeared in 77 games, and had a 1.83 ERA. He was named to the American League All-Star team and finished fourth in Cy Young voting.

He saved 22 games for the Sox in 1992, but would notch only one in 1993 before being traded to the Phillies on August 10, 1993, for Jose DeLeon. Thigpen signed as a free agent with the Mariners after the season, but pitched in only seven games for them. He pitched in Japan, but a 1996 major league comeback was derailed by back problems. Thigpen returned to professional baseball in 2007 and managed the Sox's minor league affiliate in Bristol, Virginia, at the rookie level for two seasons, then served as the pitching coach for the Winston-Salem Dash in 2009.

KENNY WILLIAMS

OUTFIELDER

1986–1988

GENERAL MANAGER

2000–Present

I WAS AN OAKLAND A'S AND SAN FRANCISCO GIANTS FAN when I was growing up, not far from Oakland–Alameda County Coliseum in the days of Reggie Jackson, Joe Rudi, Bert Campaneris, and others. It's a little different than in Chicago. In the Bay Area, you can be a fan of both the Giants and the A's. You just have to designate who you are rooting for if they play each other. I had the chance to go across the bay and root for Willie Mays, later Jack Clark, and that was my baseball upbringing.

When I showed up in Sarasota at old Payne Park as a draft pick, it was a lot different than our accommodations now. It was a little intimidating as an 18-year-old walking into a spring training clubhouse with guys like Carlton Fisk, Greg Luzinski, and Harold Baines. It was a good thing Harold was there, because he was a quiet presence on that ballclub, unlike the louder, fun guys like Marc Hill. I was taken under Harold's wing, and he taught me how to be a professional at an early age.

I think you can learn life lessons along the way at every spot. If you don't take the time to recognize when you are in an opportunity to learn one of those lessons, you are really missing out on an opportunity to grow. Those were important times for me, more so as a player, because as I moved on from the White Sox to other teams, I remembered lessons from Harold, as well as some lessons from some of the other players who maybe didn't have some of the better habits in life, and I knew to stay away from them. It was a very important time for me, and those lessons made me realize in my current capacity just how much of a role we have in the continuance of building the character of a player—not just getting them to be the best athlete they can be, but to continue on with what their parents have tried to instill in them along the way and possibly add to that.

To be sitting in the chair as the general manager is still somewhat of a surprise to me, because after I was released from Montreal in 1991, I wanted to get as far away from baseball as possible. I wanted to go back to Stanford and finish up my degree and go into finance. I had a conversation with Jerry Reinsdorf when the Bulls were coming out to Seattle, where I was living at the time, and we talked about baseball. We both recognized there was a need for inner-city scouting. He wanted to get someone into the organization who wouldn't be afraid to disagree with him, and I can certainly do that at times! It was just a match. He said I should come back to Chicago and run that particular area, so I did.

One thing turned into the next. He wanted me to run player development, but I had already experienced some of the radio and television negotiations on the business side and I didn't want to be pigeon-holed into the baseball side, so I declined that job offer. That caught Jerry a little bit by surprise, but ultimately I saw the need for some changes and I acquiesced and took the job. A few years later, he asked me if I was interested in the general manager's job, and I told him I didn't think so. He told me that he thought I'd be good at it and that I should reconsider. Again, I saw the need with Ron Schueler's resignation and thought if he wanted me to do it, I could do it in a way that could bring us a championship. As luck would have it, that's how it worked out.

I'm a planner. When I started out, the most important thing I wanted to instill was White Sox pride. I didn't believe there was that, even though the White Sox had some success through the years. I wanted to drop the anchor and bring back people whom White Sox fans identified with from the past, guys who knew and had a passion for Chicago and had a passion for the White Sox, a passion that people knew and that I knew. I wanted guys whom

Kenny Williams played parts of three seasons for the White Sox and returned to the team in 1992 in a front-office position, 10 years after being drafted. In 2000 he was named the 11th general manager in the history of the club. *Photo courtesy of AP Images*

I knew where their hearts were. Over the years, I think you can see some of that evolving. It's still continuing to evolve.

The most difficult thing for me at the beginning is still the most difficult thing for me now, and that's dealing with the media. I'm not as politically incorrect as my manager, but I do tell you what I feel. The initial shots I got upon my hiring ranged from, "He has never done anything"—even though this organization in 2000 was the organization of the year in the minor leagues—to direct quotes from people saying that the only reason I got the job was because I was black. I thought that was very short-sighted and racist. When you combine the mail I was getting, it gave me a very unsettling feeling for a long time, but ultimately I think if you focus on the job at hand and you continue to put in the work, a lot of those things go by the wayside. A lot of it has subsided, but I haven't forgotten it.

I didn't enjoy the ride at all in 2005, and I think that's a shame. I'm glad other people did, and that's more important. I did enjoy when we won it, walking off the field, and I was watching Jerry Reinsdorf. I knew how much he ached for a baseball championship and the countless hours we had talked about it. That was the driving force for me and that's what kept me up during those hard times to make sure he got one. When it happened, I just stepped to the side and watched almost every move he and his family made. It was much less about my individual accomplishment.

I almost didn't go to the parade. I told Ozzie and Jerry on the flight back from Houston, "I'm going to Arizona and I'll see you when I see you." They told me the parade was scheduled the next day, and I told them to have a good time, but I was tired and going home. They told me, "I don't think you know how big this parade is going to be." I didn't. I climbed up on the bus with my family, and we drove through the streets. It was really an expression of love from the city that I personally never thought would happen. It was an eye-opener.

A number of people had expressed to me, even before we got to the World Series, about the generations of our fans who had been lost and would have loved to have lived to see this moment. It made me sad about the futility of not being able to do it sooner, but very proud that they had such a passion for the White Sox.

I want to win again. I'm behind right now in my goals and aspirations. I wanted to bring two championships here in eight years and then I felt I could move on to do something else in life. At that point in time, people who have done it tell me you look for something else. I'd like to cross that bridge and see if I would hunger for more or if I'd be content and want to move on. Those are the sort of motivations that move me now. I want to put the White Sox organization in that elite club such as the Red Sox and Yankees. I want to build something here so that when I leave, there is a solid foundation.

We're getting there. We get our share of criticisms and we're a lightning rod in a number of ways for doing things that are a little unorthodox. People don't completely understand—that's by design. I consider our methodology proprietary information. If we are promoting how we go out and continue to bring in good young players while competing at the same time, that's information we would be giving to our competitors and would make it harder for us to succeed. I know it's better promotion and makes for better articles about the organization and me, but the bottom line for us is just to win. The other stuff is secondary.

The end of 2008 was tough, but I think the "blackout" by the fans will be our signature as a baseball organization, similar to the "Black Hole" of the Oakland Raiders. That is something that will last long past my tenure here. If we had to have that ending and that anguish of whether we would get in or not, in order to add this special part of our White Sox culture, then so be it. I would have preferred to win the division by seven or eight games and line up our pitching, plus have had Bobby Jenks, Scott Linebrink, and Carlos Quentin healthy to see if we could have turned what people thought wasn't going to be a good year into a great year. It wasn't a great year, because when you're not the last team standing on the podium, it's not a great year.

Kenny Williams was drafted by the White Sox on June 7, 1982, in the third round of the amateur draft. He played in parts of three seasons for the Sox, including his 11-homer, 50-RBI rookie campaign in 1987. On March 23, 1989, he was traded to the Tigers for Eric King.

He rejoined the Sox in 1992 as a scout and was named a special assistant to Jerry Reinsdorf in 1994. He served as the director of minor league operations from 1995 to 1996, then spent the next four years as the team's vice president of player development. On October 24, 2000, he was named the 11th general manager in White Sox history.

The NINETIES

DONN PALL
PITCHER
1988–1993

I^T WAS AWESOME. I grew up on the South Side as a White Sox fan, just like any other kid there, loving the Sox and loving baseball. I liked the team a lot, with Dick Allen and Carlos May, the "Hitmen" in '77 with Zisk and Gamble, and even Carlton Fisk. He was fabulous, and getting the chance to play with him was unbelievable.

I was probably the only future major leaguer that was in the stands for Disco Demolition in 1979. I brought my disco record and got in for 98¢. We were sitting in the lower deck on the third-base side, not behind a pole, and it was up for grabs. I was probably the only guy who was really mad that the Sox had to forfeit Game 2, because they needed all the wins they could get back then. Everybody else in the ballpark could care less about baseball. They were all in their black concert T-shirts, and there was a cloud of marijuana hanging over the stadium. People were whipping records around like Frisbees, and I saw someone get hit and leave with a gash in the face. Somebody was climbing up the foul pole from the ground. Center field was on fire— it was totally up for grabs. It was wild. I didn't go onto the field, but it was quite an experience.

I went to U of I and tried out for the team and got cut. I made the team as a walk-on the next year, got redshirted, and played a few years. I ended up having a great year my last year there and got drafted by, of all teams, the White Sox. I was such a baseball fan that to get drafted by anybody was a big deal. I remember coming home from work that day, and my mom said the White Sox had called. Oh my god, you've got to be kidding me! It was a total dream come true. My hometown team drafted me.

The scout who was watching me was Larry Monroe. He came out to U of I because we had some good players on our team—and then there was me, but I'm sure he thought that I wasn't too bad. He showed me the scouting report on me that said I would never get past A ball. It said, "We need him as a filler in rookie ball and he'll never get past A ball." It was so exciting to get drafted by them, and a couple days later to go to the ballpark and sign the contract. That was just heaven right there.

I was hoping to get a token $1,000 or something. They gave me nothing, and I was upset about it. The Cardinals were interested in me and were going to give me $1,000. Looking back on it, $1,000 is no big deal, it's the principle of it, but the Sox were like, "Do you want to play ball or not?" Okay, let's play.

In spring training I'd be with the minor leaguers and come over to watch some of the games with the big-league guys, and even then I always felt like a fan. I grew up as a fan and as a minor league baseball player, I was a huge Sox fan who got to play baseball here. I was always interested in watching the team and listening to the news about the team as a fan. It wasn't until I was in Double A that I really thought that maybe I had a chance to get there. I always felt like you had to be phenomenal to get to the major leagues. That's not me. I was just a regular guy. Then I thought, *I really have a chance, because people do get called up from Double A.*

I remember getting called up at the end of July in 1988. I was in Triple A. Our manager, Terry Bevington, who was a great minor league manager, called me into the office with another player and told us we were going to Chicago. That was awesome! I remember calling my parents at home, and my mother was crying. She said, "You better not be kidding me! I'm cryin' here." I was fortunate enough to last awhile. I'll never forget my first game in the major leagues—August 1, 1988, against Oakland. I was so nervous. This was the ballpark that, growing up, I'd always sit there and wonder what it would be like to pitch on that mound. To be playing at a ballpark where I had sat as a fan all those years was just so neat. I came in the game when we were down about nine runs in the last inning. It was, throw Donn Pall in the game and get him some work. The first guy up hit a double, and the next guy singled him in. I was standing on the mound thinking, *Great.*

225

I've faced two hitters in the major leagues and my ERA is infinity! Welcome to the major leagues. But then I got a double play and a strikeout, and it worked out after that.

In 1990 I was so hoping we would get to the playoffs. Being the last year of old Comiskey Park, it just somehow felt like fate that we would get into the playoffs. We had such a great up-and-coming team, and it was such a cool year because the fans were so into it. I'll never forget when we landed one time at Midway around 1:00 in the morning and there were tons of fans outside the airport waiting for us. I think it was after we beat Oakland a few games on the road. It was just awesome. Being able to be there during the closing of the ballpark was such an emotional thing for me. I didn't take anything, but Jerry Reinsdorf gave me a few of the old green seats. My wife won't let me put them anywhere out in the open, but they are in the basement. It was awesome to be there for the end of it all.

Tom Paciorek came up with the "Pope." Because of Pope John Paul, he called me "Pope Donn Pall." I thought that was cool, and it was kind of fitting, because I'm Catholic and Polish like the pope was. I heard about it from the TV. My parents taped every single game, and I thought it was cool. Then there were some fans who wrote in and were mad at me, giving me a hard time because they said I was comparing myself to the pope. I said if I was going to give myself a nickname, it wasn't going to be naming myself a pope.

Pitching to Carlton Fisk was a trip. My first game with him catching me, I was very nervous. I had so much respect for him. I was afraid to shake him off, because obviously, he knew all the hitters, but he didn't know me at all. I wasn't your typical pitcher. I was throwing split-fingers and forkballs. I was thinking, *What do I do?* but I was just going with what he was calling. I'll never forget, I was facing Jose Canseco, and Fisk called for a fastball in. I threw it on the inside third of the plate, and Canseco drilled it into the upper deck, foul by only two feet, and it just about put a hole through one of the seats out there. After the game, Fisk pulled me aside and said, "Hey, when I say fastball in, I mean get it *in there*!" and he was slamming himself in the chest. Yes, sir! Yes, sir! I'll never forget one of my worst feelings was when I shook him off one time in Cleveland against Brook Jacoby and threw my pitch. Jacoby hit a home run, so I thought Fisk would put the mask on top of his head and come out to call me a rookie and yell at me, but he didn't. He just knew. One time I was facing Robin Yount, and Carlton was catching. Yount was a great hitter, and my bread and butter was a split-finger fastball/forkball. Fisk gave me

Donn Pall joined his hometown team in 1988, and his best year with the White Sox came in 1991, when he was 7–2 with a 2.41 ERA.

the sign for the first pitch—fastball inside—for strike one. Then I was think-ing forkball or offspeed something, but he called fastball in again, and I threw it for strike two. Then he was all set up for a forkball and he'd be done after those two fastballs in. I wasn't even going to look for a sign, let's go. I looked in, and he wanted another fastball in. Finally, I got the nerve to shake him off, but he wouldn't let me. I never had a catcher shake off my shake-off before, so what do you do? All right, I threw the fastball in, broke his bat, and got an easy grounder to third. Fisk knows. He was awesome.

The night he was honored and got his motorcycle, I got the win. It was a memorable time, because I was such a big fan of his, and it turned out to be his last game. We were at the ballpark late after the game.

When I was traded to Philly in '93, it was crushing. We were in New York on September 1 when it happened. I grew up in Chicago, we finally had a chance because we were going to the playoffs, and to get to play in the post-season for your hometown team would have been fabulous. It was the longest flight home for me ever. I was able to put it in perspective, though. My fam-ily and friends were upset, but I told them there were worse things going on in the world. I was in the major leagues and got traded from one first-place team to another first-place team, nobody was sick or dying, so it was okay. As hard as it was, you have to move on—that's the right way to look at it.

In the playoffs Fisk and I couldn't get in to wish the team luck. I had a ticket and he didn't. I was surprised they wouldn't allow us in the clubhouse to see the guys and wish them well before the game. I couldn't understand it at all—to kick Fisk out and send him home was weird.

I was a Cub in 1994. The Cubs were the only team that offered me a job. I got released by the Yankees in July, and Larry Himes offered me a job. I was thrilled somebody wanted me, so I put all that other stuff aside and played base-ball. It was kind of tough to put that uniform on, but it was only for a week and then we went on strike. In a way, it was cool to play on both sides of town.

Two thousand five was great. Even after they won the World Series, I couldn't believe it. There were times when I was wondering if it actually happened. There hadn't been a World Series game in this town in my life-time. For the Sox to do it before the Cubs was awesome for me as a fan. I was at Game 4 in Houston. I didn't want to go on the field or in the clubhouse—it wouldn't have felt right. I played my time there and now I'm back to being a fan again. A friend of mine had a plane, and eight of us flew down for the game.

I'm very fortunate, not only to have played in the major leagues, but to have gotten to play for my hometown team. I think every team should have at least one guy on the roster who's from the hometown, just so one person knows what it is like. As a player, I always wanted to make sure I signed autographs for people, because I know what it's like as a fan to be at the park looking for an autograph. I wanted to take care of all the Sox fans I could take care of. I wish I had been a bigger name so it would have been more meaningful for the people who got my autograph! I was very, very fortunate. Playing there was like being at a fantasy camp. I tried to appreciate every day I was on that side of the fence, because I knew it wouldn't last forever. Thank God I was able to do that.

Donn Pall was drafted by the White Sox in the 23rd round of the 1985 amateur draft. The "Pope" debuted for the Sox at the end of 1988 and was a bullpen mainstay the next four seasons. On September 1, 1993, he was traded to the Philadelphia Phillies for a player to be named, who later turned out to be Doug Lindsey. Pall had stints with the Yankees, Cubs, and Marlins and retired after the 1998 season. He works in the Chicago area as a financial consultant and serves as a White Sox community relations representative.

JEFF TORBORG

MANAGER

1989–1991

I INTERVIEWED FOR THE SOX MANAGING JOB TWICE, initially down in Sarasota. I had a nice interview with [general manager] Larry Himes and Al Goldis, who was the farm director. Larry taped the interview, and I understood later on that Jerry Reinsdorf listened to the tapes of the candidate interviews. I was called back to Scottsdale, where they offered me the job.

I had known Larry just a bit on the periphery of baseball. We had both been catchers, and I knew of him, then spoke to him one time at spring training when I was coaching with the Yankees. The interview was about managerial philosophies, on and off the field, and not what I expected. I wasn't sure how the first one went but was happy to get called back. I was in the managerial sweepstakes for the Seattle and Houston managing jobs at the time, so when they offered me the job, they asked if I had to talk to the other teams again, but I said no because the Sox job was No. 1 on my list and perfect for me.

My first managerial job had been in Cleveland, and that was difficult because I replaced Frank Robinson, who had brought me back in the game on the management side and for whom I have such great respect. I knew I was replacing a guy who had worked so hard to get the position, while I hadn't made a lineup card at all. That was difficult, then I spent 10 years with the Yankees as a coach. With the White Sox, I knew you normally don't go into a situation as a new manager where everything is hunky-dory. There are problems, and you are being hired to try and remedy them. The city was special to me, and I had always loved coming to play in Chicago. I was impressed with what Chuck Tanner and Roland Hemond had done to turn the team around in the early '70s. Bob Lemon's '77 team was really something to play against. I had the feeling, sitting in the opposition dugout that year, that the city would really turn it on if you came here and did well.

I remember going to the Chicago writers' dinner and seeing Don Zimmer, who was managing the Cubs. We had coached together with the Yankees and had known each other for a long time. There was no interleague play yet, but several fans came up to me and said, "We don't care if you win the pennant, just beat the Cubs." I laughed heartily, then I realized they were serious. I smile when I think about that, because we won all three of the Crosstown Classic exhibition games against them when I was there. Zim couldn't talk to me afterward because he was so distraught.

Nineteen eighty-nine was not a good year for us. We were struggling, and I think when we got to the All-Star break, we were 32–56. We were awful and were the worst team in baseball. We had problems that ran the gamut. Right before the break, we had an off day in Kansas City, and I told the players we would have a workout there and, if it went well, I'd give them the full three-day break without a workout on the back end. It was hotter than a son-of-a-gun there then. We were doing fundamentals, doing cutoffs and relays, and reviewing things we had gone over in spring training. When you're not playing well, you have to do that. They were working, and I went into the manager's office to do my homework on the series. About an hour later I came out to an empty clubhouse and I thought the guys were gone already, but I saw their clothes. When I went out to the field, they were all still there, had divided into teams, and were playing a game. I was impressed with that—it showed me they cared about the game and one another.

I'd love to give you the movie ending and tell you we swept the series, but it didn't happen. We got swept by the Royals. But after the All-Star break, we won eight straight games, lost to Roger Clemens, then won three more. We forgot the whole first half and went from there. I think that workout and the second half that followed sowed the seeds of something better.

We made the Sosa trade, and it changed our dynamic defensively. Scott Fletcher came in and just really nailed down second base. He and Ozzie Guillen were terrific together. Sosa played right, and we moved Ivan

Calderon to left, and all of a sudden we were defending the field in the outfield and the infield. We brought up Robin Ventura to man third in September and were a much better defensive team.

We got things together in the bullpen in 1990. I could line up Bobby Thigpen as the closer, and we had Barry Jones as the setup guy and were able to shorten the game that way. We won Opening Day in Milwaukee that way 2–1. That was our formula for the entire year, because Thiggy set the record with 57 saves, and Barry won 11 games for us as our eighth-inning guy. We were a different-looking team. We didn't have a 15-game winner on the staff. Jack McDowell and Greg Hibbard each won 14. Nobody hit 20 home runs either, but we still won 94 games. It was really amazing when you think about it. We did have eight guys with at least 50 RBIs. We had team speed, so we were quicker on the bases and better defensively. That team totally overachieved. The town totally bought into it, and we could feel it. It was the start of a run of very good White Sox teams.

When Dave Stewart of the A's said we couldn't carry his jock, he was probably right. That team was full of hammers. We won 94 games, and they won 103, but we made a run at them and played them tough all year. We swept a West Coast series in June then went down to California and beat their best for another sweep. The one I remember in Oakland was in extra innings, where Dave Stewart pitched against us and went in to ice his arm after the ninth. We were ahead 3–1, but Dave Henderson hit a homer off Thiggy to send it to extras. Stewart came back out, even though he had iced his arm, and Dan Paqua led off the tenth with a homer to beat him.

We had a lot of come-from-behind wins that year, even though we didn't have a lot of firepower. What happened was guys followed Walt Hriniak's theory of making sure every at-bat is a good one and waiting out the starters. We had great leadership with Ozzie and Pudge. They were two completely different guys, different ages, different backgrounds, but they had a lot of guys who would listen to them. Oakland had the Bash Brothers, and we were the antithesis of that team.

We reaped the benefits of those four straight No. 1 draft picks by Goldis and Himes in McDowell, Ventura, Thomas, and Fernandez. I remember being in Boston and telling Himes we needed some help. He said, "What would you think if I gave you Frank Thomas and Alex Fernandez?" I said, "Are you kidding?" I wanted Frank out of spring training, but they didn't feel he was ready defensively. He had hit two home runs in spring training

Ozzie Guillen, Carlton Fisk, and Jeff Torborg pose together after Torborg declared the two to be cocaptains during spring training on April 3, 1990.

233

on back-to-back days, one off Nolan Ryan, and those things are probably still going. When they came up in August, we went to Milwaukee and won all five from them.

That last day for old Comiskey Park, was for me, by far, the most emotional day I've ever spent in a ballpark. It wasn't like I was born and raised in Chicago. At the end of the game, after the curtain calls, people were standing and holding hands, singing, the whole scene was unbelievable. After the crowd finally cleared out, I sat in the stands and did a television interview with Tim Weigel in the same seats where he had sat when he went to his first White Sox game with his dad. He still had the tickets. The two of us were in tears when he finished the interview. Both of our dads had passed away, and it brought back so many memories of bonding with my dad at the ballgame. I'll never forget that. That was the most moving day I've ever had at the ballpark.

The new uniforms were a funny story. I actually brought up the idea right after I'd been hired. We were sitting down for dinner, and I said, "Now that we've got a major league manager, can we get a major league uniform?"

There was silence, then Jerry said, "I designed it." I thought, *Uh-oh*, then said, "Can we change the hat?" It had the Campbell's soup *C* on it, and Jerry said, "Eddie Einhorn designed that." I just thought we should relate back to the last time the franchise had success in '59 with the pinstripes and old English lettering. Jerry told me, "I grew up in Brooklyn. I hate the pinstripes." Now I thought I'd really better shut up because I hadn't signed a contract yet! Rob Gallas in marketing and I spent a lot of time talking about how to convince Jerry and the organization to switch the uniforms. The new ones were great, and the look still gives me a nice warm feeling.

The next year I think we were saddled with the fact that we had overachieved the year before. We probably weren't as good as we were in '90, but a bit better than we actually played in '91. We opened the season with six wins in a row on the road, then lost the getaway game in Yankee Stadium. We came home, had a big banquet in the Stadium Club at the new Comiskey Park, then played Detroit for Opening Day in the new park. We were saying we wouldn't know how the new park would play until we got there, but the Tigers showed us how pretty quickly: 16–0. Ugh.

Wilson Alvarez pitched a no-hitter in Baltimore in August on a Sunday for our seventh win in a row. That was a wraparound series, and we had to play the final game on Monday night. We had the lead in that game, and I had to bring Bobby Thigpen in for the eighth, then in the ninth Chris Hoiles hit a home run off him to send the game into extras. Leo Gomez hit a homer for them to win it, and we proceeded to lose 14 out of 17. That's when the division went right by us.

Ron Schueler and I got along fine, but I was really wasn't his guy because I was hired by Larry Himes. I remember Ron came up to me the last home weekend of the season and closed the door. He said, "I just got a call from the Mets, and they want to talk to you." I said, "Schu, I really don't want to talk to them. I don't want to leave here." He told me to think about it and talk it over with my family, then we'd discuss it on Sunday before we left on our last road trip. When we met again, I told him I had no desire to leave, but I said, "I do need to ask you, where do I fit in in this organization, knowing you weren't the one who hired me?" His comment to me was we would both be very disappointed if I didn't listen to the offer from the Mets, then something happened down the road. I just sat there for a minute and thought, *Wow, it doesn't sound like he's really happy with what I'm doing here.* So I told him, if that's how he felt, I guess I should listen to the Mets, and that's what happened.

I ended up talking with the Mets and getting a great financial contract, but I did not want to leave the White Sox. That team was on the verge of winning. We had won 87 games, but I knew we should have been in the 90s. It doesn't take much to turn around a season when you're right there. I really thought we were ready to go and I didn't want to leave, but you have to think about your future, both financially and professionally. To this day, I have always told people I didn't want to leave the White Sox. Professionally, it was the worst move I ever made. Financially, it was not. It was really hard to leave. It wasn't what we wanted to do. Everyone was great to us in Chicago. We loved it there.

Jeff Torborg was hired to manage the White Sox on November 3, 1988. His first team struggled to a 69–92 record and finished last in the American League West. The Sox caught fire in 1990 and rolled to a 94–68 record, but still finished nine games behind Oakland. He was named American League Manager of the Year following the season. In 1991 Torborg's Sox slipped slightly to 87–75 and finished behind the A's again. He resigned on October 11, 1991, to take over as manager of the New York Mets. He also spent time as manager of the Florida Marlins and has extensive national broadcast experience. Torborg's son, Dale, is the White Sox's minor league coordinator for strength and conditioning.

ROBIN VENTURA
THIRD BASEMAN
1989–1998

THE 58-GAME HITTING STREAK [at Oklahoma State] really came out of nowhere. You go to college and don't know if you're going to start or anything, so it was really a progression that in one year you're in the spotlight. I was fortunately in a good program, and we went to the [College] World Series. It was definitely different. It was something to adjust to.

Jack McDowell ended the streak, but he never got on me about it. People brought that up more than we did. He was the one who extended an invitation when I got drafted, and it was like we were roommates from the first day on. It never came up. Other people brought it up, but we were already focused on the White Sox more than we were on what happened two or three years ago.

There were rumors I was getting picked by the Dodgers, and there were some other interested teams. At that time I was getting ready to be on the USA team, and we were going to the [1988] Olympics. It was just odd. They said you were just drafted by the White Sox. They had never come up. Back then, you didn't hear rumors of what was going on and who you were going to get picked by. I didn't really have any idea. I grew up in California, and back then there wasn't satellite TV, so you couldn't watch all the games, or SportsCenter or things like that. It was different. I didn't really know anything about the team other than Jack was picked by them the year before.

When I came up in '89, it was one of those things where the team wasn't doing real well at the major league level, and our minor leagues were really loaded at the time. We had a lot of good young players and, coming up, I think the team was 30-something games out of first place. To come up, it wasn't necessarily what you would have thought. I think the energy was kind of zapped.

That following year they brought everybody up. I just remember a lot of guys from Double A and Single A, and they kind of threw us in there to see what would happen. It was great. We were fortunate and won 94 games in a division that had Oakland and was loaded. That really set us up for the next couple years. All of the draft picks that we had at that time ended up in the big leagues that year. After Jack, I was up, and then Frank Thomas and Alex Fernandez were in there. They got the most out of their picks really quickly.

I did go 0-for-41 in a stretch early in the year. We were winning at the time, so I was lucky. Jeff Torborg had a lot of confidence that eventually it would turn around. We were winning, so I think that was one of the things. He said, "Just keep playing and eventually it will go away." It was a grind and it was a mental thing. It was the toughest stretch I had in my career. When I broke through, it was a bunt, it wasn't even a hit. I was sacrificing, and it was just a good bunt.

The Gold Glove came the next year. I think that's part of what took place during the slump that I had—I could focus on defense and get better. I think that's something that you learn. Back then, defense was important and it still is. I had a lot of work to do, not just offensively, but defensively, and it paid off. You work at everything. There's not one thing you can focus on. It's a lot of work. I had coaches who helped me, and so did other players. It was a daily effort. I think something that I'm proud of is that I wasn't brought here as a defensive player, but I turned myself into a confident defensive player.

I think to go from walking into that clubhouse at the end of '89, when they were 30-some games out of first place, to winning the division a few years later in '93 is pretty amazing. You can see how that transformation happened as an organization and with our new stadium—everything revolved around the team at that time—it was pretty satisfying.

To have the next season cut short was frustrating because we were pretty good. We had a good staff, a good offense, and everything was really there.

237

Our bullpen was great. You look at the way the Bulls had evolved at that same time, and we were kind of following that path, where you lose that first year and then you make it a little further the next. The strike stopped that, so that was probably the most frustrating.

It didn't work out after that. You're missing different pieces, and obviously Jack was gone, we lost a few guys out of the bullpen, it was just a different team. It wasn't the same team and same chemistry that were there the first couple of years.

With the grand slams, I think early on it happened just because of where I was hitting. I was getting to hit either in front of or behind Frank [Thomas]. Either way, they don't want to face him. You're going to get good pitches before him or they're going walk him to get to you. At that time, I got in good situations. [Harold] Baines was behind me, Frank in front of me, and I had Albert Belle in there, too, so I was probably the one guy where they would say, "I don't want to face those guys, but we'll go with him." I think over time you get a little confidence and learn how to hit in that situation.

The Nolan Ryan incident is still around all the time. I've never really been in a situation to talk to him about it, but it's around and it's alive. Our teams were going back and forth at the time, and Nolan was hitting a lot of guys. So it was, if he hits somebody, you've got to go. I did, and that's it.

We always had good chemistry because there were a lot of good guys on this team. A lot of them are working here now. You have Bainesy, Walker, Ozzie, and Pudge all in the organization. Kenny Williams was there as a player. You had a lot of guys who were good baseball guys who were enjoyable to be around. I think that's part of what makes watching these guys now so much fun. It feels like the same guys, just kind of extended out.

It was '97 when I got hurt. I think Herm Schneider is responsible for a lot of my being able to come back the next year. I don't think I had any idea what it was going to take to come back. I think beyond that, once I got back, I was doing what I could, but I could feel it going downhill every year I played. I was just glad I was able to play after the injury. Herm was a big reason for that.

I have an ankle transplant, which is basically taking a cadaver joint and cutting mine out and putting a new one in. It feels good. I don't do a lot of running, but I wasn't planning on it anyway at this point. I can walk and do most things. I don't think about it anymore. Before my surgery, I didn't go

Robin Ventura averaged 23 homers and 94 RBIs for the first six full seasons he was with the White Sox. He was an American League All-Star in 1992 and won five Gold Gloves while with the team.

too many places, because it wasn't that comfortable to walk around and do things. Now I can pretty much do anything, but I'm not training for any triathlons.

When I left, I think that was just a time when they had some young players they were looking at. That's just the way baseball is. I don't think, having seen it the years I was here, it was anything else. They always treated me great. It's a business decision. It's part of baseball. I was happy for the opportunity to play here and am happy just to be invited back to different things now that I'm done playing. Leaving was hard. That was the only thing we knew as a family, and then you're off in a situation where you don't know anybody and you don't know where you're going. I had some interesting things happen since then, but obviously I'm always going to be a White Sox.

It's always a family atmosphere, as far as the way the players deal with each other and former players. You obviously have that bond, and I think being with the White Sox, I don't know if it's a chip, but there's something there that bonds everybody who plays here. It's easily recognizable when you come back to Chicago for events that you're still family.

The White Sox selected Oklahoma State third baseman Robin Ventura with the 10th pick of the amateur draft on June 1, 1988, the second gem in a string of four straight winning top picks that also included Jack McDowell, Frank Thomas, and Alex Fernandez. Ventura was already a well-known name in baseball circles, having set a collegiate record with a 58-game hitting streak that was ended by future teammate Jack McDowell and Stanford in the 1987 College World Series. After being part of the 1988 U.S. Olympic team, he joined the Sox and was in the majors at the end of the 1989 season.

Ventura averaged 23 homers and 94 RBIs between 1991 and 1996 and became an outstanding defensive third baseman. He suffered a broken ankle in 1997, but returned to hit 21 home runs and drive in 91 runs in 1998. Ventura was an American League All-Star in 1992 and won five Gold Gloves while with the White Sox.

He signed with the Mets as a free agent after the 1998 season and also played for the Yankees and Dodgers before retiring in 2004. Ventura finished his career with 18 grand slams, good for fourth on Major League Baseball's all-time list. In 2000 he was named to the White Sox Team of the Century.

CRAIG GREBECK

INFIELDER

1990–1995

THERE IS A MYTH THAT I SIGNED with the White Sox after a tryout camp, but that was on the back of a baseball card or something. I'm not sure where it came from. What really happened was I was at Cal-State Dominguez Hills and I didn't get drafted. I thought I should have, because I was a first-team Division II All-American and had a great year. I had a lot of friends who were scouts, so I thought I should have been drafted, but I wasn't—maybe because of my size, maybe because of speed, I don't know. What I do know was that I had a high school coach who knew a scout who gave me a chance to play for his summer team. I played, like, 10 games for his summer team and I flat tore it up. I hit something like six home runs and drove in around 25 runs. He didn't really have the authority to sign anyone, but he convinced his head scout to give me a chance to go to spring training the following year.

They didn't want to sign me, but they let me go to spring training. I had no guarantees, no signing bonus, no nothing that everybody else got in their basic contract. I could go and I got a plane ticket. That was it. I always laughed and told people it was a round-trip ticket and they made me sign a contract in pencil in case they wanted to change their mind!

When I think back about the issue of my size, the best way I can put it is that I heard about it, but I never paid any attention to it. I just wanted to play and get a chance. I played hard, and it was never about trying to prove

Craig Grebeck is safe on a close play at first base with Toronto Blue Jays pitcher Al Leiter covering during the eighth inning of Game 2 in the ALCS on October 6, 1993, in Chicago. *Photo courtesy of AP Images*

people wrong who said I wouldn't make it because I was too small. I wanted to prove the people who believed in me right. That was the motto I used my whole life.

In 1990 there had been a lockout. What they ended up doing for the first month of the season was expanding the big-league rosters to 27 instead of 25. I had a really good spring and played really good defense. The Sox were coming off a year where they were out of it by the All-Star break and had played poorly. They were in a mode to give younger players a chance and bring them up to rebuild the organization. I had a manager at the big-league level who believed in me and trusted me and talked them into giving me one of those last spots. I did my part by having a good spring and earning a spot on the team, but that doesn't always pan out. You have to have some things go your way. It was a great spring, and I never thought I was going to make it, but I played the game the only way I knew how. I played hard, worked hard, didn't say much, and tried to learn as much as I could while I was there. I ended up making the team.

Jeff Torborg was a great manager for young players. He believed in young players and gave them a chance. He didn't put the pressure on them like some managers who are out there and only love the veteran players. He didn't put pressure on you like, "Hey, you've got 10 games to prove yourself or you're going back." He told me to relax, play the game the way I knew how, and I would be fine.

It was a great year. Not only was it the last year of Comiskey Park and people were there to say good-bye to the stadium, but it was a year built with excitement with the rivalry we had with the A's. There was also a bit of controversy with the A's when Dave Stewart said we couldn't hold their jocks. It was a real rivalry. Everything added up to make it just a great year.

My first big-league home run came that year off Nolan Ryan. I hit a three-run home run on the first pitch I saw from him, then Ozzie Guillen came up and hit the first pitch he saw for another home run. I was in the dugout shaking hands and I didn't even see him hit his. I heard everyone going crazy while I was giving high fives to people, and they were congratulating me for hitting my first one off Ryan. The next thing I knew, the crowd was going crazy again. I had barely gotten into the dugout.

The next time I came up, we had Sammy Sosa on second. My job was to move him to third, and they didn't ask me to bunt. They let me swing away, and I battled him. I got it to a 2–2 count, fouled off a couple of pitches, then hit a rocket to right-center, which was run down by Ruben Sierra. As I was running back across the field, I was running hard with my head down because I never showed anyone up. To this day, I don't know what Nolan said, but as I crossed the mound, he said something to me.

The next time we faced them was a twilight doubleheader in Arlington, Texas. They sat people in center field there, and you could not see the baseball, it was that bad. The very first pitch Ryan threw me in that game hit me right in the ribs.

The lucky part of playing with the White Sox was the opportunity to play with the veterans they had. I have to thank Ozzie Guillen and Carlton Fisk so much for what they did for me coming up. They both took me under their wings. Ozzie taught me how to play shortstop, how to prepare myself for different hitters and pitchers, and how to play the game. Carlton Fisk took ground balls with me every day and taught me mentally and physically how to prepare to play every single day. If it weren't for those two, I don't think it would have been as easy for me to do the job that I did when I first got there. Some of the best advice I ever got from Carlton Fisk was to practice like you are going to play every night. I didn't go out and look at the lineup card every day, then take my ground balls and go. I practiced like I was the starting second baseman, starting shortstop, or starting third baseman every single night, so that if something happened in the first inning or I was thrown in there, I was prepared to play day in and day out. That is what helped me to adapt to being a utility player.

When we moved into the new clubhouse at the new park, my locker was between Frank Thomas and Bo Jackson. Murderers' Row, I guess. I used to love giving the media a hard time about being around my locker, but not for me.

Hawk Harrelson gave me the nickname "Little Hurt," and I liked it. It gave some character to me, and I was out there playing hard. Frank Thomas was the "Big Hurt" and was the biggest guy on the team, and I was the littlest guy on the team. People starting bringing it up with the way I hit, and I enjoyed it.

I didn't use batting gloves, except maybe once in a while during batting practice so I didn't get blistered up. I hated them. I liked the feel of the bat. I loved that feel and felt I had better control of the bat without them. There were a very few times I used them in a game when it was freezing somewhere early in the season and I was coming off the bench. If I was starting, I didn't need them, but for coming off the bench to pinch-hit, sometimes your hands would be numb by the time you got there, so I'd give in.

When I left the Sox after '95, I really didn't want to go. The problem with the game sometimes is a lack of communication on the player's part or the organization's part. You get to where you earn a certain salary, and the organization thinks they can't pay this player any more. In my case, I would have taken a pay cut to stay in Chicago. I wanted to stay there, I loved it, and it wasn't a matter of making more money. I would have taken the same money they gave to the guy they brought in to replace me. It was a lack of communication, and then it was too late. I loved it in Chicago.

I have played in different cities for different teams, and the White Sox fans are as knowledgeable about their players as anyone. When you go out, they know you. If you go to the grocery store, kids say hello to you. The town embraces its athletes. The White Sox are great. I still see Jerry Reinsdorf and Eddie Einhorn once in a while, and they are great people. They always ask me if I need anything and, "Why aren't you back with the organization doing something?" They are great to the people who leave. It's a good feeling to know that you are still wanted.

I do a lot of coaching and teaching with kids now. Some of them know I played because of their parents. The ones who don't know me end up hearing about me from someone else, then get on the Internet. One kid came to me and showed me his iPod Touch and asked, "How does this swing look? Is it a good one?" Well, the video he was showing me was of my first career home run off Ryan! You never know what's going to come up.

If there were questions about Craig Grebeck's size at 5'7" and 145 pounds, there was never a doubt about the size of his heart. Grebeck was signed by the White Sox as an amateur free agent on August 13, 1986, and made the big-league club out of spring training in 1990. His ability to play shortstop, second base, and third base made him a valuable utility man for the team. "The Little Hurt" had his finest offensive season in 1991, when he hit .281 with six homers and 31 RBIs in 107 games. He signed as a free agent with the Marlins after the 1995 season and also played with the Angels, Blue Jays, and Red Sox before retiring in 2001.

Grebeck currently coaches AAU baseball and teaches hitting in Southern California.

FRANK THOMAS
DESIGNATED HITTER/
FIRST BASEMAN

1990–2005

I DIDN'T KNOW MUCH ABOUT THE WHITE SOX when they drafted me. I knew about Harold Baines and some of the older Sox players because I used to watch them down in Georgia every now and then. Just to come to Chicago made me very proud and very excited because I knew it was a big city.

It's kind of funny how I got called up. I had been complaining for about three weeks that I was ready to go. I was at Birmingham leading the Southern League in hitting and home runs and had had such a big spring with the team that I felt it was time for me to come up, but they had a plan for me. Fortunately, Alex Fernandez was there at the same time and was mowing people down, so they had a good reason to bring both of us up at the same time. It worked out great. It was time. My manager told me I had finally gotten my wish, and they were bringing us both up. I said that was great.

They put me right in the starting lineup, and I had a lot of butterflies. I was a little overwhelmed. I wasn't nervous about the fans—I was used to big crowds from playing college football. I wanted to do so much on that first day, but I didn't have a good first day at all. About the fourth or fifth day, things started to settle down for me, and I was back to playing the game I always played.

My first home run was in Minnesota. I had been in the big leagues for a few weeks or so and hadn't hit a home run. The fans were expecting me to start hitting home runs right away. I was happy, and it was great to hit the ball hard. I was locked in at the time because I had Walt Hriniak as a hitting coach, and he didn't put up with much. So I was putting in my work, and he had me locked in.

When I came in, the team was not that good and they had a lot of players they wanted to replace. When we all broke in—Robin Ventura, Alex, myself—it was perfect timing. Things worked out for us. We were able to put some great years together and bring this organization up to the top of the charts with everybody else.

Nineteen ninety-three was an unbelievable feeling. It was like being in the World Series, just getting to the playoffs, because the South Side wasn't known for being able to get that far. With four straight great draft classes, we got there. Add Jack McDowell in when you talk about those drafts. We all became All-Stars, so I guess we were in the right place at the right time.

The next year was really the year for us to win the World Series. We were experienced, and the hunger was there. Unfortunately, sometimes business gets in the way of baseball, and that's what happened that year. It was nice to be the MVP that year, but my goal was to win a ring. I had won the MVP the year before, but I wanted that ring. To get it early in my career, when I knew we had the best team in baseball, would have been the time to get it.

I had this iron bar I used in the on-deck circle. Back in the day, Chicken Willie Thompson and Vinnie Fresso, our clubhouse guys, were rebuilding something, and they had those bars out and just brought one over. I picked one up and swung it around and thought it was a great weight. I started carrying it, and from that day forward I had it in my bag every year.

I had three or four nicknames, but Hawk Harrelson always seemed to find ones that stuck on people. He's good at that. When he broke out "the Big Hurt" for me, that was the first nickname I really liked besides "the Hammer" that I had in high school. It worked, and I had no problems with it.

Two thousand five was very bittersweet because I really wanted to play, but I wasn't even close to being healthy. Things happen for a reason, and I was proud to play at all that year. I got in there and hit some big home runs for the team. I had a small impact, though not the same impact as usual. I helped that year. One of the biggest moments I ever had in my life was throwing out the first pitch at the World Series. I wasn't playing, but I

248

Frank Thomas hits a two-run home run, scoring Ray Durham in the fifth inning against the Chicago Cubs on June 29, 2002. Thomas is the Sox's all-time home run leader with 448. *Photo courtesy of AP Images*

remember the way I was accepted by the crowd—it still sends chills down my spine. It was good to be embraced that way.

Baseball has always been defined by the home run. It's just one of those offensive categories that people pay attention to. They don't care what guys are hitting, what they're going through, if a guy hits big home runs, fans feel he is getting the job done.

A lot of things have to go your way to hit a home run. That's what I tell people. It's the most difficult thing to do as a hitter. You have to be perfect, you have to get the perfect pitch, make the perfect swing, and most of the time, those things don't add up. Hitting a home run is a special moment every time. If you allow your mind to think base hits, the proper mechanics will go through the swing, and that's what generates home runs when you're trying to do the little things at the plate. That's why most hitting coaches and people who teach hitting just focus on getting you to hit the baseball hard. If you do that basic, simple thing, then bigger things will happen.

I take a lot of pride in the fact that now this organization is known for winning, not just silly gadgets. For many years, the team was known for a lot of things, but not for winning baseball games. Ozzie Guillen as a manager and Kenny Williams as a general manager want to win. It's about winning over here now.

I spent 16 years here in a real nurturing, growing part of my life. I came here as a young kid and left here as an older man. Being here, staying here, and being part of the history here—I'm very proud of all that. Jerry Reinsdorf has always been great about bringing guys back and keeping guys involved who meant so much to the organization. We had a little tiff for a couple of years, but it wasn't really that big of a deal. I just knew I had a lot of baseball left in me and I wanted to prove it. I still have a lot left, I'm just not playing anymore. I'm proud and happy any time I'm back here.

The White Sox drafted Frank Thomas out of Auburn with the seventh pick of the 1989 amateur draft, and he was in the everyday lineup just a year later. For the next 10 seasons, he was the most feared hitter in the game, hitting .320 and averaging 34 homers, 115 RBIs, 104 runs, and 114 walks. Thomas won back-to-back American League MVP awards in 1993 and 1994 and was selected to the All-Star team five years in a row, starting in 1993. After an off year in

1999, Thomas was the Comeback Player of the Year in 2000, leading the Sox to a division title with 43 homers, 143 RBIs, and a .328 average. He was injured in 2001, but had 28 homers and 92 RBIs in 2002 and 42 homers and 105 RBIs in 2003. Injuries curtailed his final two seasons with the White Sox, and the Big Hurt was not on the 2005 Sox postseason roster. He signed as a free agent with Oakland in 2006, spent 2007 in Toronto, and split 2008 with the Jays and A's before retiring.

Thomas is atop almost all of the Sox's career hitting categories, including homers (448), RBIs (1,465), runs (1,327), walks (1,466), on-base percentage (.427), and doubles (447). He finished his career with 521 home runs, tied for 18th place on the all-time list. In 2000 he was named to the White Sox Team of the Century.

JOEY CORA
SECOND BASEMAN
1991–1994

WHEN I WAS TRADED TO THE WHITE SOX, I didn't know what to expect. All I knew was the Padres, and they told me I was traded, so I thought, *Well, we'll see what happens.* I flew all the way to Sarasota without really knowing what to expect there. Baseball is baseball. You hit the ball, you catch the ball—what's the big deal? American League and National League, it wasn't a big deal, because at the end of the day, I had to play.

The team in 1993 was a really good one. We had everything, and I'm a little surprised we didn't win it. We had a great year and great players. Frank Thomas was the best player in the game at that moment, and we had Robin Ventura, Lance Johnson, and Tim Raines on that team. Unfortunately, we didn't win it all.

That team was special, but the '94 team was the best team I ever played on. Because of the strike, we'll never know. I thought we were better than the year before, because we had all the pieces together and we were playing really well. We'll never find out, but we'll have to let history tell, I guess. I thought we were the best team in baseball by far. Even though Cleveland was there with us, we really thought we were going to win it. It was tough to be the best team and not get to finish the season. How many chances are you going to have to assemble that talent? We had no injuries and we really had everything going. It's tough to know that you had it all and that might have been the shot at a World Series, but it is what it is.

Ozzie Guillen was always sure that he was going to be a manager, and he and I always talked about that. When he got the job, he gave me a call. I don't want to say I expected it, but he did call me right away and said, "Joey, be ready. I'm going to be the manager of the White Sox, and let's see what happens. Let's see what we can do."

Ozzie wanted to change the culture. In '04 we had a lot of pieces on the team that probably didn't fit Ozzie's mentality. You have to play with what you have and you have to coach the players they give you. Once he found out the way things were, he let everybody know what he wanted to do, and it all happened in 2005.

We won the first game of that season 1–0, and that said it all. That's the way we played all year. Mark Buehrle pitched an unbelievable game, and it was scoreless for a long time. Paul Konerko was at third base and went on a ground ball that the shortstop missed. We won 1–0. Ross Gload made a great play to finish the game, and that's the way we played all year. We won so many one-run games, and, looking back, that first game of the season was a sign that we were going to be playing that way all year.

You can have a great regular season and bomb in the playoffs, so you have to wait to see it play out. We won so many close games that year and went from wire to wire in first place, but once the playoffs started, we didn't know. We played Boston and had a great first game against them, but then the next two were really close. Against the Angels, all the games were close. In the World Series, we could have easily been the ones who got swept, because that's how close all the games were. You have to play the games, and, once the season is over, then all of a sudden you're world champions and you go to a parade.

I didn't go to the parade. As soon as the season was over, I went to winter ball and managed. For me, I never got the chance to enjoy the World Series or the parade. I don't know what it feels like to really celebrate a World Series.

At the Series, I never really said, "I made it." The Series is about the players. They win it and they lose it. The players are the ones who did it. I'm glad I was there for the ride, but I really wish I could have been there as a player instead of as a coach. Playing the games is what it's all about.

I've been in baseball all my life and I knew I could never play forever. I knew I wanted to stay involved somehow. When you have played the game as a big-leaguer, you've gone through all the things the guys you're coaching go through. They have some tough times, and I went through those, too. I don't like to say, "Back when I played…." That's the worst thing you can do

Bench coach Joey Cora looks on prior to a spring-training game against the
Oakland Athletics on March 4, 2009, in Phoenix.

as a coach, personally. In the back of my mind, I know I went through the
same situations, so that really helps.

　　When we won the division in 2008, in some ways it was more satisfying
than 2005. We went through so many injuries, where in '05 everything always

worked out. Crede, Quentin, Contreras, Linebrink, Konerko—so many guys were hurt. We made it, but in the back of your mind, you say, *Boy, I wish we could have had everyone healthy the whole year or at least at the end*. I wish we'd have had that and then gotten to see what would have happened in the play-offs. Tampa was playing great, and I can't take anything away from them, but you want to take your best shot with your best players, and we didn't get to do that. Maybe things would have changed. It was satisfying that our team kept fighting and went through every kind of situation. They kept fighting and fighting and fighting and, all of a sudden, we won the division. That was a great accomplishment.

It was tough to win those last three games that year. Every day you had to make every play. At the end, it was satisfying to win the division on a 1–0 game. If everybody was healthy, maybe we wouldn't have had to play those last three must-win games and would have had the time to set up our rotation for the playoffs. That will always be in the back of my mind.

Ozzie has his style and he sets the tone. We're always going to compete and we always have a chance no matter what. We're going to play hard, and that comes from the top. Jerry and Kenny are like Ozzie. They want to win and play the right way.

I love baseball and I love to watch games. I watch TV all the time, even when we're done, I'll watch all the way through the World Series. There's always something that other teams do that maybe can help you. It's true about baseball—that you learn something every day. You learn about other players, other managers, other teams. I love the intricacies of the game. It's the greatest game on earth.

Joey Cora was traded from the San Diego Padres along with Warren Newson and Kevin Garner to the White Sox in return for Adam Peterson and Steve Rosenberg on March 31, 1991. He was the Sox's regular second baseman on the 1993 division-winning team when he hit .268, scored 95 runs, hit 13 triples, and stole 20 bases. Cora left via free agency after the 1994 season.

He rejoined the White Sox as their third-base coach on November 7, 2003. After three seasons, he moved to the dugout as Ozzie Guillen's bench coach.

GENE LAMONT

MANAGER

1992–1995

I THINK JIM LEYLAND HAD A LOT TO DO with me getting hired here. He had worked here and knew Ron Schueler and the owner. I came here for an interview, and it was kind of secretive. When I was announced, I don't think anybody knew for sure that it was going to be me.

Our club in '92 wasn't a really good team. We weren't strong up the middle, and our starting pitching wasn't quite ready. I'm sure I had some growing pains, too. I don't think anybody managing for the first time in the major leagues is as good as he is going to get. We got hurt in the fourth or fifth game of the season when Ozzie Guillen tore his knee up and was done for the year. We went through some shortstops, and when you have a big part of the team like that go down—because Ozzie was a veteran guy—it really affects your team. When I look back, they talked as though our pitching were really ready to compete, but it wasn't.

The next year Jason Bere and Wilson Alvarez came on the scene in a very strong way. I've heard that we really did a good job with them, but we really didn't have a whole lot of other choices. We put them in there, and they pitched really well. Roberto Hernandez really came on as a prime-time closer, and that really helped. I think you always enjoy it when you're winning. We had a lot of good players. It was fun.

Bo Jackson was with us and wasn't a distraction. He wasn't the player that everyone wished he was going to be before he hurt his hip, but he still could run decently for a guy who had had a hip replacement, and he had a good arm. He added some good things, and I don't think it bothered the team. Bo contributed and hit the home run that clinched for us against Seattle.

When you're ahead like we were in the division, you just want it to get over with and clinch. Nobody wants to say we didn't get it done. It was a big time for us. We knew we had a good team. Winning against the Mariners was a great night, but I wish we could have celebrated a few more times that year.

I think if you look back at our playoff series, Toronto was a really, really good team. Maybe if, in our first time, we hadn't been playing such a good team, we might have fared better. When you look at the Jays, they have quite a few guys who are Hall of Famers. We had some of those guys, too, but they were playoff-tested and we weren't. That probably hurt a little bit, but they were just a really good team.

The team in '94 was the best we had. I think our bullpen was better with Dennis Cook and Paul Assenmacher down there to get out the lefties. We had Roberto to close again and added Scott Sanderson along with our starters. There was Ozzie, Frank Thomas, and Robin Ventura, then we added a really good DH in Julio Franco. If you look at his numbers, he had as many homers and RBIs in early August as he ever had in his career. It was so frustrating that I don't even like to think about it. When they went out on strike, I was told we'd get right back. They kept saying, "They'll settle it, they'll settle it." The longer it went, I was pretty sure we weren't going to get back. We really felt that we had the team with the experience from the year before, but it just didn't happen.

The Indians were getting there at that time, and the next year you could see they had become really good. They had their young guns, but we had a good mix of young guys and veterans. We really had good players, the chemistry was great, and we were hungry to get back to the playoffs and hopefully the World Series.

When I asked the umpires to check Albert Belle's bat that year, I had a tip. I'm not going to go into it too much, but we were pretty sure that his bat had been altered. The whole thing got really crazy when they stole the bat from the umpires' room. When we got to Cleveland that year, they also wanted me to check Kenny Lofton's bat, but I wasn't going to do it. It will all come out at some point—we knew Albert Belle's bat was corked. We had to check it, and we did. [Albert Belle was suspended for 10 games after the incident, reduced to seven on appeal.]

Manager Gene Lamont talks with Michael Jordan in February 1994 during the White Sox spring-training camp in Sarasota, Florida. Jordan attended camp and then played in the minors that season.

Nineteen ninety-five eats at my craw a little bit still. We probably wouldn't have gotten it going because our team was different. For some reason, it seemed like the hierarchy didn't think we were going to come back, but we didn't have nearly as good of a team. Jack McDowell was gone. We decided that Ray Durham, who later became a great player, would replace Joey Cora, who was a really important part of our team. We lost the two lefties in the bullpen and were a different team, not close to the team we were the year before. We lost Franco, and it was frustrating that I didn't get the chance to right the team. It was only 30 games, and while some people might think that was fair, I didn't.

I can't be a White Sox fan because I work in the same division. I loved the time I was here and thought we were starting to get some of the Chicago faithful over to the South Side. I think the strike might have made it worse. We were winning fans over, and I don't know if they've come back. I loved the years I had here—and I had some great players. Ron Schueler and I had a great relationship, even though he ended up having to let me go. I just wish we could have finished '94.

Gene Lamont replaced Jeff Torborg as White Sox manager on November 26, 1991. Lamont's first team went 86–76 and finished third. In 1993 he led the Sox to a 94–68 record and the American League West title before losing to Toronto four games to two in the ALCS, and was named American League Manager of the Year. The Sox were in first place at 67–46 the next year when the remainder of the season was cancelled due to the strike. He was fired early in the 1995 season when the Sox stumbled out of the gate to an 11–20 start. Lamont managed the Pittsburgh Pirates from 1997 to 2000 and has been the third-base coach for the Detroit Tigers since the 2006 season.

DARRIN JACKSON

OUTFIELDER

1994 ★ 1999

BROADCASTER

2000–Present

I NEVER HAD A MULTIYEAR DEAL IN MY CAREER. Nineteen one-year contracts makes you work very hard every off-season. Fortunately, you have to know that nothing is given to you. You show up every year with the opportunity to play in spring training and you run through the process. Every year, you realize if you do a good job this year, you'll get a raise next year through arbitration, free agency, or your agent doing the best he can for you. In the end, when I look back after 19 years of doing it, I got paid. I made the money I was supposed to make. It definitely made me stay hungry, and I never took anything for granted.

Having some medical issues really put things in perspective. I was fortunate to play baseball since I had loved it as a kid and always wanted to be a big-league baseball player. It made it that much more that I had to focus. I had to take care of my family and I had things I wanted to do. I never took it for granted. I came across and played against so many great players who didn't have the focus they needed. That was inspirational to me in its own way. I'd see guys going out and doing things where it was more important to them to have fun

Darrin Jackson played two seasons with the White Sox, in 1994 and 1999. Since 2000 he has been a part of White Sox broadcasts, both television and radio. *Photo courtesy of WGN-TV*

wherever they were playing and they didn't take the job as seriously as I needed to. I saw some short-lived careers because of it. I realized I needed to pick my moments. If I was going to enjoy the big-league life or wanted to go have a few pops with the boys at night, in my case, there had to be an off-day the next day. I never did it if it was going to affect me the next day at work.

In 1993 I had gone to arbitration against the San Diego Padres and ended up winning my case. Right then and there, they were interested in trying to trade me. I told myself that it didn't matter, and I would just get ready to play baseball. In spring training I had some time at home in Arizona and got food poisoning not long after I had the flu, so I lost a lot of weight. I ended up getting traded to the Blue Jays about four days before the end of spring training and I hadn't been able to put the weight back on. I joined them in British Columbia for some preseason games. I was skinny as a rail, down to 175 instead of 192. I knew there was something wrong because I couldn't put the weight back on. A few weeks into the season, I was still off and got myself checked because I had a history of cancer. It was hard tracking it down. I got traded to the Mets in the middle of the season, and after a month and a half with them it was discovered I had Graves disease, which is a thyroid condition. I went on the disabled list and got everything in order.

I was released by the Mets. Because of that terrible season, I was invited to White Sox camp in 1994 as a non-roster invitee by Ron Schueler, who said if I could show myself and show I was healthy, I'd be on the team. We shook hands and moved on from there. Fortunately for me it opened up the door to become part of the White Sox family.

You had better believe we were the best team in baseball in 1994. Having been with the Blue Jays the year before, I knew the talent that it took to win a world championship. To come here and then have the strike take place so that it was the only year with no postseason was very frustrating. I knew that team had as much talent and probably more than the '93 Blue Jays team I left that went on to win the World Series. We were in first place at the time of the strike, and it was very disheartening not to come back and play ball.

The situation was such that when I got here, the blend of guys on this team—both old and young—made me feel part of the program right away. Walt Hriniak was a great leader with his hitting program, and you knew what you were supposed to do hitting-wise every day. For the first time in my career, I was actually pushed to focus on the daily routine with my swing and use the same approach. It made me a better hitter. I hit over .300 that year thanks to my teammates and Walter.

The next two years I played in Japan and really embraced it. Some of the guys I played with over there really enjoyed it. They were usually not the big-name players, but guys who played a little bit in the majors here, then went over and had success and were treated like gods. The guys who had problems were big names here who got over to Japan and thought it was bush league. They didn't appreciate it and thought it was beneath them. I didn't see it that way and liked learning the new culture. I accepted the way they played the game and never took it for granted. I wanted to do something new. I wouldn't trade that experience for anything in the world.

I loved the way the game was played in Japan. It was their game, not ours. They bunted in the first inning, and that sometimes led to a 1–0 win. I think they recognized their limitations with power and how good the pitching was.

They played to ties, and we weren't allowed to play any more than 10 innings. It felt incomplete, but everything was different. On the road, you got dressed in your hotel, not in the locker room, then went back to the hotel after the game. I got back to the States because I had a reputation for playing hard and being a good fourth outfielder.

I was actually thinking about staying at home and shutting it down in 1999, but Chris Singleton had just been traded to the White Sox. We worked out together in Arizona during the off-season, and he talked me into coming back to the White Sox. I talked to Schueler, and he told me he'd give me an invite and that I'd be competing for an extra outfield job. I'd heard that before and really had a good spring training to be the lucky one and make the club. The big key was that I knew I wanted to work for this organization some-how when I was done playing. It worked out perfectly because it led me to broadcasting after that season.

Schueler called me during that off-season and usually when you hear from the GM, it's not a good sign, but he told me Jerry Reinsdorf wanted to meet with me and I'd like what he had to say. I met with Jerry in Scottsdale, and he proposed an opportunity for me to get into TV broadcasting. When Jerry said that this was something that would be good for me, I knew him well enough to know that I needed to think about that over trying to play another year. It was the right thing for me to do at the right time. It's one of the best decisions I've ever made.

The game definitely looks slower up in the booth. Going upstairs was the first time in my baseball career that I could see the whole field, because you sure can't from the dugout or outfield. You see everything, and it looks so much easier, but thank goodness I played the game a long time and I know it's not. You can never forget that as easy as it looks, it's not, and there may be a good reason why a guy didn't get the job done, because they certainly are not trying to mess it up.

It took me a couple years to transition from being a player. I went from the judge of the kangaroo court my last year as a player to going to the tele-vision booth and analyzing my former teammates' play. It's a forced separa-tion, because the players look at you differently, not unlike when a coach becomes a manager. The relationship changes.

The transition to the radio side has been very enjoyable. It's a pure form of broadcasting, and you are the eyes of the listener. I am enjoying it a lot. Television has a certain prestige and, yes, you are on camera, but I do enjoy the radio work. Ed Farmer is great and sets me up to look and sound good. He brings me into everything.

I want to make sure our guys are playing the game the way they should. I will be sure to point it out if they don't. I don't have a hard time critiquing anybody as long as they are playing hard. The "grinder" ads they've had here are very apropos. They are fitting, and our guys should buy into it and play the game that way.

Chicago is a special city. I grew up in Southern California, where everything is much more laid back. These fans love their baseball and want us in the booth to say it like it is. I will always be as honest as I can.

Darrin Jackson batted a career-high .312 in 1994 for the Sox with 10 homers and 51 RBIs. Jackson spent the next two seasons with the Seibu Lions in the Japanese Pacific League, then returned to the U.S. and played with the Twins and Brewers from 1996 to 1998. D.J. rejoined the White Sox for his final season in 1999 and moved to the television booth as a broadcaster to work with Hawk Harrelson beginning with the 2000 season. After nine years on TV, he moved over to the radio side to work with Ed Farmer before the 2009 season.

JERRY MANUEL

MANAGER

1998–2003

I WENT THROUGH THE INTERVIEW PROCESS with the White Sox and was rec-ommended for the manager's job after an interview by Kenny Williams to Ron Schueler. I met some tremendous people there, and they gave me the opportunity to talk about my philosophy and thoughts.

Jerry Reinsdorf was tremendous, just tremendous to me my entire time there. He'll always have a place in my heart and so will the White Sox for giving me my first managerial job. I thought the city gave me a chance to grow as a manager. It didn't work out, but it was a tremendous opportunity.

We had talent, and when you have that, you have the chance to build something and program that talent into what you think can be a champi-onship team. Unfortunately, I didn't get the chance to be a part of that, but I feel that I played a small bit in all that and they were able to take it to another level, which you have to do.

In 2000 we put together some good players on that team. Some of the young talent was evolving and maturing at that particular time. They made strides, and those pieces became a foundation. Once they were in place, we knew it was only a matter of time for adding and taking away certain pieces to make that a championship club. That's what the White Sox did.

We ran into a little trouble with Detroit early in the year at home. I think it was Carlos Lee and Jeff Weaver, then Parque and Dean Palmer. We went out there and shed a little blood together, and it really brought us close as

Jerry Manuel led his first two teams to second place, and he was named AL Manager of the Year in 2000, the year the White Sox captured the AL Central title. He was replaced two seasons later, with a White Sox record of 500–471.

265

brothers. Unfortunately, those things happen, but if you can make them a positive, which is what we did, and go on to play extremely good baseball, then it happens for the best.

Our clinching was a little odd. There were two teams celebrating on the field at the same time in Minnesota. They had a walk-off home run to beat us, but we could see what happened in the other game on the scoreboard. It was a tremendous feeling to have finally gotten to that particular part of championship baseball. Everything went well for us that year. It really did. The young players developed and came along. Some of the players we had developed at the major league level took it to the next step and played really well. Everything that had a chance for us to go right went right.

We played Seattle, a very good team managed by Lou Piniella, in the play-offs. They were playing extremely well at that point, and we had run into a little trouble with our pitching. We didn't actually know whether we'd have enough pitching to compete there. It turned out that pitching wasn't our Achilles' heel in that series, it was our offense, which had been so great during the entire year. They really stifled us offensively.

It was frustrating the next few years. We felt we knew what the formula was for a winning team, and it was just a matter of trying to get that back together. Once you get to a certain level, the expectations are heightened, and rightfully so. We didn't fulfill those expectations, at least I didn't as a manager.

I think, to a certain degree, there have to be some people who walk in patience in order for an organization to get to where they want to get. If that's what you are called to do at a particular time, I think you have to do it with class and grace.

When the White Sox won the Series in 2005, I was able to enjoy it. It was tough, because, selfishly, I wanted to be the guy who made it happen. The unselfish part of me was very happy for the people I had come to know in Chicago, especially people like the grounds crew guys, Roger Bossard, all the people in the front office. I was extremely proud of the entire organization.

Jerry Manuel was a surprise hire by the White Sox as their 36th manager in 1997. His first two teams went 80–82 and 75–86 and finished second both seasons. Manuel was named AL Manager of the Year when his 2000 team went 95–67 and captured the AL Central title before losing in the American League Division Series to the Seattle Mariners. The Sox couldn't get back to the postseason in Manuel's tenure, going 83–79 in 2001 and 81–81 in 2002. In 2003 the White Sox faded down the stretch to finish 86–76, and he was let go after that season. His career mark with the White Sox was 500–471. Manuel is currently the manager of the New York Mets.

The
NEW
MILLENNIUM

PAUL KONERKO
FIRST BASEMAN
1999–Present

WE'VE HAD GREAT TIMES HERE. The clincher in 2000 was kind of a weird day. We got walked off and lost at Minnesota, but Cleveland had lost, so we won the division anyway. You had both teams celebrating on the field in the Metrodome at the same time, which was kind of weird. Clinching is clinching, and you'll take it any way you can get it, but if you had a choice, it's much better to have a magic number of one and just go out on the field and do it yourself.

When I look back on 2005, it's easy to enjoy a lot of the memories that go along with it, but at the time, I was so focused on the job at hand and who we were facing. It was so intense that it was hard to enjoy it. On game day, maybe during batting practice you do and certainly after the game, because in those playoffs, we won almost every single game. When you're playing, you get very focused. When you look back and see the highlights, it looks like a lot of fun, but when we were going through it, it definitely was a grind, no doubt.

We knew it would be a big deal if we won it, but if we had known how big it was to so many people—what we've learned since—we might not have been able to do it, because we would have felt so much pressure when we were going through it. I think we have all had thousands of people come up to us and tell us all their wild stories. Throw in all the excitement of the parade, and it's probably good that wasn't connected to it until after we had won. There are people who come up to me all the time and talk about where they were and all the crazy stories about that season, the playoffs, and the World Series.

I had caught the last out in all of our victories in the postseason that year, both the division series and the ALCS. Both times, I gave the ball to the winning pitcher of the game, which I felt was the right thing to do. I didn't think about it too much before the game because I didn't want to get too far ahead of myself. When we were up 1–0, then 2–0, I didn't want to think about it. Then we were up 3–0, so before Game 4, I did say to myself, *Hey, if I get the last out, what am I going to do?* I definitely knew I'd keep it, but I knew there would be a celebration. I didn't want someone to take it, so I hid it in my bag.

After the game, I had to make sure I got it to the clubhouse, then took it with me so I had it all the time. I didn't want to leave it alone in a bag or anything like that, because you hear crazy stories about people stealing stuff, and I didn't want someone to seek that thing out. I made sure it was in a safe place. I had a jacket on and kept it right in the inside pocket.

I knew that I would give it to Jerry, but I didn't know when. It actually worked out that I didn't really see him. I saw him a bit the night we clinched, but the next time I saw him wasn't until we were on the stage at the rally. I was leaving on a plane right after that, so it just worked out that I could give it to him there. It wasn't like it was all preplanned. In my mind, that's who it should have gone to. It wasn't mine, it wasn't for anybody on the team. Maybe I could have thrown it to the fans and let them have at it, but I thought it belonged to the guy who runs the show.

I take almost as much pride in our team and our 2008 season as I do in the year we won the World Series. We got everything we could out of it, especially because we had some injuries down the stretch. There comes a time in every season when a club faces a fork in the road in July, then August, then September, and you see clubs take the wrong way and fall to the side. We saw those forks many times, from early in the season on, but every time we kept battling and kept choosing to go at it and battle hard, all the way up to the end and all the way up to the 163rd game.

We constantly could have chosen to give up, and I think people would have been fine with that. We had injuries, with Carlos Quentin going down and our bullpen went down. People wouldn't have had much to say, but our team really battled and made it to the playoffs. It didn't end the way we

269

Above: Paul Konerko hits a grand-slam home run off Chad Qualls in the seventh inning of Game 2 of the World Series against the Houston Astros on October 23, 2005. The drive helped lift the Sox to a 7–6 win over the Astros.

Left: A plaque marks the spot where Konerko's grand slam hit, on a seatback in the bleachers at U.S. Cellular Field. *Photo courtesy of Bob Vorwald*

wanted, but I'm proud of that group as much in some ways as when we won the World Series.

The big thing for me is to show up and be consistent in preparing to do my job. All the vocal stuff and how you talk to other people if you are a leader is important, but if you show up to play every day and play hard, that's the best way to show leadership. My dad taught me to be on time, or early if possible, and stay late, no matter what sport you are playing. Practice at game speed, treat your teammates well, and conduct yourself as a professional. Whenever my career ends, I hope the lessons I've learned in baseball will serve me well.

Paul Konerko was acquired from the Cincinnati Reds on November 11, 1998, for Mike Cameron. The first baseman averaged 26 homers and 95 RBIs in his first four years on the South Side. After a down year in 2003, he was the AL Comeback Player of the Year in 2004, when he hit 41 homers and drove in 117 runs. Konerko followed with another big year in 2005, with 40 home runs and 100 RBIs.

He was a key figure in the Sox's 2005 postseason run, starting with two home runs in the first-round sweep of the Boston Red Sox. Konerko hit two homers and drove in seven runs against the Angels in the ALCS and was named the MVP of the series. His grand slam in Game 2 of the World Series off Houston's Chad Qualls is one of the most famous home runs in Sox history. "Paulie" capped the season in grand style at the team's victory rally when he presented Jerry Reinsdorf with the baseball from the last out of the Series.

He followed with a 35-homer, 113-RBI season in 2006 and averaged 27 homers and 80 RBIs while battling some nagging injuries the following three seasons. Konerko was named to the American League All-Star Team in 2002, 2005, and 2006. He is active in a number of charitable activities, including the "Bring Me Home" campaign in support of foster families he founded with former teammate Jim Thome.

MARK BUEHRLE
PITCHER
2000–Present

WHENEVER YOU GET DRAFTED BY A BIG-LEAGUE TEAM, it's a dream come true, and you want to do whatever you can to make it to the big leagues. I was picked in the 38th round, but had heard if I went back in the next year, I would move up to something like the third or fifth round. I ended up signing with the White Sox and was lucky to move up fast through the organization.

The way I got to the big leagues in 2000 was that there was a confrontation between one of our pitchers and a hitter. The pitcher said he meant to hit the opposing player and was going to get suspended. Instead of letting this guy get suspended, they sent him down and called me up. I've been here ever since.

My first appearance was against the Brewers. I got the call to come up on a Saturday night and got here Sunday morning in time for a day game. I went down to the bullpen in what turned out to be a blowout, so I got to pitch the ninth inning. I don't remember much about the pennant race because it was my first year in the big leagues. I was trying to figure out what to do, where to go, and just figure out my role. I didn't soak it all in as much as I'd have liked to. I do remember facing Seattle in the playoffs. I came in for one-third of an inning and gave up a couple hits, then struck out A-Rod. It was a blowout game, too, but I did get in.

I've always been more of a pitcher than a thrower, because I have never been a hard thrower. So I have to pitch, keep guys off balance, and hit my spots. From Little League to the minor leagues to now, I've been the same. I'm not going to go out there and throw the ball by guys. I'll be around 85 mph and maybe hit 90 occasionally, but my game has always been finding a way to keep hitters off balance.

Any time you have success, you start to feel more comfortable. At the same time, when you are failing, you wonder if guys have started to figure you out, if maybe you are tipping your pitches, and you wonder in the back of your head if you can do it anymore. Once you have a few good years in the big leagues and have been getting guys out, you know you're still going to have some bad outings but still have your confidence because you know you've done it before.

My first All-Star Game in 2002 was weird, being in the clubhouse with so many big-name guys. I sat next to some of the guys in the clubhouse and then looked up at their names on their lockers. I realized that just a couple years before, I had been at home watching them play in All-Star Games and in the World Series. It was definitely an experience where I took a step back and looked around to try and let it sink in. I was really there.

The second time I went was as the starter in 2005. I was a little more comfortable because I had pitched a few years and knew more players I could go up to and say hi. The first time I thought some of them might have said, "Who is this young guy coming over and talking to me?" I was more comfortable and was able to get some autographs and get to know them better.

It seemed like that year we couldn't do anything wrong. A lot of stuff has to happen to win a World Series. Guys have to have career years. Scott Podsednik would get on base with a walk and would end up scoring without us getting a base hit. It seemed that every ball that landed and every bounce went our way. That's what it takes to win a World Series.

We enjoyed the ride for the first five months, but that last month, it did get kind of tight. We just had to sit back and realize what a good team we were. Obviously, once we got into the playoffs, we felt we were a good team and took it one game at a time. We all know what happened then.

I had a complete game in Game 2 against the Angels, but that was the night A.J. Pierzynski ran on the third strike, and Joe Crede got the game-winning hit, so we laugh any time the highlights are shown because I was forgotten! Seriously, I was fortunate to be able to start that game and keep us in it. We won the game, and that's what really matters.

It was a thrill to come in and get a save in Game 3 of the World Series. When you are a starter, you know you will get a start, but to come in two days after I got to start Game 2 and get a save in that long game means a lot. There's a lot of great closers that can say they got a save in the World Series, but I can say I started one game and got the save in another. I'd like to have gotten the win in my start, but that save meant more.

When we came back for the rally, I didn't know there were that many people who lived in Chicago, let alone that many Sox fans. When we got on the bus and left the park to drive around the neighborhood a little bit, I didn't know where we were going, but there were tons of people around the stadium. When we got downtown, the crowd just blew my mind away. Looking down the street, you couldn't see the end of the road because there was a sea of people everywhere you looked. All those people came out to support us and made it such a memorable experience. Hopefully we can do it again.

If you ask me what my goal is coming in to spring training each year, obviously as a starting pitcher you want to win every game and hopefully get to 20 wins, but I think my main goal is to get to 200 innings. If you get to 200 innings, that means you are getting deep into games and giving your team a chance to win. You can't always control wins because you have to get run support, the bullpen has to hold your leads, and there's a lot of stuff that comes into play to get a lot of wins. I set my goal to pitch 200 innings and go deep into every start, because that's how you give your team and yourself a chance to win.

When I got my no-hitter against Texas, it was just one of those times you come close, and I had to finish it. To get through a big-league lineup three times without giving up a hit, I still can't believe I did it. I can see how some people do it with some of their stuff, like Justin Verlander, because he can throw 100 mph, but to go through a lineup like that probably still hasn't sunk in to this day. Maybe once I retire and look back on what I did in my career, it will sink in a little more. My teammates talked to me some, but I did what I always do. I went up in the clubhouse when we were hitting and talked to some guys. I even said to some of them, "Why are you guys staying away from me now? You talked to me for the first five innings. Why aren't you talking to me now?" I just wanted to keep everyone loose. There was one ground ball to Konerko where he looked more nervous than I was. I just told myself, *Hey, if it happens, it happens, and if it doesn't, I just hope we win the game.* I bought everybody on my team watches after that one.

I was thrilled to be picked for the '09 All-Star Game in St. Louis. Everybody knows I grew up a Cardinals fan. It was kind of like a home game, and any time you get to represent the White Sox, it's a huge honor. I had a lot of

Above: Mark Buehrle pitches against the Tampa Bay Rays as he throws a perfect game at U.S. Cellular Field on July 23, 2009. The The White Sox defeated the Rays 5–0.

Left: Center fielder Dewayne Wise leaps over the wall to catch a ball hit by right fielder Gabe Kapler of the Tampa Bay Rays, preserving Buehrle's perfect game in the ninth inning.

family there. Even though I had been picked before, I always feel like a rookie coming into the clubhouse, trying to meet people, figuring out who to play catch with. Meeting President Obama was great. When he threw his first pitch and had on his Sox jacket, I was like, *Holy cow, he's actually doing it.* Everybody around me was giving me a hard time, saying, "What the heck, he's wearing White Sox stuff." It's great to have the president behind us.

The perfect game against the Rays came right after that. As each inning went, it built up. When you get through about the sixth inning, you think, *There's only one time through the lineup left, and if I don't screw up or make a bad pitch, I have a chance.* So much has to happen. You can't let the crowd get you too crazy, though, or get too amped up. I was talking about it, because you have to soak it in and just have a good time with it. On [Dewayne] Wise's great catch, when it was hit, I was just hoping it would stay in the park so he had a chance to catch it. I knew he would do anything he could to get that one.

It was funny that A.J. said he predicted it. A.J. and I talk before the game, and if we add a catcher, he always claims it's my personal catcher. That was the first game [Ramon] Castro caught me, and before that A.J. said, "Hey, why don't you go out and throw a no-hitter for him." I said, "I already have one of those." He told me I should go and throw a perfect game then. That all happened even before I went out to warm up.

The president called me after the game and told me he was taking some of the credit for it since he wore the White Sox jacket to the All-Star Game. He was on Air Force One at the time. I never thought I would throw a no-hitter, or throw a perfect game, or hit my first home run. In this game, you just never know.

My next start I was perfect into the sixth and got the record for most batters retired in row, which surprised me. Considering how long the game has been around, it's really special to have that one. It's just me. For me to have something over all the great pitchers in this game is really, really special.

I'm a baseball fan. If we don't make the playoffs, I go home, and if St. Louis is in it, I'll get tickets and go to the Cardinals games. I watch all the playoff and World Series games on TV. When I get home from our games, I turn on ESPN and watch all the highlights. I have always been a fan of the game and, even though I play it, it's not like I go home and don't pay attention to it. I watch as much baseball as I can.

At our park, I catch a lot of the "first pitches." I guess it started because I was asked to a few times a while back, then I started doing it all the time and I've done it ever since. It only takes two minutes of your time, and you get to meet some special people. It's not that big of a deal. If it means a little more to them, I guess that's great, but I just go out there and enjoy meeting and taking pictures with different people. Just because I've got more time in the big leagues doesn't mean I've changed and won't do something like that.

I don't feel like I'm a good teacher as far as learning how to pitch. I do have some younger pitchers who come up to me and ask me questions. I help them out as much as I can, but I tell them I don't know how I do it. A.J. puts his finger down, then I try and throw to his glove.

It's funny how it works most days. It seems to be the opposite of what you warm up with versus what you have in the game. If you're lights out in the bullpen, you worry a little bit going out to start the game, because you don't have stuff that's as good. But if you don't have good stuff in the bullpen, I don't know if you concentrate more because your warm-up wasn't good, but you are sharper.

You always keep setting goals. On a personal note, I would like to win a Gold Glove, because I do take pride in fielding my position the best I can. [Buehrle was awarded a Gold Glove following the 2009 season.] Certainly, we always want to get into the playoffs and win another World Series here. That was a special year. It was so much fun. I tell the guys who weren't here how much fun it was and how much fun it would be to get back. That's always the biggest goal.

277

Mark Buehrle was drafted by the White Sox in the 38th round of the 1998 amateur draft. The left-hander rose rapidly through the Sox's system and made his debut on July 16, 2000, finishing with a 4–1 record. Buehrle moved into the starting rotation the next year and quickly established himself as one of the best and most reliable pitchers in the game, while logging at least 200 innings every season through 2009. He is a four-time All-Star (2002, 2005, 2006, 2009) and posted a high of 19 victories in 2002. Buehrle went 16–8 for the 2005 World Champions, earning wins against Boston and Anaheim in the playoffs. After starting and pitching seven innings in Game 2 of the World Series, he came out of the bullpen in the fourteenth inning of Game 3 and got Adam Everett on a pop-up to save a 7–5 White Sox win.

Buehrle threw a no-hitter against the Texas Rangers on April 18, 2007, at U.S. Cellular Field, allowing only a walk to Sammy Sosa, whom he promptly picked off. He topped that feat on July 23, 2009, when he threw a perfect game at home against the Tampa Bay Rays, a performance highlighted by Dewayne Wise's home-run-saving catch in center field in the ninth inning. In his next start, he took a perfect game into the sixth inning at Minnesota and set a major league record by retiring 45 consecutive hitters. He won his first Gold Glove after the 2009 season.

AARON ROWAND

OUTFIELDER

2001–2005

I WAS A BASEBALL FAN GROWING UP. I also grew up a Bears fan. When the White Sox drafted me, Ron Schueler was the general manager, and he called me up to tell me they had taken me with the 35th pick. I really didn't hear much else for the next 20 or 30 seconds because all I could think about was going to the city where my favorite football team played. The first thing I did was get on the computer and look up all the minor league stops, then I looked at the guys on their team like Ray Durham, Robin Ventura, and Frank Thomas.

After I got called up, we were down 8–3 in the ninth inning with two outs, and Jerry Manuel put me in for my first big-league at-bat against Dave Veres. He had that great sinker, plus a slider and a splitter. I got to two strikes and swung at one of his sinkers. It busted my bat in half on a little pop-up back to the pitcher to end the game. After the game, Boomer Wells started it, and all the guys glued toothpicks and wrote all sorts of nasty sayings on the ball I hit. That ball is in my trophy case now.

When I had my accident before the 2003 season, the first thing on my mind was baseball. [In November 2002 Rowand was seriously injured in a dirt bike accident but recovered in time play a full season while splitting time between the White Sox and the minors.] I was lying out there in the middle of the desert and, when I came to, the first thing I asked my brother-in-law was how many days we had until spring training. It was difficult. It was a

Aaron Rowand safely slides home under the glove of Boston Red Sox catcher Jason Varitek during the sixth inning of Game 1 of the American League Division Series in Chicago on October 4, 2005. Rowand scored on teammate Juan Uribe's single.
Photo courtesy of AP Images

long rehab, eight hours a day, six days a week, trying to get back to being healthy and ready to play, especially since that spring was going to be my first opportunity to start every day as the center fielder. There was a lot of pressure on me after that. In this game, you only get so many opportunities. If you waste your opportunities, you may never get another one.

They sent me down that year. I wasn't completely healthy, and the Chicago weather in April didn't help, especially after I'd had surgery. I was still having some problems, and the mechanics in my swing were sideways because I was compensating for my injury. I went to the minors with the mindset of trying to get my mechanics right and get healthy. The only thing it was going to take was time. I was lucky enough to have Greg Walker down there with me at the time, and he helped me shore up my swing. When I got the opportunity to come back up and play in Chicago, I tried to take advantage of it.

I really had the opportunity to play every day in 2003. Before then it was a platoon or play here or there. I'd had that accident before 2003, but the second half of that year was when I gained confidence to know I could play here as a regular and not be an extra outfielder. I took that into 2004 and had a good season.

One of the things Ozzie brought up when he took over as manager was the possibility of bouncing me around in the batting order. I told him he could hit me anywhere he wanted. I didn't have a preference and I could hit first, ninth, fourth, seventh, because it's not where you hit that dictates what you do at the plate, it's the game situation when you come to bat. That is what sets up what you are able to accomplish.

Everybody had a good ride in 2005. The team enjoyed our games, and we played a lot of close ballgames, games where we came back. Every day was exciting and fun to come to the ballpark. We had a lot of characters on that team, starting from our head "Jefe"! It was fun to be at the park with a close-knit group of guys who did everything together, not just at the ballpark.

I came up as more of an offensive player than defensive. It's something I really worked hard on. I do my homework on the hitters and try to learn what their tendencies are. Center field is a technical position from that standpoint, then you can add to your performance by just being able to go out and run some balls down. You never give up on a ball, because there have been many times where a ball was hit in the gap or over my head and I thought I had no chance, but I was able to get it with a good jump.

The catches I made in the Yankees series in New York that year were really a matter of the ball being hit in the right spot at the right time. They did it a number of times that series. I look back on that as sheer fun, and wish I had the opportunity where balls were hit in the right spot for me to do that more often. The stars were aligned, and they hit some shots just within my reach. Another couple of feet, and those weren't outs.

Greg Walker is the one who coined the phrase "the Three Stooges." Joe Crede, A.J. Pierzynski, and I were pretty much attached at the hip and did everything together. Not that we didn't all hang out as a group, but the three of us were always around each other. We liked to clown around, and finally Walker said, "You know, you guys are just the Three Stooges. Larry, Mo, and Yo." We had fun with it, and it came out in the media. It caught on with the rest of the team, too.

"Don't Stop Believin'" came from the three of us in Baltimore. We were there for an off day and were in the hotel having dinner and drinks. They had a lounge singer who was singing some sort of jazz in French, and somebody hollered, "Sing some Journey!" The next thing I knew, A.J. brought the CD in the next day, and we started playing it in the clubhouse. It was just a joke that caught on and was the kind of thing that happened on a daily basis that year in our clubhouse with that group of guys. Everybody was funny, everybody was a comedian, and "Don't Stop Believin'" just caught on.

Because we played so many close games that year, everybody had been put in a pressure situation. It seemed like that was a daily occurrence, so when we got to the postseason, it wasn't that much different than what we had been through during the year. At the end, Cleveland made a run, and we had to step it up. We did and started playing really good baseball, swept that last series from the Indians, and carried it on.

The whole experience of the World Series was great. I was on the foul line during introductions for Game 1, and it was 30 degrees, drizzling, and nasty, but you couldn't feel the weather because the excitement and adrenaline were huge. It was all about baseball. Of course, the last out of Game 4 in Houston will always be my favorite moment.

The rally that followed was amazing and will always stick out in my mind, especially because it was so emotional for all of us to see the turnout. The outpouring of love from a community that had been starved for a championship for so many years in baseball was something else. It gives me goosebumps just thinking about it because of all the people that showed up downtown.

It was a shock to be traded after that season, and I don't think it matters whom you were traded for. *Shocked* is the only word I can think of. I really enjoyed my time here and loved the people in this city. They were always wonderful to me, whether I was doing well or not. I grew up in the White Sox organization and I didn't know anything else. They were my family and the only thing I'd ever known. When you get traded and have to go somewhere else, it's culture shock and a disbelief. The reason Kenny traded me is that he thought he was bettering the team and the organization. If there's one thing that the fans may not totally know, it's that Kenny wants to win baseball games, and I can't blame him for that. I was disappointed to be leaving, but I never blamed the organization or Kenny for doing it—I understood why. I understood they want to win.

I was able to go to a lot of Bears games and get to know a lot of their guys. One of the most special moments in my life was after I was traded, I had planned to go to the Bears–Packers game and I still went. They had me out there as an honorary captain and, when they announced my name, I got a standing ovation from the Bears fans. Walking out to the middle of the field with the players and having the fans show me that appreciation for the time I spent here was one of the most special days of my life.

The Phillies had an off-day when the White Sox held the ring ceremony, and I was able to come. I was glad I was wearing sunglasses, because that was a very emotional time. The outpouring from the fans, seeing my teammates again, getting my ring, having the chance to say good-bye to Jerry and Kenny and all the people in the organization—it was great. I had been traded in the off-season, so it was nice to come back to say good-bye to my teammates and the fans.

What I had here was very special. Starting from Jerry Reinsdorf to Kenny and on down through the organization, including people like our great training staff, it meant a lot to me. A lot of the fans will always see me as a White Sox. This city, the fans, and the White Sox organization will always hold a very special place in my heart.

Aaron Rowand was drafted by the White Sox with the 35th pick in the first round of the 1998 amateur draft. He won a regular job in center field in 2004, when he hit .310 with 24 homers and 69 RBIs and followed up with 13 homers and 69 RBIs in helping the Sox win the 2005 World Series. Rowand's take-no-prisoners play in center field made him an instant fan favorite at U.S. Cellular Field.

On November 25, 2005, Rowand was traded along with two minor leaguers to the Phillies for Jim Thome and cash. After an All-Star season in 2007, Rowand signed a free-agent contract with San Francisco.

DON COOPER
PITCHING COACH
2002–Present

WHEN I STARTED, MY GOAL WAS TO HELP the team win a world championship. That was always my goal. The first part of that goal is to make the playoffs each year. I was named pitching coach in 2002 and can remember driving around, thinking to myself that this would be a hell of a place to win the World Series. The fans were hungry for it, and that was always my goal. You have to get into the playoffs for that to happen, though.

A lot of guys influenced me, but the main one was Sammy Ellis. He brought me here 23 years ago and was my mentor. Pat Dobson, Hoyt Wilhelm, and Johnny Podres were all coaches I ran into, and I've plagiarized all their stuff. I'm not bright enough to think up on my own all the things I learned from them. I've learned a lot of things from a lot of people and then tried to put my personality with those things and be myself. Luckily, things have worked out for me. I still talk with other pitching coaches like Dave Righetti, Roger McDowell, and Leo Mazzone. Sometimes when I talk to them, it's almost like therapy, because they know what I do and what we all have to work on.

Sammy Ellis was the best delivery and mechanics guy I've ever been around. When I got into pro ball, I looked up to the coaches and listened to them, because I wanted to hear everything they had to say. I would say, "Give me help," and I wanted to learn things. Sammy was that guy for me, and I looked up to him. One day, I heard him talking to another pitcher in

Don Cooper, here talking with Jose Contreras during a game in August 2009, has counseled pitchers for the White Sox organization since 1987. He has been the major league pitching coach since 2002. *Photo courtesy of AP Images*

Spanish and I was in awe of him. I learned Spanish because of that. I wanted to be in coaching and saw how valuable he was. I saw how important the role was, and that's one thing that guided me in the direction of being a coach. It's an important job, because you have people's careers in your hands. I don't want them to have a career like I had. I want them to have good careers. Sammy Ellis was the best at that. I later found out that he knew only those two sentences of Spanish!

We have always had open, honest communication and a lot of it. I happen to think that's the key to any relationship. I don't care what relationship you are talking about—boss to employee, coach to player, husband to wife—they are all important. I want to hear what the pitchers have to say because they are going to hear what I have to say, regardless. It's better and more enjoyable when you have a relationship with each guy. Continuity comes in when you're with a guy longer, like I have been with Mark Buehrle. Each one is different depending on how long guys are around.

One of the most fun parts of the job for me is that everybody is different. I want to get to know them and where they are coming from. What makes them tick and what buttons can I press? My wife tells me I'm not a great listener sometimes, but it's because I don't really care what she's telling me. Fortunately, I'm a good listener with the pitchers because it's interesting to me and I want to hear what they are saying. If you can listen to them closely and let them have their input, you can hear the answers. Don't try to cram things on people. I don't want it crammed on me, so I won't cram it on them.

I enjoyed the whole 2005 season, the beginning, middle, and end. I enjoyed all of it. It was wonderful, and I'd love to be able to be blessed to do that again. It was a wonderful season, and it's one we will always be trying to duplicate. Once you're a part of that, nothing less than that is acceptable. That's a good thing because the bar for the Chicago White Sox has been raised. We're doing an awful lot of winning on the South Side since Ozzie Guillen became the manager and we're looking to continue that. We want to add on to our résumé and get some more championships. Once it's all said and done, I'd like to say that, while I was here, the pitching was good and our team went out, won ballgames, and made the fans proud. It's nice walking around when you're winning and you see the White Sox fans coming out of the woodwork. You see them everywhere. They've made us all feel special over the years for what we did in 2005.

Looking back on 2005, getting into the playoffs was the toughest thing for us. Once we did, things went pretty smoothly for us. In 2008 we got into the playoffs, and I felt good about that. If the only thing you do is raise a division banner, that's pretty good, and let me tell you, that one was hard-fought. We had to fight 163 games to do that and we maxed out everything we could get out of our guys and pitching staff.

Make no mistake about it, the ultimate prize is a World Series championship, and we were fortunate enough to do it in 2005. Looking back on it, to be the last team standing is quite an accomplishment. Getting to the playoffs is too, but it's not the ultimate one. I thought we missed out in 2008, even though we won the division. Something was missing.

The last out in 2005 was the moment I will always cherish. I can still see Bobby Jenks jumping to try and get that ground ball, and you couldn't slide a slice of American cheese under his feet. Jose Uribe came in out of nowhere and threw the batter out at first base.

I remember saying, "World champions!" and I just kept repeating it. Not the state, not the district, not the diocese, not the borough, the whole world. For one moment in time, we were the world champions. Not a lot of people get to say that. You do learn so much from going through that process. I don't think that anything else can come your way the rest of your career that you haven't run into before because of that. It was the one time I didn't go out after we won. Every other time, I was out there going crazy. This one was more humbling. I went back to my room with my family and just kept thinking about being a world champion. The next day when I woke up, I had to think to myself whether that really happened, and the answer was, "Yes!" We did it, and it was an unbelievable sense of accomplishment.

The rally was surreal. I can only imagine now if we hadn't done it how many people we would have let down. Everywhere I go in Chicago people will come up to me and say, "Thank you." They tell me stories about leaving things on a grandfather's grave. It reminds me of how important that was. Thank God that we didn't let anybody down.

There used to be a flower commercial on TV that talked about the gift that keeps on giving. Winning a World Series for me has been that gift because of the people of Chicago. They are very special.

Don Cooper was hired as the Sox's pitching coach for the South Bend Class A affiliate on October 11,1987. He was the team's minor league pitching coordinator from 1997 to 2002 and was named the major league pitching coach on July 22, 2002.

A.J. PIERZYNSKI

CATCHER
2005–Present

I'VE ALWAYS BEEN A CATCHER since I was seven years old. I tried to get out from behind the plate a few times, but always ended up staying there. I went to practice one day when I was a kid, and the regular catcher wasn't there, so I said I'd do it. I've been a catcher ever since.

When I came to the White Sox in 2005, I was a free agent looking for a place to go. Hawk Harrelson pulled some strings and got me to come over here. I definitely was at a bit of a crossroads. I had a bad year the year before in San Francisco and took some unfair abuse from some guys who should have kept their mouths shut. I was at a point where I needed a place to go, and the White Sox welcomed me with open arms. It obviously worked out great—we won the World Series that year, and things have been great ever since.

You're never sure what it will be like coming to a new team. I was lucky I knew a lot of the guys like [Paul] Konerko, Frank Thomas, Jermaine Dye, and Mark Buehrle from before. I had played against them and had been around them doing different things. It's hard to get a sense of when you belong. Spring training is so hard because there a lot of things going on. After a couple weeks with the team and having won some games in the season, guys started asking me to join them at dinner or do some stuff. That's when I got the feeling this was a good place and I had made the right choice. I was fitting in, and we were winning. Being in first place, I wasn't going to complain.

The fans were great to me from day one. They accepted me right away, which was great. I couldn't ask any more from the fans and the people of Chicago. The media, everybody, they all accepted me right away, and it was nothing but the best.

I was in the middle of a lot, and I have no problem with that. I always tell people I'd rather have it on me. Things like running on the strikeout in Game 2 of the ALCS, the weird plays in Games 4 and 5, some of the crazy things that happened during the Series, it just seemed like I was always there to take the brunt of it and take the spotlight off my teammates. It didn't bother me, and I'm used to it. It's fine.

Our guys threw four straight complete games in the ALCS, and I didn't think about it at the time. Don Cooper mentioned something about it to me afterward, and I hadn't thought about it. We had just won and we had dominated, so then I looked back and thought, *Wow, all four guys finished those games!* You will never see that again. Managers have a lot of pressure to get their closers in the game. With the money closers are paid and the money set-up guys are paid, no manager is ever going to be comfortable letting their starters go the way we did and have it work out the way we did.

I always tell people I'd like to do that season again and this time, sit back and enjoy it a bit more. It was going a million miles an hour in the postseason—you're trying to plan, get tickets, get flights for your family, and figure how to get everybody into the ALCS or the World Series. You had to line up hotel rooms, too. There were so many things going on, I'd like to be able to have that run again and be able to sit back and enjoy it.

I never got to do the postseason introductions because I was always in the bullpen warming up the starting pitcher. I do remember after we won that long Game 3 in the World Series, I went home with my family and said, "We're going to win the World Series tomorrow, and it's going to be awesome!" You're in the moment and you certainly don't want to give anything away or let your guard down, but when you get up 3–0, you definitely say, "We're gonna do this tomorrow and we're going to win the World Series!" Everyone was there, and it was great.

You see the videos of the moments and the celebrations, and you say, "I forgot about this," or, "I forgot about that." You forget about all the little things you got to enjoy at the time, and when you look back on it you do wish you would have had more time to enjoy it. It's just that you are so caught up in what's going on, and it's over so fast, you never really get to

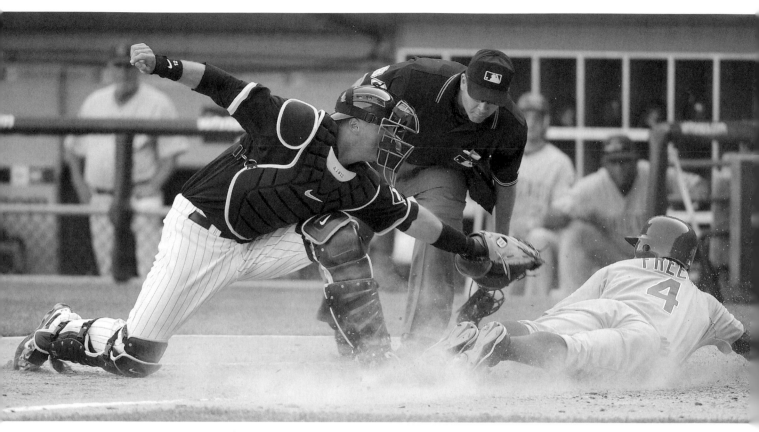

A.J. Pierzynski attempts to tag Cub Ryan Freel at home plate in the eighth inning on June 27, 2009, at U.S. Cellular Field.

enjoy what is happening. You still have a lot of memories of what happened, especially with guys who are still on the team. We still talk about some things that happened that year, and it's great.

The rally was the coolest part of the whole thing. Going down through the neighborhoods and streets, seeing the people who were outside their homes and businesses was great. They were waving, saying thank you, and they took the time to come and see us. When we got to Wacker Drive, stood up on the bridge, and looked across at all the people, it was one of the coolest things I've ever been a part of or probably ever will be a part of. To see the support, emotion, and energy that were brought to that one little area is something I'll probably never be a part of again. It was incredible.

Coming off what I had been through before Chicago, to come here and win the World Series, then have the fans vote me onto the All-Star team the next year was great. The public relations staff of the Sox was great with the "Punch A.J." campaign. It was perfect timing after the fight we had with the Cubs. To have it all come together and be able to go to Pittsburgh for the All-Star Game with seven other teammates and coaches and Ozzie was fun. I didn't get to play, but that was even better. There was no pressure. Ozzie told me before the game I wasn't going to play, so I got to enjoy it.

In 2008 we worked hard to get in a situation to win. Those last three games were as pressure-packed as could be, and we found a way to win all three against three different but very good teams. When we got to the playoffs, it was a disappointment the way it ended. It was still a great year and something I'll never forget. That "blackout" game was cool. I walked out to warm up John Danks before the game and looked around and saw all the people wearing their black and waving their black towels. That was really cool.

To get through the season, I have to stay on top of my routine. I work out almost every day, usually four or five times a week during the season. I get my sleep and make sure I get that rest every night. It's a bigger challenge mentally because you have to let go of games and let go of pitches. I can always go home and think, *Man, if I had done this or called this, could we have won that game?* There are so many games and so many plays throughout the season, mentally you have to be able to let some things go.

Having a relationship with the pitcher makes our job easier. Spring training is very important because that's when you get to know the new guys. You get that familiarity and not just with the major leaguers. I also get time with the younger guys, so if they get called up during the year, I know what and how they throw.

I don't mind being booed. I always say I feel sorry for whoever is hitting behind me in the lineup, because no one hears their name when they announce the lineup since they're still booing me. I understand why they boo me in places like Anaheim, because of the playoffs, and Wrigley because of the things with the Cubs. It's led to a lot of things for me I wouldn't have gotten to do otherwise.

We're still in the building process. We won one and really want to win another. It's just a challenge, because baseball is so hard. People don't understand how hard it is to win every year. You have people moving on, coming and going, getting hurt, and you have to be really good as a front office and an organization. We have been very fortunate to have young guys who have stepped up.

The White Sox signed catcher A.J. Pierzynski as a free agent on January 5, 2005, and he hit 18 homers and 56 RBIs in his first season with the team. He helped launch the Sox's postseason run by homering twice and scoring four runs in a Game 1 win over Boston in the ALDS. A.J.'s signature play in the postseason came in Game 2 of the ALCS against Anaheim, when he alertly ran to first on a dropped third strike with two out in the ninth inning, which led to the winning run in the Sox's 2–1 win.

He was voted by the fans to the 2006 American League All-Star team as the 32nd player after the White Sox set up a "Punch A.J." campaign. Pierzynski hit .300 in 2009 and has been one of baseball's most durable catchers, averaging 130 games behind the plate in his five years with the Sox.

JERMAINE DYE

OUTFIELDER

2005–2009

WHEN I WAS DECIDING WHERE TO SIGN after becoming a free agent after 2004, my agent and I took a lot of things under consideration. I was very happy when things worked out with the White Sox to get a deal done there. It really worked out well for all of us when we had the season we had and won it.

It was a very exciting but very exhausting year. There was a lot of hard work and grinding it out through all those one-run games. In the end, if you can hold up that trophy, it's all worth it. It was an unbelievable season from start to finish.

In the World Series, it was great in the very first game to go up against a guy like Roger Clemens and hit a home run in my first at-bat. It not only gave us as a team and an organization some confidence, but it got everybody going and everybody excited, the fans included. We really rode on through it from there the rest of the Series.

After we won it, I was in the pile celebrating with my teammates when somebody pulled me out of there and told me I needed to go to a special room because I had won the MVP award for the World Series. It was very exciting, but I kind of missed out on a lot of the celebration on the field with the guys. I got the chance to go into the clubhouse afterward and continue to celebrate with them.

Jermaine Dye celebrates after hitting an RBI single in the eighth inning against the Houston Astros during Game 4 of the 2005 World Series.

You look at Ozzie as a manager who understands the game and who has played the game before. He knows a lot of the things we are going through. He's great with taking a lot of pressure off us and letting us go out to play and perform. He gets the best out of us.

My commitment comes from my parents. My parents taught me how to be who I am now. They wanted me to respect others, take care of my family, and respect my elders. In baseball, when I came up with the Braves in my rookie year, I was around guys like Marquis Grissom, David Justice, Fred McGriff, Tom Glavine, Greg Maddux, and John Smoltz—all those guys paved the way for me and showed me how to be a professional on and off the field. It's something that you carry on as you go through baseball and try to show others as you become the older veteran. You try to show the younger guys how to play the game and how to be a professional.

Winning is what it's all about. Jerry Reinsdorf, Kenny Williams, the whole organization, their job is to put together a winning product on the field. Year in and year out, they find a way to do that and give us a chance to win. It's a matter of us going out on the field and making it happen. The White Sox are a great organization, not just for baseball but also for families. It's really close-knit here, and that's something you appreciate as a player.

Jermaine Dye signed with the White Sox as a free agent on December 9, 2004, and was a vital cog in the championship season of 2005 with 31 homers and 86 RBIs. The right fielder was named the World Series MVP after hitting .438 with a home run and three RBIs in the four-game sweep over Houston. Dye followed in 2006 with his best all-around season, posting 44 home runs (second only to Albert Belle's 49 on the Sox's single-season list) with 120 RBIs and a .315 batting average. He averaged 30 homers and 85 RBIs in his next three seasons with the Sox.

SCOTT PODSEDNIK

OUTFIELDER

2005–2007 ★ 2009

WHEN I WAS TRADED TO THE WHITE SOX, at that point, I'd been around long enough to understand that is the nature of the game. Both the Brewers and White Sox were trying to improve their ballclubs, and that move was one that both sides decided to make. I was excited about the new opportunity to come over, bring my game to the American League, and join my new club.

The big question going into the '05 spring training was whether my game would mesh with this team. Kenny had the idea of changing the offensive philosophy somewhat. We wanted to manufacture some more runs than they had in the past. It seemed like in the years before, the Sox relied solely on the home run. It was kind of new to everyone. No one knew how that club would jell together. Chemistry is obviously a big part of the game. That was a big question as to how our club would come together.

If you would have asked me earlier in my career about chemistry, I wouldn't have known what you were talking about. All of a sudden, that group got together, and we started taking the field with a swagger and the right attitude we needed each and every night to go out and battle and win. We gained some momentum early and continued on. When we took the field, we had an air about us and an attitude that we were there to battle you. We were able to carry that momentum and that attitude all throughout the '05 season.

It was exciting, and there was so much energy in our park. When I'd steal a base, the fans just loved it. What that did was provide energy for our offense, and not just that club. If you look at any team, if the leadoff guy at the top is getting on base, it sets the table for the hitters in the middle. [Tadahito] Iguchi and I did a pretty decent job of getting on base that year for those guys. Iguchi did a great job of getting me into scoring position most of the time, and that set the table for Jermaine [Dye], Paulie [Konerko], and all the hitters behind us.

When the fans elected me to the last spot on the All-Star team that year, that was incredible. I understand that none of that would have happened without the support of our great fans and my family and friends. That campaign for the last spot took on a life of its own. It was a special year for me being able to make the All-Star team. I'll always be able to reflect fondly on that.

Our games revolved around our pitching staff, and they set the tone from day one. Mark Buehrle threw a shutout on Opening Day, and that set the tone for the rest of the year. As an offense, we knew that if we could show up to the ballpark and score two or three runs, maybe manufacture one here and get a big home run from one of our guys there, we were going to be on top of a lot of ballgames. We won a lot of close ballgames, and that set us up for all the close, intense games we had in the postseason.

There's nothing like postseason baseball. After being able to experience it, it is like a wolf getting his first taste of fresh meat—all you can think about is getting it again. There is a sense of preparation, and you have to under-stand each game is just another ballgame. You have to go out and not try to do too much and remember the things that got you to that situation. After it was all said and done and we had won the World Series, you almost pinched yourself and understood that was a lot of craziness and fun we had just gone through.

When I hit the home run against the Astros, I was probably just as shocked as any of my teammates or any of my fans here at the park. What can you say? I put a pretty good swing on that ball and I didn't miss it. I was just trying to reach base. I was ahead in the count 2–0 and was able to put a pretty good at-bat together from there. It was the biggest hit of my career, and it's going to be tough to top. I don't anticipate getting a bigger hit or home run ever.

Scott Podsednik connects on a game-winning, walk-off home run in the ninth inning off Brad Lidge during Game 2 of the World Series against the Houston Astros at U.S. Cellular Field on October 23, 2005. The White Sox defeated the Astros 7–6.

I have the World Series DVD at our house, and I go back and watch that periodically. Every time I watch it, it brings tears to my eyes, and I get goosebumps just thinking about it. It was a special year—a lot of things went our way. We caught a lot of breaks and made the most of them.

The next two seasons were tough for me because I just didn't have the ability to play the running game that I wanted to play. I had the two operations that just didn't allow me to play the game I was accustomed to playing. I lost that snap in my step and my explosiveness, and when I did, I lost some value. Since then, I've conditioned myself and have gotten myself back into shape. I feel like I can go out on a baseball field and make an impact again.

I was home golfing when Kenny Williams got in touch with me about coming back to the Sox. The Rockies made some decisions and brought in some different personnel in the spring, so when they let me go, I went back to my house. My agent and I continued to monitor the league and looked for some potential spots for me to play in. The White Sox had some unfortunate injuries, and one thing led to another. Kenny and I did have a couple of conversations, and I told him that I was in good shape. I still think there's a lot of gas left in my tank. I was fortunate that he considered it and allowed me to come back here and play.

It was really exciting to come back. My wife and I love the city of Chicago. I spent three years here from '05 to '07 and created a lot of relationships. You create a special bond with a group of guys when you battle and win the World Series. It was special to come back to the city and rejoin the organization, plus see a bunch of the guys again.

You can't help but learn each year you spend in the big leagues. That's the thing for me every year is that I learn so much more about the game and about myself, how I react to the game, and how the game is played. I have learned quite a bit over the last few years and hope I can use that knowledge when my body starts slowing down a little bit. Perhaps I can rely on my smarts and some of the things I've picked up.

With what we accomplished in '05, we've kind of raised the bar. As an organization, we expect big things. That's what it's all about. You want to raise the bar, you want to be a championship-caliber ballclub each and every year. I think we did that.

Outfielder Scott Podsednik was acquired by the White Sox along with Luis Vizcaino from the Brewers for Carlos Lee on December 13, 2004. "Pods" immediately jump-started the offense that season with 59 steals and 80 runs scored and was an immediate fan favorite, as evidenced by his selection by the fans as the final All-Star on the American League squad that year. After going homerless in the regular season, Podsednik keyed an opening-game win over Boston with his first of the year. In Game 2 of the World Series at U.S. Cellular Field he drove a Brad Lidge pitch through the rain into the right-field stands for a walk-off blast that stands as one of the most memorable homers in team history.

Podsednik was hampered by injuries his next two seasons and was released by the Sox prior to the 2008 season. He spent that year with the Rockies and was released at the end of spring training in 2009. He rejoined the White Sox organization, was called up from Triple A Charlotte on May 1, 2009, and hit .304 in 132 games. He signed with the Royals as a free agent on January 8, 2010.

BOBBY JENKS

PITCHER

2005–Present

WHEN I FOUND OUT I WAS COMING TO THE WHITE SOX during the off-season before 2005, I was excited to have a change of scenery and to be working with some new people. When I got called up in July, I showed up at the ballpark a good two hours before anyone else did! I was sitting there in my uniform waiting. I was obviously excited to be there and looked forward to my chance.

My first week up here, they let me get my feet wet before I got too deep in the water. As the weeks went on, they threw me out there in the ninth with a big lead a few times just so I could get a feel for it. They told me in September I was the guy for the ninth inning, then I went out and blew back-to-back saves against Cleveland when the Indians were making their run.

I didn't really have a big adjustment for my mindset. I've always had a pretty short memory anyway, so I guess I was a good fit for the role. Dustin Hermanson was pitching relief for us that year and really helped me a lot with that role. We talked about the mental aspects of being a closer, how to forget and focus on certain things during the game, and then what to focus on when I was out there on the mound. As a closer, I guess it's the closest thing to being a starter as far as pitching goes. You are in the spotlight more. You can't close unless the guys in front of you are good. It's always about the whole bullpen.

I definitely knew what was going on in the pennant race. I'm no dummy to baseball, but it was nice to go out there knowing if something went bad, it was easily forgotten because we were in first place. Having that cushion was kind of nice.

The postseason for me that year was one big blur. I've watched the DVDs a few times since then to find out what happened. Playing in the World Series was a great feeling. The only thing I could compare it to was my first Opening Day, that chance to be introduced and walk out to stand on the foul lines. It was a situation just like you imagine as a kid when you dream about playing baseball. To live out that fantasy was an incredible feeling for me.

Since it was my first year, I was still fine. I didn't let it get to me as much as I thought I did when I think about it now. I guess I was young and dumb. I'll tell you, though, up until that ninth inning, my stomach hurt every day.

I was lucky to be on the mound when we beat the Astros to win the World Series. I tell people the one thing I do remember is that when Orlando Palmeiro hit the ball to shortstop on the last out, everything went silent for me at that moment. Then, it was pure excitement when Paulie caught the ball and we won it. But for that one moment, I really didn't hear a thing.

When we got back to Chicago, that parade downtown was just something else! Going down the street was just awesome. I get excited just thinking about it. Obviously, you're not thinking about the celebration when you're still playing and trying to win it, but afterward we knew there was going to be a nice parade with ticker tape and the whole works. That was as close to the perfect end to the World Series as you could ever get.

In 2006 I was still a little nervous because I didn't know for sure if I had the closer's role or not. I knew I still had to go out there and compete for a job. Once spring training was over, it was okay again, but that year the preseason was a really nervous time for me about my role.

I had the record 41 guys in a row retired the next year. Earlier that year Mark Buehrle had thrown his no-hitter against Texas. After I threw a ninth inning later that year, one of our beat writers came up to me and was laughing when he told me I had just thrown a perfect game that beat Buehrle's no-hitter. At that point, I had 27 in a row, but I just laughed it off and didn't think about it again until it was brought to my attention when I was in the mid-30s. Somebody told me about it then, and it was still two or three more outings until I tied that record.

Bobby Jenks throws in relief against the Tampa Bay Rays on April 16, 2009, at Tropicana Field in St. Petersburg, Florida.

303

The two All-Star Games I've been selected to have been a lot of fun. Unfortunately, I didn't get to pitch in either one, but I had a great time. Hopefully, there will be more chances in my future when I actually get to pitch. My first full year was 2006, so I kept my mouth shut. It was just fun being in the clubhouse and seeing everyone. In 2007 in San Francisco I knew more people and had been in the league, so that one was even more fun for me.

I don't have a big routine. I get here early to do my work, but beyond that I play a lot of cards. I pride myself on pitching more as I get older, not just throwing. One of the biggest things I've learned is how to pitch. Obviously, you can go out there and throw 98 mph by guys, but this is the big leagues, and if they see 98 enough, they are going to turn on it. I've learned how to pitch to their weaknesses instead of just going with my strength all the time. You certainly get more outs more quickly that way.

Art Kusnyer was the bullpen coach at the time I came up and really helped me. He was a big influence on me in helping me get ready when I was in the bullpen. He had a lot of good advice and had worked with a lot of great pitchers in the past. He was very helpful to me when I was starting out.

It's not just about throwing hard. I did throw 102 at Safeco Field in Seattle once and 103 unofficially when I was playing winter ball in Puerto Rico. Now I'd rather see 94 to 96 with movement on the ball instead of just seeing how hard I can get it there straight. That's more effective.

We're lucky to play in front of some great fans. When they had that "blackout" at the playoff game with the Twins, that was really something. I didn't know anything about it until that day. Just walking out and seeing a packed stadium with that look was an incredible thing to see. It was really cool. I won't forget it.

I can't look back and be satisfied with how far I've come yet. There is still too much I want to do. I want to be a part of another World Series–winning team again, this time start to finish instead of coming in at the halfway point in the season. I'll cherish my career a whole lot more then.

Bobby Jenks was selected by the White Sox off waivers on December 17, 2004, from the California Angels. He joined the team in July and took over the closer's role in mid-September, posting six saves and a 2.75 ERA in 32 appearances. Jenks picked up two saves in the Division Series against the Red Sox, then added two more to his postseason total against the Astros in the World Series. He was on the mound to nail down the save when the Sox won Game 4 to complete their Series sweep.

Jenks saved 41 games in his first full season in 2006 and had a stretch in which he tied a major league record by retiring 41 batters in a row. He was named to the American League All-Star team that year and followed up with another All-Star selection in 2007 to go with his 40 saves. Jenks saved 30 games in 2008 and 29 more in 2009.

JIM THOME
DESIGNATED HITTER
2006–2009

I LOVED BASEBALL GROWING UP. I didn't have one particular player I loved, I just loved baseball. I loved playing it, I loved watching it, and, growing up in Illinois, we were fortunate because you could watch the Cubs and the Sox on TV. It was great.

The White Sox fans treated me great from the start. It was the same way when I went from Cleveland to Philadelphia. The fans in Chicago have treated me with a lot of respect. I think that works both ways. As a player, when you see that, you want to give back to them, as well. I appreciate them because they are passionate, very loyal to the players, and it's been so cool for me to come home and play.

My first game for the Sox was Opening Day at U.S. Cellular in 2006, and I hit a home run, so it was all great. Just think about it—Opening Day with a new team and to hit a home run, especially against the Indians, was just great. It was all so much fun. Coming home and doing that in the first game was really cool. Having my family there made it just that much more special.

To be Comeback Player of the Year that year was special. Any award you get is special. At some point, you will either get hurt or have that mulligan-type year, and that's what happened to me in 2005. Then I got traded, and everything was great, so to win that award was even more special. Let's face it, you never like to get hurt, but if you do, you want to win that award. It's pretty cool.

I enjoy being a DH. I had to sit down and learn my routine when it first happened. Once I got that routine down, learned it and got accustomed to it, it became second nature. I go out and do my routine now that I know it. I'm just like an everyday guy who plays defense. I know where to go to stretch, where I need to go to hit during the game, and I want to be on the bench as much as I can to watch our guys. I've got work to do in the meantime, so I try to even those out in a team-oriented sense.

I learned my own routine, but I picked Harold Baines' brain the first year, and it helped me watching Eddie Murray do it in Cleveland. Like anything, I think I had to learn through experience.

When you're struggling, it's a gradual process to get going. The one thing you have to learn as you play is that you can't make it all up in one day. It's a grind. One of the best pieces of advice I was ever given was from Eddie Murray. He said try to get a hit a day, not go out and press to get three or four. If you do more, great, but get a knock a day and mix in a few walks, and that will build your confidence—you'll be off and running. It's a game of confidence, and you can never let yourself get down.

My 500th home run was very special. To do it at home in Chicago and have it be a walk-off was great, plus I got to watch the fans celebrate and have fun. I was greeted at home plate by my teammates, and it really was a surreal experience. You really don't imagine it, maybe you do as it gets closer, but I never dreamed it would be a walk-off. The whole thing came together and was so special. It's a moment I will never forget.

We won our division in 2008, and that meant something because it was so competitive. Each team that year had a lot of talent, and we played very hard all year long to win it. To accomplish that was really a great thing. The ultimate would have been to go to the World Series, but it didn't happen. We had to feel very good about what we did accomplish because no one picked us to win the division.

The wild-card game that year had an incredible atmosphere. The fans with the "blackout" certainly lifted all of us up before the game even started. John Danks for us and Nick Blackburn for Minnesota threw great games. To win 1–0 showed it was just such a clean game. There was good pitching, good defense, and a good bullpen on our end. We got some good hitting, and I hit a home run to help us win.

You are who you are, and I was fortunate to have great parents, a great family, and great teammates. You learn that at a young age through good

Chris Getz, Paul Konerko, and Jim Thome get ready in the dugout before a game against the Oakland Athletics during the 1929-themed turn-back-the-clock game at the Oakland–Alameda County Coliseum on August 16, 2009.

veterans and good baseball people like Buddy Bell and Charlie Manuel. Each organization has someone like Harold Baines. You take little bits and pieces from the Hall of Fame–type people and you add it to what you're trying to do by treating people with respect.

I love Chicago and I've never tried to hide that. It really is my home, even though I grew up downstate. My four years with the White Sox were some of the most special years I've ever had as a player. It gave our family an opportunity to be close to home, so it was tough to leave. You realize as you get older that baseball is a business. I didn't expect to be traded, but the situation came up. It was a tough decision, because I had about 45 minutes to decide. I didn't want to look back and find out I missed a chance to go to the World

Series with the Dodgers. I've got nothing but good things to say about the Chicago White Sox organization. They treated me great.

Left-handed slugger Jim Thome was acquired by the White Sox on November 25, 2005, from the Phillies along with cash in exchange for Aaron Rowand and Daniel Haigwood. Coming off back problems, he paid immediate dividends with 42 homers, 106 RBIs, and an American League All-Star selection. Thome was honored as baseball's Comeback Player of the Year for 2006. He hit 35 and 34 homers the next two seasons, and on September 17, 2007, Thome hit his 500th home run, a walk-off shot off the Angels' Dustin Moseley.

Thome's other signature home run with the Sox came when his 461-foot blast won the wild-card playoff game 1–0 over the Twins on September 30, 2008. After slumping to 23 homers with a .249 batting average, Thome was traded to the Los Angeles Dodgers on August 31, 2009, for minor leaguer Justin Fuller.

JERRY REINSDORF

CHAIRMAN
1981–Present

I HAD THE CHANCE TO INVEST as a limited partner in a number of ballclubs before 1981, but none of those transactions ever worked out. When the last one didn't, I thought to myself, *Why do you want to be a limited partner when everything you've ever done you've been in charge of, and why do you want to invest in a team that doesn't even play in the city where you live?*

My son, Michael, was a huge White Sox fan, and we had gone to a lot of White Sox games. Bill Veeck's group had owned the White Sox for five years, and his history was that he didn't hang on, that he sold teams. Through a contact that I had, I contacted him, and the rest is history.

Bill did a great job in other eras, but the reason he got out was that he realized things were changing. Free agency had come about, and it was going to be very hard for him to compete. He was excellent at day-of-game promotions and things like that, but he just didn't want to fight the fight anymore. We realized that the future of sports was in television, in generating more TV revenue and doing more sophisticated things.

Eddie Einhorn had the idea that if we got all the teams together and started a pay television service, we could really have something. We were too early, because Chicago wasn't cabled at the time, and we had to deliver our programming over the air with a scrambled signal. We really weren't giving value, and it didn't work out. Years later, Eddie's vision proved to be correct, and that's where we are now with Comcast SportsNet.

When we took the team over in 1981, we said we were not going to be in the free-agent market. We were going to build a farm system and do this the right way. It was just one big collective yawn among our fan base. Carlton Fisk just fell into our laps. Boston lost him on a technicality, and we thought we had a great opportunity to get a great player. The White Sox hadn't had a great player in a long time, and we went after him.

The most fun I ever had has to be 1983. Obviously, the most satisfying thing was winning the World Series in 2005, but '83 was a lot of fun. It was our third year, and we had the greatest collection of ballplayers. They were great human beings—[Greg] Luzinski, Fisk, Ron Kittle, Jerry Koosman—it was just a great bunch of guys. They all got along with each other. After the lousy start, we just never lost any games. We started 16–24, then won 99 games that year. It was a tremendous amount of fun. We thought, *Well, we've got this figured out.* Even though we didn't get to the World Series, we thought we were pretty smart in putting that team together and that the next year we'd be back. Little did I realize it would be 10 years before we got to the postseason again.

Everybody was so happy when we clinched. It had been 24 years since the White Sox had been in the postseason and even longer than that for the Cubs. It was a wonderful night. It almost happened the night before, and I was praying it wouldn't happen, because it was a Jewish holiday and I wouldn't have been able to be there.

We definitely went from the top of the mountain in '83 to the outhouse for the balance of the '80s. We did have a decent team in '85, and I think we won 85 games that year. After that, things really got bad, and we realized we didn't have much talent in the farm system and would have to retool. I made the dumbest mistake of my life in hiring Hawk and letting him fire Tony La Russa. We struggled through the '80s, but as we got to '89, that's when it started to turn around. We actually finished last in '89, but in the second half of the season we were over .500, and that set the stage for a pretty good run. In 1990 I think we won 94 games, although the A's won 103 games that year, but that was the start of a pretty good run.

It was very hard to get our new ballpark built, but it had to be done because the old ballpark was going to fall down. It truly was at the end of its useful life, and it was well beyond the end of its economic life, because with the salaries escalating the way they had, you had to have new sources of revenue from a ballpark and you couldn't find them in the old Comiskey Park. Also, physically, it wasn't going to last much longer.

When I walked into the new ballpark, I thought we had created something really wonderful. There were no obstructed seats, terrific sightlines, wide aisles, wide seats—I thought everybody was going to love it. I obviously miscalculated. People wanted something more intimate. That took us a while to be able to do, but now we've achieved what everybody likes.

The '94 team might have been the best team that we ever had here, although at the time of the strike, we were only one game ahead of Cleveland. It was an awfully good team and had a really good chance to go to the World Series. The strike came along and just devastated us. It took us a few years to recover from that. I know that I got blamed for the strike, but the only one to blame for the strike, in my opinion, was Don Fehr. He's the guy who called the strike.

You can't kid yourself in this game. What you don't want to do is get caught in the middle. What we saw in '97 was that we were three games out of first place, but we were under .500. We knew Cleveland had a much better ballclub than we had. We knew we had players who we were going to lose at the end of the year. They were going to get big contracts, and we couldn't afford to bring them back. We decided that we'd bite the bullet and try to go younger. It worked. The players that we got at that time really were key in winning the division in 2000. You can't think like a fan, unfortunately. Sometimes you have to do what you think is right. Sometimes you have to be willing to take a hit but be judged in the end on the results. I think the results of the '97 trade were pretty good.

I had known Kenny Williams since he was 17 years old. He was the only player drafted who I ever had anything to do with signing. Roland Hemond came to me and said, "We just drafted a guy in the third round, but he's a first-round caliber player. He dropped to the third round because he's going to go to Stanford and play football." So I went out and visited with the family and convinced them that he should still go to Stanford, play football, but give up the scholarship and play baseball in the summertime, which he did initially, but then he dropped out of Stanford, which annoyed me to no end. I wanted him to graduate.

As it turned out, Kenny had some injuries and never turned out to be the player we all expected him to be. After his career was over, Kenny contacted me about getting involved in scouting. He wanted to scout the inner cities. We hired him that way but discovered, at that time, there really wasn't a lot of talent in the inner cities. I said to Kenny, "Why don't you move to

Jerry Reinsdorf headed the limited partnership that bought the White Sox from Bill Veeck in 1981. He has been chairman of the team since then, guiding the team through the construction of a new ballpark, a World Series victory, and the support of numerous charities.

Chicago, be my assistant, and I'll teach you the baseball business?" He came here and worked very closely with me on a lot of things that I was doing. We got to the point, though, where I felt we needed to change something in the farm system and needed a new head. I looked around, and the only one I thought would have a chance was Kenny. I said, "Kenny, you are going to have to be farm director." And he said, "No, I don't want to do it." I said, "Okay, then tell me who's going to do it?" He didn't have another name, so we made him the farm director. He did such an outstanding job there, and

I realized what good judgment he had and how organized he was, that when Ron Schueler decided he wanted to step aside as GM, it was a no-brainer. Kenny was right there.

In 2005 the last month was a little bumpy when we went from a 15-game lead to a game and a half! I thought we were going to win the division in 2005, but I had gotten to the point where I didn't know if we would ever win the World Series. I really didn't. I truly enjoyed it after it was over more than I enjoyed it while we were going through it.

That team had pitching and defense, but it didn't lack for power. We had some boppers in Dye, Konerko, and Pierzynski, but there were players that Ozzie could do things with. There was strong pitching, with four complete games in the Championship Series to show how strong our pitching was. It was gratifying to know that we won it with the kind of team we wanted to have.

When we won the third game in all those extra innings well after midnight and went up 3–0, at that point I said, "I think we can win this thing!"

I never could have imagined what happened on the parade day. I was obviously very happy when we won the last game, but it was only afterward that I realized the impact that winning the World Series had on our community. You could have gone to any cemetery in the Chicago area the next day and found graves decorated in White Sox paraphernalia. I don't know how many people came to me and said they had to be sure that their father or mother or grandfather knew that the White Sox had won the World Series.

The parade was phenomenal. The mayor himself planned the parade, so it went through six or seven different neighborhoods. The city estimated there were close to 2 million people on the parade route, and there wasn't one arrest. There wasn't one incident. The signs that were held up along the way were just phenomenal. I had women come up to me after that with tears in their eyes, telling me how happy they were and what it had done for their families. I even had one gentleman stop me the following spring in the parking lot to say that his father had died 15 minutes after the last out, but he knew and he died happy. That's the kind of impact that winning the World Series had on this community.

Paul giving me the ball kind of stunned me a little bit. I hadn't given any thought to where the ball was. If somebody had asked me, I would have said, "I guess Paul has the ball." The year before there was a dispute with the Red Sox and Doug Mientkiewicz, and they ended up in litigation. [The

Red Sox and Mientkiewicz were suing each other because he had kept the ball from the last out of the World Series, while they felt it belonged to the team.] When Paul handed me that ball, it just choked me up. It was a tremendous feeling. It got me in a little bit of trouble with my wife, because I think I said it was the most emotional moment of my life, and she pointed out there was a time when we got married and had some children, so maybe I should have said it was close to the most emotional moment of my life!

We think we have a great family here. I can never get rid of anybody. Nobody ever seems to leave. Peter Gammons once said to me, "Is there anybody here who answers the telephone who hasn't been here for 20 years?" It's a great thing. We've all been together for a long time. We've had the ups, we've had the downs, and that's great. The kind of people we get here and the fans who come out are families. The area we have in left field where we have instruction for the kids is great. We have really developed our young fan base. We've also developed a great fan base in the minority community. Where typically in baseball 5 to 6 percent of your attendees are African American, we're at 12 percent, and we are at 12 to 13 percent in the Latino community. We are a team for everybody in this area, not just the typical white male. We get women, we get children, we get blacks, we get Latinos, we get everybody here.

I think it's important to have people in the farm system who are White Sox people. They are able to transfer that love of the organization to the kids they are training. It took me years to get Greg Walker to come back here. I worked on him for a long time, just like Richard Dotson, Bobby Thigpen, all of those guys. I think it's part of the education of our young players to know that there is a White Sox way and a White Sox feeling and we are a family organization.

I think we're in great shape now with Kenny, Rick Hahn, and the crazy guy we have managing the team, and I expect that everybody will be around for a long time. The satisfaction I have really comes from knowing that this team makes so many people happy. I've often thought about growing up in Brooklyn and sleeping on a cot in a hallway. I never could have dreamed that something like this could have happened. Originally, it was all about trying to win for us, for the people who work here. What it really became was winning for everybody. This is all about the fans.

Jerry Reinsdorf has been the chairman of the Chicago White Sox since heading the limited partnership that bought the team from Bill Veeck in January 1981. The Sox made the postseason in 1983, 1993, 2000, 2005, and 2008 under Reinsdorf's guidance and won the franchise's first World Series in 88 years in 2005.

Under his watch, new Comiskey Park, now U.S. Cellular Field, was built and opened in 1991, and in 2009 the Sox and Dodgers moved into the state-of-the-art Camelback Ranch spring-training complex in Glendale, Arizona. He established White Sox Charities, which has donated more than $12 million to Chicago-area organizations since its inception, and the Chicago Bulls/White Sox Training Academy, which promotes and teaches sports to thousands of children each year. Reinsdorf purchased a controlling interest in the Chicago Bulls in 1985 and has been chairman of the team since then.